Brain-Based Learning

Third Edition

To all the teachers who thoughtfully struggle and strive to be better and more aligned with how the brain works. The more you know (and apply) about how the brain works, the better your job keeps getting every day.

Brain-Based Learning

Teaching the Way Students Really Learn

Third Edition

Eric Jensen

Liesl McConchie

FOR INFORMATION:

Corwin

A SAGE Company

2455 Teller Road

Thousand Oaks, California 91320

(800) 233-9936

www.corwin.com

SAGE Publications Ltd.

1 Oliver's Yard

55 City Road

London, EC1Y 1SP

United Kingdom

SAGE Publications India Pvt. Ltd.

B 1/I 1 Mohan Cooperative Industrial Area

Mathura Road, New Delhi 110 044

India

SAGE Publications Asia-Pacific Pte. Ltd.

18 Cross Street #10-10/11/12

China Square Central

Singapore 048423

Publisher: Jessica Allan
Senior Content Development
  Editor: Lucas Schleicher
Associate Content Development
  Editor: Mia Rodriguez
Project Editor: Amy Schroller
Copy Editor: Will DeRooy
Typesetter: Hurix Digital
Proofreader: Dennis Webb
Indexer: Jean Casalegno
Cover Designer: Scott Van Atta
Marketing Manager: Deena Meyer

Printed in the United States of America

ISBN 978-1-5443-6454-4

This book is printed on acid-free paper.

MIX
Paper from
responsible sources
FSC® C008955

20 21 22 23 24 10 9 8 7 6 5 4 3 2

DISCLAIMER: This book may direct you to access third-party content via web links, QR codes, or other scannable technologies, which are provided for your reference by the author(s). Corwin makes no guarantee that such third-party content will be available for your use and encourages you to review the terms and conditions of such third-party content. Corwin takes no responsibility and assumes no liability for your use of any third-party content, nor does Corwin approve, sponsor, endorse, verify, or certify such third-party content.

Contents

List of Illustrations

Chapter 5: The Power of Neuroplasticity

Chapter 6: How Emotions Impact Learning

Chapter 7: Physical Movement and the Brain

Chapter 8: Motivation That Works

Chapter 9: The Non-Conscious Learning Climate

Chapter 10: Better Classroom Learning—Easy as R-C-C

Chapter 11: Getting Your Brain to Work With You, Not Against You: Self-Care

Preface

What's Different in This Edition?

This new edition is more like an overhaul than an incidental revision. Both authors are quite excited about what's in this book, and we're confident you'll feel the same. *Brain-Based Learning* reminds us that if we want better learning and more savvy teachers, we'll all need to be up to speed on how the brain learns. That means we'll be doing things differently, and we'll be doing them better. We will also be invited to stop doing things that have little or no value.

What's in this for you and your students? First, you'll get relevance—everything in this edition applies to the real world and gives you tools to be more effective. Second, this edition is highly readable. The language is learner-friendly, and the text is chock-full of illustrations. Finally, the content is credible. Every claim is backed up by peer-reviewed, evidence-based studies. You can be confident that what you learn and apply will work. Here's how each part of this book will make a difference in your students' lives.

In **Part I**, you'll get a brief overview of the fundamentals of brain-based learning. The first chapter, on how your brain learns, is clear, straightforward, and easy to digest. Yet it distills the entire process of learning. The second chapter addresses one of the biggest challenges in education: How do we teach such a wide variety of learners? We know that everyone is unique, but is that a result of our genes or our environment? The answers may surprise you.

In **Part II**, we'll dig into the main factors that impact learning. They are your senses, your relationships, and the role of neuroplasticity. Each of these plays a unique and vital role in learning. More importantly, you can influence each of them in ways that contribute to learning and help learners get "unstuck."

A core part of learning is the enhancers or accelerators to the process. In **Part III**, you'll learn about the brain's learning strengths. A big part of the discussion involves shaping and engaging emotions for learning. Active movement also improves learning; we'll explore the question, "How much physical activity do my students need?" Finally, we'll help you crack the "Big Why," to give you biologically based motivation that works in the real world.

The final section (**Part IV**) puts all of this together for you. We know that the learning climate matters, but in what ways, and how much? From a practical point of view, how do we promote better classroom learning? Are there secrets to lesson planning based on how the brain learns? The final chapter invites every teacher to invest in getting their brain to work with them, not against them. Self-care helps educators maintain their vitality and contributes to student success.

Acknowledgments

Props to all my own teachers, professors, and scientists for their decades of support. Always a big debt of gratitude for the never-ending support from my wife, Diane. And, finally, I owe a big debt to the cognitive engine and emotional support of my writing partner on this book, Liesl McConchie. Thank you.

—*Eric*

A huge thank-you to my husband, James, for supporting me in all my professional dreams, including this book. I have immense gratitude for all who have mentored me in my teaching, writing, and speaking endeavors. Your investment is greatly appreciated. And to the brain-based learning guru himself, Eric Jensen—thanks for believing in me. It has been a learning-filled pleasure.

—*Liesl*

About the Authors

Eric Jensen is a former teacher who grew up in San Diego, California. With a PhD in human development, he synthesizes brain research and develops practical applications for educators. GlobalGurus.org lists him among the top 30 educators in the world.

He has authored more than 30 books, including *Different Brains, Different Learners*; *Teaching with the Brain in Mind*; *Teaching with Poverty in Mind*; *Tools for Engagement*; *Engaging Students With Poverty in Mind*; *Turnaround Tools for the Teenage Brain*; and *Poor Students, Rich Teaching*. He co-founded an academic enrichment program conducted in 21 countries and which has produced more than 85,000 graduates. He is a member of the invitation-only Society for Neuroscience, the President's Club at Salk Institute of Biological Studies. To book him as a conference speaker or for trainings, visit jensenlearning.com or email eric@jensenlearning.com.

Liesl McConchie is a former secondary math teacher from San Diego, California. With 20 years of experience training school leaders and teachers across the globe, she has partnered with hundreds of schools and districts to understand the science behind what *really* improves achievement for all students.

She spent over three years in Denmark learning and working within the Scandinavian school system, known for decades as one of the best in the world. She helped create a brand-new school, True North Efterskole, founded on the most evidence-based pedagogical principles. She continues to visit Denmark several times a year to deliver trainings to the staff, consult with the leadership team, and provide individual classroom coaching to teachers.

Today, she speaks at conferences and conducts trainings at schools internationally. Email her at liesl.mcconchie@gmail.com or visit her website at www.lieslmcconchie.com.

Introduction

For many teachers, every day is a bit of a coin toss. Some wonder, "What kind of day is it going to be?" Maybe they hope that today will be one of those "good days"—a day when they actually get through the prepared lesson, they don't have any emotional babysitting to do, and, if it's a really good day, the students actually learn something.

If only there was more to it than just having a "lucky day" every now and then. The "not-so-lucky" days leave teachers wondering whether all the work is worth it. The good days fuel their passion for teaching and the love they have for the students. The question asked the most usually starts with "why."

Understanding how the brain works may be one of the most relevant areas of knowledge for educators today. Everything you do uses your brain, and everything at school involves students' brains. And, luckily, our old way of schooling is fading fast as our understanding of the brain increases. This is great news for tired teachers whose passion and efforts don't always yield the results they want. The more you understand about the brain and how it works, the better you can be at the profession you care so deeply about.

This is also great news for students. Humans are born with a deep curiosity and a drive to learn new things. Unfortunately, our old way of schooling typically squashed much of this drive, which is probably why you don't see too much of it in your students today. There is hope for a return to a way of schooling that embraces students' natural curiosity and way of learning. It is called brain-based learning, and it begins with understanding the organ that drives all learning: the brain.

Brain-based education is learning in accordance with the way the brain is naturally designed to learn. It is based on solid research from brain-related disciplines. It is not "tips and tricks," methodologies based on myths, a well-meaning mentor teacher, or "junk science." It is a multidisciplinary approach built on the fundamental question "What is good for the brain?" It is also a way of thinking about learning. It is a way of upholding your responsibility as an educator.

Brain-based education considers how the brain learns best. The brain does not learn on demand according to a school's rigid, inflexible schedule. It has its own rhythms. If you want to maximize learning, you first need to discover how your students' natural learning engine operates. Many classroom elements we used to think were critical to learning may, in fact, not be very important at all.

Why This Matters

The brain is poorly designed for formal instruction. In fact, it is not at all designed for efficiency or order. Rather, it develops best through selection and survival of, first, what is *effective*, and, then, over time, what is *efficient*. If a particular knowledge, skill, or attitude serves your survival and prosperity, your brain will prioritize that knowledge, skill, or attitude over another, less successful one.

Teachers and school leaders across the globe are rethinking our old models of instruction, which proposed that the best means of molding individuals was operant conditioning (through rewards and punishments). This line of thought was popularized in the 1950s and is still promoted in some schools today. As an example, some school leaders believe the best way to reduce school violence is to build high fences, install metal detectors, reduce student-to-student contact, stiffen the rules, and have a police presence on campus. The associated "three strikes and you're out" type of policies have been shown to be dangerously short-sighted. In 2007, a school in Fairfax County, Virginia, banned all physical contact, including high-fives, between students. The school did not permit a student to touch another, or a teacher to pat a student on the back, or anyone to get a hug. This is an example of a good intention gone horribly wrong.

But humans are creative and emotional; some kids will try to beat the system, and others will just plain get resentful or shut off any love of learning. A more brain-based approach would be to increase classroom engagement, greet all students with a smile, increase (not decrease) social connectedness, and boost involvement in school activities like martial arts, theater, music, and ballroom dancing.

Adamant "old school" policymakers still insist that achieving the highest possible rank in test scores (instead of producing happy, well-adjusted human beings who can think critically, care about others, and innovate) should be the top priority in our school systems. This means that, as teachers, we *must* be able to care for our students better and help them succeed with less wasted effort, fewer distractions, and greater focus.

Brain-based learning reminds us that if we want things to be better, we'll need to be better informed about the brain. We will need to see what happens when we do *this* instead of *that*. Brain research can help us understand learning at a much deeper level. We'll show you what we mean. A student whose brain activity matched the image on the right in Figure A.1 would likely be acting de-motivated. Teachers who didn't know better might assume the student was disinterested. But this type of brain inactivity may be consistent with chronic stress disorder. That's a far cry from being lazy or disinterested.

Our students are not lab rats; they are, of course, human beings. To account for their human propensity to be creative, depressed, oppositional, and motivated, as well as to make conscious choices, we have to take a more sophisticated approach. Consideration must be given to these factors and the diversity of our students' experiences and backgrounds. How, then, would you integrate a simple behavioral reward/punishment system with such diverse human learners? Shouldn't the student who is living with abuse, rage, brain insults, or distress, for instance, be evaluated on an individual basis? How can educators possibly account for all of these differences? The answer is that we

A.1   Stressed Brains Underperform

Impact of Acute Stress on the Underside
of the Brain as Seen with a SPECT Scan

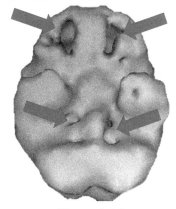

Resting state
(smooth activation)

Stressed state
(gaps in activation)

can't—at least, not with a simple model that uses either a carrot or a stick to motivate learning. The vast range of learners in today's classrooms are subjected typically to one of the following three models.

Survival of the fittest. "You can lead a horse to water, but you can't make it drink." This old adage reflects the thinking of some educators that their responsibility ends at leading the proverbial horse (their students) to water. Thus, if children don't learn to read in the standard program provided, then the children are deficient. The thinking is that if students can't cut it (or don't want to), that's *their* problem. This model reduces the teacher's accountability and allows many learners to "fall through the cracks."

Determined behaviorist. "With enough punishment and rewards, you can get any behavior you wish." This model basically views learners as rats to be manipulated by the whims of the establishment. If test scores are too low, teachers can essentially bribe students into achieving higher ones. If school violence is a problem, then what we need is more guards and metal detectors. This way of thinking manipulates learners and reduces the classroom to a place where students have little voice or choice.

More thoughtful and brain-based. "How can we make the horse thirsty, so that it will *want* to drink from the trough?" This shift in thinking reflects the approach of brain-based educators. A teacher following the brain-based model would ask herself, *How could I discover the learner's natural impediments and built-in motivators so that desired behavior emerges as a natural consequence?*

Give the Brain a Balanced, Healthy Learning Environment

Nature's biological imperative is simple: No intelligence or ability will unfold until, or unless, it is given the appropriate environment. From a biological perspective, it is important to realize that the human brain, like the immune system, is designed solely for survival. Thus, students will do what they need to do to "survive" in the "schoolyard jungle." The negative behaviors they learn—put-downs, deceit, attacking, avoidance, and peer pressure—are to be expected as long as students perceive that their survival is at stake. This precept calls for dramatic changes in the way we organize formal teaching and training. As you continue to read this book, keep in mind this basic brain-based principle: The brain is designed for survival, not typical formal instruction.

Having said that the brain operates naturally on a selection principle, can it still learn through instruction? Of course it can. Every day, learners worldwide develop new skills and knowledge based on a brain-compatible model of instruction.

Brain-based education is about knowing why certain strategies work better than others to create an optimal learning environment. Using research-based practices is a responsibility of any professional. Keep in mind that if you don't know why you do what you do, it's less purposeful and less professional. Relying on common wisdom or experience—while there's nothing inherently wrong with that—may lead to ineffective teaching.

When you embrace the principles in this book, your professional life will change. You will feel more energized, because you will experience more success on a daily basis. You will find it easier to teach your students challenging topics. You will have fewer behavior challenges to deal with. You will prepare lessons more purposefully, and it will become easier. You will design assignments that feel meaningful to both you and your students. You will better know what to teach, how to teach it, and why it is important. As you read this book, you may notice that certain topics and strategies crop up in more than one place. Influences on learning can and do overlap, due to the highly interconnected nature of the brain.

You are not the only one who will benefit from this journey toward a more brain-friendly approach to teaching. Your students will ultimately be the grand beneficiaries. As you embrace and teach in ways supported by our current knowledge of the brain, your students will be more motivated to learn, give more effort to learning tasks, and retain information better. Ultimately, when they are taught in a way that is aligned with their brains' natural way of learning, they will connect with an old, yet familiar feeling: the joy of learning.

Great things are in store for you and your students; let's get started.

Fundamentals of Brain-Based Learning

How the Brain Usually Learns 1

It's likely you have planted something in your life. I have been through my "trial and error" share of flowers, bushes, trees, fruits, and vegetables. Some have been a success, and others were a spectacular failure. My wife says I am a plant hobbyist (vs. a farmer), and she's right.

There are a surprising number of similarities between plants and the brain.

If you're an amateur horticulturist like me, in order for your plants to flourish you need the right **context** (good soil, good weather, the right surrounding vegetation, your well-being). You also need the right **triggers** (e.g., water) to start the growing process, **ongoing processes** (the seasons, pest eradication, fertilizer, etc.), **systems** (routines and devices to automate the watering, managing the sunlight and frost), and **structures** (the sturdiness of the plant itself, staking up the plant, pruning, fencing, grafting, harvesting fruit or vegetables, etc.).

Every time I write all these out, it gets overwhelming. I can see why many of my gardening "adventures" end up with dismal results. It's not easy. But most successful farmers just had to learn one at a time.

Now, given the complexity of this chapter's title, it would be easy to overwhelm even the most determined reader. Toward that end, this chapter will be a bit unusual and even more practical than you imagined. After all, you're more interested in how to help your students learn better than you are in getting your plants to grow well. So, for starters, let's define learning.

What Is Learning?

Learning is the process of acquisition of new (or the modification of existing) knowledge, behaviors, skills, values, or preferences (Gross, 2012). This definition does two things. First it reminds us that there must be *some evidence of the learning*, even if the evidence is a quiet, implicit bias.

Second, it allows for a portion of the learning to be beyond our cognitive awareness. Any given experience may influence our values, behaviors, or preferences, even if we don't recognize it at the time. As an example, a student may dislike a teacher but not always be able to tell you why he or she feels that way.

When someone says to you, "This is how the brain learns," specificity is critical. Putting your hand (accidentally) on a hot stove is one form of learning. Hopefully, you would not do that again. Shaking someone's hand can be a learning experience. Maybe they squeeze too hard or their hand is a bit sweaty and you wonder why. Drawing a hand by tracing it is also learning. Explaining how a hand works to an infant is pretty difficult, so you demonstrate. Doing surgery on a hand is a learning experience in the early days of a doctor's residency. In short, there are many, many ways to learn. This chapter will focus on the core processes typical to learning of any kind.

Third, the complexity of the brain can be overwhelming. Over time, researchers have discovered that greater, not less, complexity is the rule. And since all learning is connected to the brain in some way, it is tough to encapsulate a brain-based approach. Maybe the best way to define brain-based education is through three words: *engagement*, *strategies*, and *principles*. Brain-based education is the engagement of strategies based on principles we currently believe to be true about the brain.

1.1   Brain-Based Learning Is E-S-P

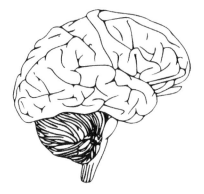

Engagement
(of)

Strategies
(based on)

Principles
(of how the brain learns)

Learning's Big Five Players

Since we all want better strategies for learning, now you see that we have to back up a bit to learn the principles. The foundation to this chapter is your understanding of how five "players" in your students' brains can help inform your understanding of their learning. These five players are **context, triggers, processes, systems,** and **structures**. In its most simple form, here is how we commonly (but not always) learn:

All learning happens somewhere **(the context).** You are with friends, or not. You are indoors or outdoors. You are in school or at home. You are feeling healthy, or not. In short, the "place" you are in is a huge regulator of the learning process. If you are sick, angry, hungry, and feeling hopeless, that is a socio-biological context for poor learning. At school, we hope to always influence the environment (and the student) to be in a positive context for the brain to grow.

The next "player" in the learning "chain" are the **triggers** (internal or external) that activate a **process** (e.g., listening to a conversation, recoiling from a loud sound) that involves one or more **larger systems** (emotional, cognitive, sympathetic and parasympathetic pathways, etc.) running through **multiple structures** (peripheral nervous system, prefrontal cortex, hypothalamus, amygdala, etc.) in the brain (Dang, O'Neil, & Jagust, 2012).

Since the "learning" has obviously been simplified here, let's dig down a bit to make some sense of it.

The end "product" of this five-player sequence is learning, a physical change in the brain that typically constitutes a memory. When it comes to certain types of learning (e.g., the development of a subtle bias), however, we are not sure how and where that learning is stored (Robertson, 2018). Learning may manifest itself as a new skill, new content, or fresh insights (i.e., something new that the learner is now consciously aware of), or it may be an implicit shift that is stored until it gets triggered someday. To ensure we can connect all this better to our workday and the students we serve, let's unpack this "five-player" sequence just a little more.

Context Situates the Learning

The list of potential influences on the learning that is about to begin is huge. The following questions that may arise beneath learners' consciousness hint at the vast number of internal and external conditions that can either enhance or inhibit the entire learning process:

1.2   Learning's Big Five Players

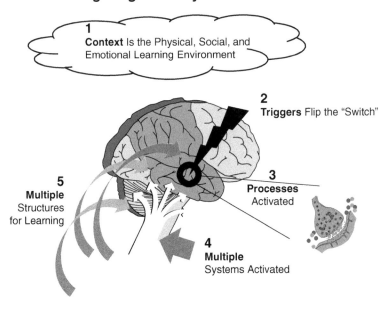

1
Context Is the Physical, Social, and Emotional Learning Environment

2
Triggers Flip the "Switch"

5
Multiple
Structures
for Learning

3
Processes
Activated

4
Multiple
Systems Activated

- Is the learning relevant?

- Is there an urgency to learn it?

- Are my friends here for support?

- How do I feel today? Am I in peak health, or am I a bit under the weather?

- Is the environment well-lit, is fresh air available, and are nearby noises at a minimum?

- Do I have background knowledge on the topic?

- Is there water for hydration?

Triggers Start the Learning

The most obvious of the five players is the appearance of one or more **triggers**. A trigger is a stimulus that may be internal or external. Sometimes triggers arise within our own minds—for example, in the form of a reflection, an insight, or an aha moment. Other times, they come from outside. For example, the trigger for learning might be a student seeing a poster, hearing a loud bang, asking a question in class, reading about the subject, trying an experiment, music playing, hearing a brief lecture, a curiosity "prompt" about new learning, sharing and listening with a partner, joining a new social group, or writing a summary. Any of these events may initiate a change in the brain.

We say "may" initiate a change, because the brain typically gets exposure to countless bits of sensory data (from multiple sources), and much of it is daily "noise." The things that are most likely to get your attention or even "stick" relate to what you perceive as important in your life. For our survival, the brain is designed to respond best to the environmental signals that seem the most relevant (Ritchey, Murty, & Dunsmoor, 2016). Something may stand out because it is fresh or novel. But that won't evoke change in your brain unless there is an added "kicker" to it: relevance. Thus, many effective teachers use a constant stream of relevance to hook their learners.

Classroom examples of triggers are countless. Greeting students at the door can be a trigger for an upcoming good experience. Maybe you lower your voice to draw in the students or tell a compelling story. You might have a noisemaker to get attention (I often use a wooden train whistle). You may flick the lights off for a moment. You might play music when students arrive or use an energizer. You might change your appearance with a hat or scarf, or you might play the role of a famous (or infamous) person for a lesson. You might get extra attention with a suspenseful pause, increased buy-in, or extra relevance.

In short, nearly everything you do can be a trigger, if used properly. Relevant content is a clear trigger for your students' brains (Oudiette, Antony, Creery, & Paller, 2013). The classroom triggers you provide minute after minute, every day of the school year, are influencing what you see and hear from students; and, just as important, their brains are likely changing, too. Some of the changes are temporary, and others may be more lasting. Embrace this new "superpower" as an educator, and make it your goal to be more purposeful about what triggers you employ, how, and when.

Processes Work Within Systems

The next part of the five-player process begins as your triggers activate a **process** within a **system**. Critically, there is no one way that all learning occurs. Some learning is nonconscious, like putting your hand on a hot stove; some learning is like throwing an object to score points; other learning is like listening to a conversation or reading. In short, every different way the brain learns stimulates *a different process in the brain for learning.*

The most common and primary process for learning is the creation of new connections between neurons. The trigger stimulus activates an electrical signal, which originates in the cell body of the affected neuron and runs down through the output (the axon). That electrical signal stimulates the release of neurotransmitters from the end of the axon out into the space between it and other neurons.

This space, known as a synapse, is a highly charged area where those newly added neurotransmitters (serotonin, dopamine, glutamate, etc.) create a powerful messaging system. Those molecules are attracted to, and may land in, the appropriately matched receptor sites on nearby neurons' "feelers," known as dendrites for their tree-like shape.

At this part of the process, there is evidence for genetic contributions to learning. For example, there is some (but not dramatic) evidence of heritability for memory (Barr & Brito, 2013). There is evidence that a genetic variation to increased dopamine at the synapses can induce better learning (Pearson-Fuhrhop, Minton, Acevedo, Shahbaba, & Cramer, 2013).

In summary, the most common form of learning is a perturbated, stimulated cell that dispenses a message to another nearby cell via the interactions in the synapse. So, the activity goes like this: output axon (part of a neuron) releases a message via the synapse to a nearby dendrite, which sends the new signal to its cell body.

Other processes might also include activating the somatosensory pathways (a new thought may activate a "gut feeling"), the stress-response pathway (an energizer activates heart rate, the hypothalamus, adrenals, and gross motor muscles) (Herman, 2012), or attentional pathways (a new thought in the prefrontal cortex, and multiple parietal areas within cognitive systems that help the brain create working memory) (Anderson et al., 2018). Or, maybe the change is a sharp, new attentional orientation or an energizer activity (either may raise norepinephrine and dopamine, along with increased blood flow) (Chaddock-Heyman et al., 2016).

Each process that is activated above works within the confines of a pre-existing system with the brain. But, as an educator, how do you know what to do? You'll want to be mindful of the *brain's process* that you're triggering. Think through (in time, this will become automatic) which pathway you want.

Let's say you want to foster sharper, more focused attention among your students, to activate the brain's own source of focus and long-term memory. That means focus on activating your students' *sympathetic nervous system.* Norepinephrine is the primary neurochemical used by the body's sympathetic nervous system (Hamill, Shapiro, & Vizzard, 2012). It is a catecholamine (in the family of "uppers") that functions to get the brain and body ready for serious, urgent business. So, the actions you use to initiate this process in students' sympathetic nervous system will be ramping up norepinephrine with triggers such as urgency, risk, or excitement (e.g., a timed assignment or energizer). Focus on the specific triggers for this compound (excitement or urgency) and let the magic begin. As you grow, you are going to initiate much smarter, more specific kinds of input to impact *a specific process you want.*

As a counterexample, let's say you wanted a student to calm down. You could make a very subtle change, such as using a quieter, soothing voice, or you could organize a positive change in seating, which may trigger the release of serotonin which is correlated with less aggression, less anxiety and improved learning (Carhart-Harris & Nutt, 2017).

Here are descriptions of a few of your "systems." These include (but are not limited to) your attentional system, your emotional pathways, your stress response system, your gut biome, and your cognitive processing pathways.

1. Your digestive system helps you turn the food you eat into energy. This can affect your thinking and focus.

2. Your respiratory system helps you breathe. This can affect your state of relaxation or anxiety.

3. Your nervous system (including your brain) controls other body systems. For example, your cognitive capacity is part of your nervous system.

4. Your circulatory system includes a transport system (blood) and a pump (the heart) that keeps the blood moving.

5. Sympathetic and parasympathetic pathways typically function as opposites. The sympathetic pathway "sympathizes" with the "moment" and excites the nerves, to enable quick responses to situations requiring immediate attention. Parasympathetic pathways serve to maintain the status quo and promote rest and relaxation.

6. Most of your body and mind systems work together. (Examples are the respiratory and circulatory systems, the muscular and skeletal systems, the digestive and circulatory systems, and the nervous and digestive systems.)

Systems Run Through Structures

Let's begin with what you already know about structures. You may have colleagues that assert their beginners' knowledge about the brain by rattling off words like "neuron," "synapse," "hippocampus," and "prefrontal cortex." Sorry, but that knowledge is rarely useful in the classroom.

Yes, the brain does have mostly stable (but somewhat modifiable) (Oakes, 2017) structures (cerebellum, frontal lobes, amygdala, temporal lobes, gyri, nuclei, etc.). But there's a *lot* more to it, so let's dive in.

Most every **process** runs through multiple systems (sympathetic, digestive, immune, etc.) and engages not one, but multiple **structures** (prefrontal cortex, hypothalamus, amygdala, etc.) in the brain and body (Bogdanov et al., 2017). This is why it is often a fool's game to try to play "Where in the Brain?" when talking about a process like learning or memory.

As an example, if you have eaten something that did not agree with you and you have a rumbling, upset stomach, can this make it hard for you to pay attention? Of course. No doubt you see it happen throughout the year with your own students. So, where then is the problem—in your stomach or your brain? In short, yes, the mind/body structures are the source of the processes, but no single structure

1.3   The Brain's Four Primary Input Pathways

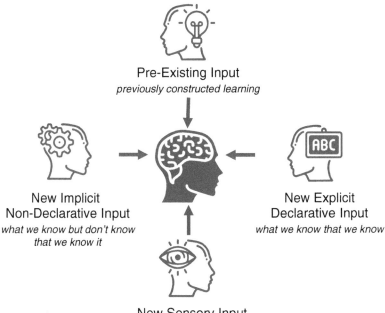

Pre-Existing Input
previously constructed learning

New Implicit
Non-Declarative Input
*what we know but don't know
that we know it*

New Explicit
Declarative Input
what we know that we know

New Sensory Input
what we feel and sense

tells the story. It's a bit like a huge traffic pileup—it can be difficult to know for certain which car caused it all.

Learning (and Transfer) Is Our Goal

Figure 1.3 is an overview and simplified adaption of a commonly held model of how the brain stores what we learn (Camina & Güell, 2017). We have made some modest additions to the model to update it. Later in the chapter, we present a more detailed version. But for the moment, check out the ways the brain's input starts to get learning activated. As you can see in the illustration, there are only four known ways for the brain to get or generate learning.

Four Types of Input: A Deeper Dive

Let's take a look at where the learning starts and walk through the process to find out what happens in students' brains. We will focus on four of the main types of input, or starting points, for an experience that results in some form of learning.

As far as scientists know (at least as of today), input to the brain consists of:

1. existing input,
2. new sensory input,
3. new explicit declarative input (words and pictures), or
4. new implicit non-declarative input (Kump, Moskaliuk, Cress, & Kimmerle, 2015).

Each of these types of input engenders a fully different learning experience, and each has advantages and disadvantages in a school setting.

Pre-Existing Input

The first of the four input sources is simple: Use what you already have in your brain and work with it to come up with something different or better. Imagine you are quietly sitting on the couch, when somehow your thoughts turn to the weird sounds your car has been making for the past several days. As you sit reflecting on this, you eliminate a handful of possible causes—it's not this, it's not that . . . maybe it's the. . . . Because you have a decent consumer's understanding of cars, you are able to do some simple problem-solving or "learning" within the confines of your own brain, without any "outside" support or stimuli. New learning can begin when you simply think about something, reflect on an experience, or reframe something you already know. In the overstimulated world we live in, this form of input is often overlooked and undervalued. A tremendous amount of brain activity and learning happens in the quieter moments of reflection. Pre-existing input simply means you are using what you already know to generate new insights, solutions, or action steps.

IN THE CLASSROOM

How can you maximize this form of input in the classroom? Here are a few suggestions to get you started:

- Have students brainstorm all the things that come to mind when they think of _____ (your current topic for learning). Then have them reproduce these associations in some sort of graphic organizer or visual collage.

- You can even orchestrate the use of pre-existing inputs in a social way: A student can tell a partner something they already know (or think they might know) about a given topic. Their partner then responds with something they think of on that same topic. This verbal back-and-forth with pre-existing inputs reengages relative neural networks and primes the brain for further learning.

- Have students engage in a reflective free-writing activity in which they list all associations they have with a particular topic.

Sensory Input

Sensory input refers to all of our senses—and some people believe there are more than our famous five of touch, sight, hearing, smell, and taste. Remember walking into your grandmother's home when you were little and being met with that familiar smell that told you, "Yep—we're at Grandma's house"? That "learning" first occurred at an earlier visit to Grandma's and was reinforced every subsequent time you visited. Yet you may have also experienced thermoception (sense of temperature), nociception (sense of pain), or equilibrioception (sense of balance) that same special day. Much of what we learn is prompted by some form of sensory input. Many parts of the brain are responsible for sensory reception, including the hypothalamus. The job of the hypothalamus is to assess the body's condition (stress, hunger, lighting exposure, thirst, etc.) and signal the needed changes (Xie & Dorsky, 2017).

You may look out the window in the morning and SEE snow on the ground. BAM! You just learned something about the weather for the day. You walk back into your house after working on something in the garage and SMELL dinner burning. BAM! Next, you just HEARD that you're going out to dinner tonight! Your brain is constantly receiving input from sensory stimuli all around you. It is the context and intensity of those sensory stimuli that impact the kind of learning they produce.

There was a prevailing theory in education for a while that students learned best when material was presented to them in their dominant sensory style, often called their "learning style" (Dekker, Lee, Howard-Jones, & Jolles, 2012). At first, there were only a handful of learning styles—visual, auditory, tactile/kinesthetic, and blends of these three. Yet as of 2013, educators had gone on to identify a total of 71 learning styles (Coffield, 2013)! Yet many educators still adhere to the practice of labeling students (Newton & Miah, 2017), even though the claimed benefits of this approach were never supported (Dekker et al., 2012) and we now have substantial evidence to support a simple but profound idea: Learning is improved when students receive input through *multiple sensory channels* within the same learning experience (Schneider, Beege, Nebel, & Rey, 2018).

Here are a few ways you can utilize sensory input in your classroom.

- Maximize your physical learning space with purposeful visual input: Write questions on the board to stimulate thinking; hang posters summarizing previous lessons; provide a graphic overview of the entire unit to give students the "big picture."

- Use a variety of sounds in your instruction—music, vocal accents. Pause for emphasis before relating an important piece of information; whisper occasionally to pique students' interest.

- During instruction in special subject areas, use special scents (cinnamon, lavender, pine, etc.) that may invite stronger associations.

- Bring props (puzzles, items that reflect a particular period of history, objects that enhance math understanding such as manipulatives, etc.) for students to hold, examine, and figure out. And, yes, there are times when tasting can fit right in with a lesson (such as a science lesson on acids, which taste sour, and bases, which taste bitter) or a special time of year.

IN THE CLASSROOM

Two Types of Explicit/Declarative Input

Recall the last time you sat in a workshop, watched a tutorial video online, or listened to someone give you directions to a restaurant. These are all declarative, or explicit, inputs (Eichenbaum & Cohen, 2014). They consist of facts, knowledge, stories, or experiences. They are often categorized as either *episodic learning* or *semantic learning*. Let's start with episodic learning.

Episodic learning (the "where") means your brain is designed to remember the "address" where you experienced something (Moscovitch, Cabeza, Winocur, & Nadel, 2016). From a survival perspective, the location of the event—Are you with friends or not? Are you near food sources or not?—may be relevant. And if you ask someone, "What did you have for dinner three nights ago?" the usual response begins with, "Let's see, *where* did I have dinner that night?" As this example illustrates, our brains often encode the content of *what we did* with *where* we had the experience. Thinking back to the place can help us remember the particulars of the event. And the more intense our sense of that place or the stronger our associations with it are, the better our recall is (Zeidman & Maguire, 2016).

Our brains form stronger memories of the "where" when it is less "diluted." For example, you probably recall the first time you rode a

IN THE CLASSROOM

Episodic learning is continually occurring for you, because no matter where you are, you're in a specific place. That place might be at home in your kitchen, at school at your desk, or in your car. So how do you take advantage of the episodic capacity of the brain?

Stop "contaminating" the locations your students learn in and provide more variety with greater distinctiveness and do it more often. To your students, the "where" memory cue is not just a "what," such as "I was at school today." It can be more precise: "I sat *with my team* and worked on our math problems." Or, it could be, "I was *up in front of the class* today sharing my story about how my grandparents from Vietnam were involved in the war decades ago." To engage this capacity within your students, periodically rotate *where they sit in class*. Use learning stations. Ask students to take seven steps, partner up, and talk while standing (vs. seated most of the time). Allow students to recreate scenes from history or literature, or have them create skits in their foreign language class. Any time students are acting something out, they are engaging in episodic learning.

bike better than the 389th time you rode a bike (unless there was an emotional event). Novelty was key on the first bike ride, but much less so on the later rides. Some might call this life-learning, or learning that happens as you go about your daily activities. Literally everywhere you go and everything you do is *some sort of* episodic input.

Semantic learning (the "what") more closely resembles the structured learning of facts, concepts, and knowledge about the world we have acquired by means other than personal experience (Osada, Adachi, Kimura, & Miyashita, 2008). These inputs—the names of state capitals, elements of the periodic table, math facts—if not well "packaged" with other forms of input, often stand alone as isolated inputs in our classrooms. As a result, they are not very meaningful to students, and recall tends to be weak.

All of this particular type of learning (declarative, semantic, explicit) is word and picture-based. It means, "What did you see and hear?" It is also the type most talked about, researched, referred to, and, of course, tested. Why? *It is the easiest to measure.*

To support your students' word-based learning, use what the brain does well. Teach students simple memorization skills. Teach students to act out the content. But maybe the best technique (the one that is most interesting to students and a strong aid to memory retention) is the use of stories. Any time you can tell a story (especially an interesting one) about the content you're teaching, you feed the brain's hunger for meaning and tales. Have students create a story that personifies things they're learning about in their math and science class (". . . and then the electron said to the proton . . .") to embed learning in an episodic make-believe narrative. Students are traveling their semantic pathways when they read a text or when they use flash cards to take in new math facts, spelling words, or foreign vocabulary.

IN THE CLASSROOM

Implicit/Non-Declarative Input

You might be surprised how much "learning" is happening outside of your conscious awareness or without direct instruction (Yang & Li, 2012). A student who unconsciously perceives a teacher's tone of voice and body language to lack warmth has "learned" to not approach that teacher for help. That is implicit learning. You are constantly picking up on cues from your environment and the people around you as to how you should feel or behave. For example, the darkness of an alley may give you a twinge of apprehension and prompt you to take a different route. Or the sound of laughter from the other side of the room may make you curious enough to try to see what's so funny. Or walking in on two people having an intense conversation may make you feel uneasy and want to head right back out.

IN THE CLASSROOM

Play-embedded learning is a powerful way to utilize implicit learning. Search the internet, or your colleague's repertoire, for activities and games that facilitate learning. Students playing a dice game might not recognize they are actually learning addition, multiplication, or patterns. Have students compare, contrast, and discuss two similar objects. They will implicitly be building their vocabulary and literary skills. Teach students a song or a dance embedded with content knowledge, life skills, or procedural tasks (e.g., the five steps to cleaning up after group work).

Researchers have labored for decades to sort out each of the many types of learning (there are more than a dozen). The problem with nearly all of the learning categories is that there is overlap (Wang, Mao, Li, Lu, & Guo, 2016; Taylor, Krakauer, & Ivry, 2014)

As soon as you think you know *what type of learning* occurred, you can label it. It was "another day at the park" (It was an environmental experience, so it was episodic. Right?). Naturally, you can find it also has qualities of another types of learning—definitely sensory, procedural, implicit, and so on. By now you may have gotten enough clues to realize that when someone uses the phrase "how the brain learns," your first question might now be, "Learns what?"

The difficulty in labeling a specific type of learning (and hence describing the specific pathways it takes) is akin to trying to nail Jell-O to a tree. In addition, the learning ages, too. Some of what we learned when we were younger (about monsters, Santa Claus, etc.) gets replaced with updated or more sophisticated models of understanding. Other early learnings (e.g., a traumatic experience) may lie dormant yet still shape the rest of our lives. Some memories simply fade due to lack of use. This is another way of saying that there's a timeline to most of our learnings as they become dormant, disappear, or get revised as we move through life.

For now, let's accept that most types of learning also include other types that often "go along for the ride." So, for the moment, we can say that the general "map" of types of learning might include multiple

1.4   Learning Happens Almost Everywhere in the Brain

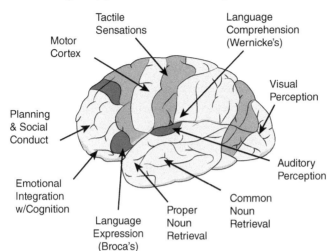

types. Now it becomes more obvious that *what* we learn is a lot easier to understand than *how* we learn. This is because we often have no way of knowing when exactly learning is happening; we simply know later that it did happen somehow (Loonis, Brincat, Antzoulatos, & Miller, 2017).

What we can confidently say is that multiple inputs can create change in the brain, indicating learning of some kind (Zatorre, Fields, & Johansen-Berg, 2012). Knowing that every form of input is creating change and learning in the brain is the beginning for you. You are now learning how to be purposeful with the inputs you orchestrate for the students in your class. Having said that, we all have to keep in mind the bigger picture. The brain works like a world-class orchestra; different instruments working together to produce the astounding effects. In fact, under certain circumstances, learning involves nearly every part of the brain. Figure 1.4 reminds you of how many areas of the brain can learn.

Putting It All Together

Now that you have a basic understanding of the inputs, let's walk through the process again and see how the other players we mentioned earlier (context, input processes, systems, and structures) become involved in a learning experience.

Let's take a look at sensory inputs and how the other players interact with these kinds of triggers. You generate or receive sensory input in the form of something you see, smell, taste, hear, or feel; your sense of balance (proprioception), your sense of comfort, such as your level of hunger (or satiation); and others.

These triggers activate a complex process that involves your sensory systems sending information to your central nervous system. The processes might involve somatosensory pathways, the stress-response pathway, attentional pathways, or cognitive systems that help your brain create working memory. As you have learned, these systems employ multiple structures in the brain.

The occipital lobe is primarily involved in processing and storing visual sensory information (de Schotten, Urbanski, Valabregue, Bayle, & Volle, 2014). The auditory cortex, temporal lobe, Wernicke's area, and Broca's area are involved with language, speech, and sound (Friederici, 2017). The parietal lobe and cerebellum are active during physical movement. The olfactory cortex is the brain structure most associated with smell, while the gustatory cortex is the center for processing and storing information relating to taste (Fletcher, Ogg, Lu, Ogg, & Boughter, 2017).

Beyond Explicit/Declarative Input

Remember that explicit inputs are initiated by life experiences—or what we, as educators, might call direct instruction. Episodic learning is usually rich in sensory information, and therefore our discussion of sensory inputs involves the processes, systems, and structures outlined above. It also often includes the brain's emotional systems, headquartered in the amygdala. Semantic learning, on the other hand, is often less sense-enriched unless a teacher is highly skilled in the art of differentiated instruction. A traditional lecture will only involve the language systems and structures of the brain (i.e., the parietal lobe, the auditory cortex, Wernicke's area, and Broca's area), with the occasional inclusion of visual systems and structures (the occipital lobe) when visual presentations are used.

All explicit and declarative memories are made through the hippocampal areas in the medial temporal lobes. All explicit learning involves the conscious attentional systems of the brain. Implicit learning relies on the brain's ability to make associations between unrelated inputs (Carpenter, Wills, Benattayallah, & Milton, 2016), like when you first connected the three letters C-A-T to a four-legged fuzzy animal with a long tail. Implicit and non-declarative inputs work with the brain's unconscious systems, moderated mostly by the frontal cortex and basal ganglia (Reber, 2013).

Summary

In its most simple form, here is how it generally works. Learning always takes place somewhere, so it all starts with **context**. Then, **triggers** activate a **process** that involves one or more **systems** operated by various **structures** in the brain. Now, in the upcoming chapters, you'll be able to place this better into context and see how the many types of learning, in the many circumstances, play out. More important, you'll learn how you can become far more effective in your work by working with the brain, instead of against it.

Why Each Brain Is Unique 2

Let's say you are falsely accused of a crime. One of the first things an investigator will do is check out the crime scene (maybe your house or place of work). Of course, the investigator wants to find fingerprints. Your fingerprints are the impression left by the friction ridges of your fingers. They are unique to you. Your fingerprint may be used as a security access point to your smartphone, a safe vault, and other high-security systems. It is a valuable piece of evidence at a crime scene, so if your prints are found, the police can likely build a case against you. Let's hope that never happens.

But just as your fingerprints are uniquely yours, your brain is equally unique. The old belief was that most brains were "typical," with the rare exceptions of those with "biological differences." Current research says only about 10% of human brains can be categorized as "typical" (Mazziotta et al., 2009), and even those have varying features. Decades ago, we thought most kids were "typical" and just a few had measurable brain differences.

But the scientists (like Dr. John Mazziotta, founder of UCLA's Brain Mapping Center) who study tens of thousands of brain scans will tell you that most of the brains are "atypical" or have "issues" or might not be accepted into a typical research study looking for "healthy" brains. In fact, the whole paradigm is now turned upside-down.

2.1   The Old Paradigm vs. the New

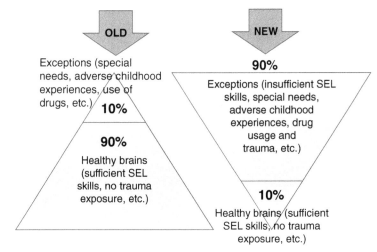

Source: Mazziotta et al., 2009.

With fingerprints, it is your finger that leaves an impression on a surface. Your prints are always the same and will be for the rest of your life. Your brain, however, works differently. There are many influences that make an "impression" on your brain and contribute to its uniqueness. This chapter will introduce you to five of the most prominent factors that make an impression on each person's brain, with the result that there are differences among all of us. These five factors are age, genetics, environment, gender, and luck. Figure 2.2 reminds us that there is no way to rank these factors; each of them can be a deal-maker or deal-breaker when it comes to how we turn out.

Age

It probably comes as no surprise to you that the brain of a 4-year-old is vastly different from the brain of a 74-year-old. As we grow, develop, and age, our brains undergo a lot of change, especially during the years we are in school.

From your own experience in the classroom or with other children, you might intuitively know that our attentional systems expand as we age. In most cases, a 14-year-old can focus on a task for longer than a 4-year-old can. A rule of thumb is we can focus on a task for approximately the length of time (in minutes) equal to our age, with some variance of course. As adults, we tend to reach a maximum attention span of around 20 minutes. There are exceptions, of course.

2.2   What Makes a Brain Unique

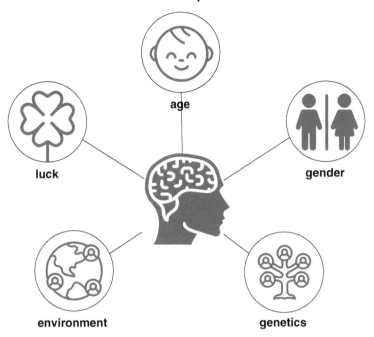

Our age also impacts our motivation. Since we are highly motivated by topics that are biologically or behaviorally relevant (Oudiette, Antony, Creery, & Paller, 2013), you can see how age influences our motivation in terms of pursuing rewards. This is why, as a reward, stickers might work for a 4-year-old, but they won't do the trick with young adults in a university class. If you had to choose whether to relate your lesson to a video game or the stock market, I trust you'd make the right choice for a classroom of 8-year-olds and go the other route for a classroom of 40-something adults.

Other changes happen to our brains as we age. First, an older brain has far less gray matter than a younger brain. This result of aging supports our understanding of cognitive decline in later life. Our brains also decrease in volume as we get older (after growing into adulthood), with some areas shrinking more than others. Working memory seems to be one area that keeps most of its size, losing only approximately 5% of its volume. On the other hand, the nucleus accumbens—the headquarters for the brain's motivation and reward systems—experiences an average decrease in volume of 25% (Jäncke, Mérillat, Liem, & Hänggi, 2014). What does all this variance by age have to do with teaching? Well, it should guide you, as a teacher, to learn what is relevant for the developmental age of your students.

Ask your colleagues, your friends who have children, and your students themselves: "What is the hottest trend for 13-year-old kids right now?" Or "What does every 6-year-old want to have?" Do your research, and then find a way to connect those topics to your subject matter.

In working with young learners, try to limit content, lectures, and cognitive activities to periods of 5 to 8 minutes each. In working with adolescents, try to keep content-input sessions to no more than 15 minutes long. And with adults, no more than 25 minutes in length is recommended for content sessions. After each focused learning period, conduct an elaboration activity, such as mind mapping, pair shares, or model building. Provide downtime by granting a recess or by leading students through a light physical activity such as walking, stretching, deep breathing, or cleanup.

Genetics

How much do your genes impact your brain structures and functions? Although the exact answer depends on which scientist you ask and what structures and functions you are talking about, the consensus is that our genetic makeup plays a major role in forming our unique brain structures and cognitive functions.

A study of 10,000 twins showed that identical twins were far more similar in terms of brain structure than fraternal twins were, with correlations of 0.85 and 0.60, respectively (a correlation of 1.0 would mean they were 100% matching). In another study of twins, it appeared that the volume of gray matter and white matter in specific brain regions was highly heritable, at 82%–90% (Gu & Kanai, 2014). "Heritability" refers to the likelihood or degree of genetic "transfer" from parent to child.

Heritability of certain genes can increase our susceptibility to heart disease, some forms of cancer, Alzheimer's disease, depression, ADHD, and more. But remember, susceptibility does not equal causality. Most cancers (including breast cancer) have a genetic heritability under 5% (Anand et al., 2008).

There is no doubt that our genetics can predispose us to exhibit certain mental, as well as physical, traits. Even our IQ is influenced by our genes. However, genes can also be modified through our experiences. Many of our lifestyle choices (diet, exercise, stress, etc.) can modify our genes. For example, chronic inflammation can tamper with your genetic makeup. Because of this and for other reasons, according to some of the most liberal estimates, our genetic makeup is only 30%–50% inherited from our parents (Plomin, DeFries, Knopik, & Neiderhiser, 2016). Thus, the role of genetics in our lives is not as large as you might have been led to believe. Your DNA is not your destiny.

The heritability of your parents' IQ, for example, may be influenced by your socioeconomic status. The higher your socioeconomic status, the greater the likelihood that you will have a similar IQ to that of your parents. Why? Well, greater wealth can be seen as providing a greater protective factor against adversity and stress, as well as ensuring a good education and access to more robust health care. Thus, our genetics lay the foundation for our unique brain, but our environment shapes a good portion of the rest.

In your classroom, if you currently are or will be working with students from poverty, remember that the heritability of those students' parents' IQ is low; it's actually under 10%. This means that, if a student comes from poverty, no one on your staff should think that because the student's parent is "not very bright" there is any reason to assume the student will underperform. Environments (which we'll discuss next) matter *more* to students from poverty than they do to middle- and upper-class students (Tucker-Drob & Bates, 2016; Tucker-Drob, Rhemtulla, Harden, Turkheimer, & Fask, 2011).

Environments

Nearly 20 years ago, a now-famous study revealed that London cab drivers, who possessed a highly developed memory of the streets and routes around their sprawling metropolis, also possessed a large hippocampus. The hippocampus is one of the most critical structures for learning and memory in the brain. The longer a cabbie had been in the profession of navigating London's 25,000 roads, the bigger his or her hippocampus, suggesting the importance of complexity, relevancy, and repetition of this particular type of task to "growing" the corresponding area of the brain (Maguire et al., 2000). This proved not only that our brain structures can change, but also *how* they can change and that the changes can make us smarter.

There is now an exciting field of study that bridges the "nature versus nurture" debate. This new science, epigenetics, explores how our environment *can influence our genes* (Gottesman & Hanson, 2005). Early research suggested that environmental triggers only either suppress genes or allow them to express their message. But researchers now

2.3 Genes or Environment? Both!

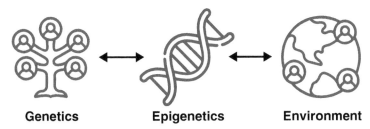

Genetics	**Epigenetics**	**Environment**
Over 99% of your genes are the same as those of everyone around you.	Your lifestyle, behaviors, habits, and events can modify, alter, or damage your genes.	Your social, physical, emotional, and cultural world is unique.

know that some types of environmental-impact messages are passed from parent to child. For example, pregnant rats that were exposed to a toxin gave birth to male offspring with significantly reduced fertility. That defect persisted among the rats' descendants for four successive generations, even though only the first generation's mothers had been exposed to the toxin (Crews et al., 2007).

The current research is showing that the old question of "nature versus nurture" (i.e., "Which factor is more dominant in human development—our genes or our environment?") is usually answered with a resounding *both*! Looking at the nurture side, there are several ways our environment impacts the uniqueness of our brains. Three important categories consist of (1) experiences outside our control, (2) experiences within our control, and (3) experiences in a social culture.

Experiences Outside Our Control

It is an unfortunate reality that some of us (and thus our brains) are simply born into tough circumstances that influence the uniqueness and functionality of our brains. For starters, we may have been exposed to toxins—from air pollution or unsafe drinking water to any substance (alcohol, nicotine, or drugs) a fetus might be exposed to in the womb. Other factors include the food we eat as children, the safety of the neighborhood, the randomness of acquiring certain congenital diseases—the list goes on. Some of these influences (e.g., fetal alcohol syndrome) have long-term effects on our brains. Others can have less of an impact if we adopt new, healthier lifestyle habits, such as a better diet.

Experiences Within Our Control

As we age, we develop more autonomy over our life choices and thus have more control over the factors that continue to make our brains unique. Eventually, we determine our nutritional habits, substance use, sleep patterns, stress levels, work environment, living conditions, exercise routines, and many other influences. Each of these has neurological effects that impact our physical health and our cognitive functioning. This is where we can leverage our brain power.

Some experts say that 40% of your daily life experiences are your habit choices (Wood, Quinn, & Kashy, 2002). Being intentional with these choices can help mitigate some of the effects of the environmental influences outside your control. Let's briefly explore four major factors that impact the brain: drugs, sleep habits, diet, and exercise.

Drugs (Prescription, Street/Illegal Use, and Over-the-Counter)

Most every drug, prescribed or not, can damage your brain. Be sure you understand what's happening to the brain with substances most commonly used by students. Many drugs are addictive by definition because they initiate the release of dopamine from the brain's reward centers (headquartered in the nucleus accumbens) (Volkow & Morales, 2015).

The danger is, any time you ingest a product that mimics your body's natural responses, you risk dysregulating your existing healthy systems. For example, with continued use, you may become more tolerant of a certain drug until you need far more of it than you bargained for originally. That increases the risk of side effects that you may have dismissed at first.

The most purchased over-the-counter products are NSAIDs (Nonsteroidal Anti-Inflammatory Drugs). These include aspirin, naproxen, and ibuprofen, with brand names like Aleve, Excedrin, Motrin, and Advil. NSAIDs are an example of common interventions that can, for some people, entail serious risks. The risks include heart attack, Reye's syndrome (potentially fatal encephalopathy), adverse stomach and intestinal reactions, bleeding, liver disease, ulcers, kidney failure, and perforation of the stomach (Ong, Lirk, Tan, & Seymour, 2007). If pain or inflammation is an issue for you, it might benefit you to consider other sources for pain relief, shorter time frame usage, or much lighter dosages.

Alcohol is a central nervous system depressant that depletes brain function. In fact, having three or four drinks per day can decrease the production of the number of new cells *by nearly 40%* (Anderson, Nokia, Govindaraju, & Shors, 2012). Also, alcohol turns into sugar, which will be discussed later in this chapter. Alcohol can be addictive, and addiction creates greater risk of damage to brain functioning (Sachdeva, Chandra, Choudhary, Dayal, & Anand, 2016).

Tobacco products continue to morph into new and attractive options for young people. The traditional cigarette or tobacco chew have seen new players, like e-cigarettes, enter the field. Vaping, Juuling, and whatever methods of nicotine delivery will come next introduce harmful, addictive substances to the brain. Using tobacco increases the risk of at least 14 types of cancer. It also accounts for about 25% to 30% of all deaths from cancer and 87% of deaths from lung cancer (Anand et al., 2008). As you can see, the influences on the brain that are non-genetic (environmental) can have a continuous impact. Figure 2.4 highlights the breadth of that lifelong impact.

Sleep

Sleep matters! You've likely been there before—after a night (or two, or three) of little to no sleep, your energy levels are low, you struggle to focus, you can't remember things as easily, and you're in a bad mood. And then there are the secondary effects—reaching for sugary foods or drinks to compensate for the lack of energy and skipping your exercise due to feeling so tired. These are all things you can feel and are aware of when you get insufficient sleep. But there are also effects on your brain that you might not notice.

Poor sleep patterns reduce the ability to focus on a task (Ma, Dinges, Basner, & Rao, 2015). The prefrontal cortex, a key brain region for

2.4   Our Experiences Often Modify Our Genes

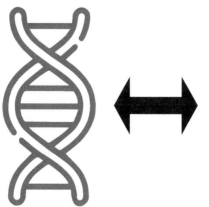

- ✓ Diet
- ✓ Exercise
- ✓ Disease Exposure
- ✓ Homeopathy
- ✓ Social Contact
- ✓ Microbiome
- ✓ Therapeutic Drugs
- ✓ Toxic Chemicals
- ✓ Psychological State
- ✓ Seasons/Weather
- ✓ Drugs of Abuse
- ✓ Economic Status

Source: Kanherkar, Bhatia-Dey, & Csoka, 2014.

higher level cognition, seems to become a major casualty of sleep deprivation (Killgore, 2010). Sleep deprivation affects emotional regulation, fostering depression and unhealthy reward-seeking tendencies (Goldstein & Walker, 2014). Poor sleep habits also decrease neurogenesis, the brain's ability to produce new brain cells (Mueller, Meerlo, McGinty, & Mistlberger, 2013). To sum it all up, sleep impacts the cellular, molecular, and network systems of the brain that are involved in learning and memory formation (Abel, Havekes, Saletin, & Walker, 2013).

Diet

Everything you know about a healthy diet for physical well-being is also true from the perspective of mental functioning. Fruits, vegetables, protein, and other foods rich in omega-3 fatty acids, folic acid, and antioxidants, are great for learning. Proper hydration has been connected to better cognition and even improved mood (Masento, Golightly, Field, Butler, & van Reekum, 2014). The foods that especially benefit the brain are those that are packed with medium-chain triglycerides. These "good" fats are found in avocados, cold-water fish (e.g., salmon), macadamia nuts, Brazil nuts, and coconuts. Your brain is over half fat (Chang, Ke, & Chen, 2009) and uses fats for many functions, including energy (Ota et al., 2016).

Sugar, and foods that metabolize into sugars (white bread, white rice, and other carbohydrates), might create a short-lived "high" that leads to briefly increased cognitive functioning. But this is definitely a case of the short-term benefits not being worth the long-term consequences. Aside from increasing our chances of diseases such as diabetes (Anand, Nath, & Saraswathy, 2014), cancer, and heart disease, too much sugar slows down our production of new brain cells (Beilharz, Maniam, & Morris, 2015). It also slows down our brain functioning, which can ultimately lead to neurodegenerative diseases such as Alzheimer's (Matos, Macedo, & Rauter, 2017).

Exercise

Students who are physically active have better memory, better attendance, better classroom behavior, and better academic performance (Michael, Merlo, Basch, Wentzel, & Wechsler, 2015). The good news is we only need 20 minutes of high-intensity exercise daily to reap the benefits of neurogenesis (Jeon & Ha, 2017), but getting more than that throughout the day can help improve attention and learning.

We will be unpacking all the research on the importance of physical activity for learning in a later chapter, but for now we'll just say that (a) schools should make physical education a priority and (b) teachers need to use more active learning in their classrooms. You'll get dozens of movement ideas in Chapter 7.

Experiences in a Social Culture

If humans happily existed in total isolation from one another, we might be able to pause our conversation on environmental factors here and move on to our next topic. However, we are social and communal beings, and our interactions indeed affect our brains. In brain scans, a "lonely" brain looks and acts differently than a brain with strong friendships or a tight family connection. When you experience strong social connections, your brain releases oxytocin—a hormone that facilitates feelings of safety and trust (Stanley & Adolphs, 2013). Both the oxytocin, and the brain structures that are activated when you feel socially connected, improve cognition (Hutcherson, Seppala, & Gross, 2014). One of the reasons this helps cognition is that someone who feels connected and safe is more likely to turn to others for help—in students, being so inclined can provide a huge boost to their level of achievement (Ryan & Shin, 2011).

This is a stark contrast to the cortisol released in the brain of someone who is feeling isolated, bullied, or simply not accepted by others. Cortisol is a stress-related hormone that has been linked to negative physical and emotional health (Stanley & Adolphs, 2013). A student who feels alone or unsupported by his or her peers in a classroom might be dealing with the fear and anxiety of dealing with classmates' sarcasm, teasing, or bullying. All of these factors guide our understanding as to how our social culture contributes to the uniqueness of each and every brain.

IN THE CLASSROOM

Learn about your students' family life and home environment. Understand what they bring with them to class every day from their family of origin. Teach them the importance of a well-balanced diet, daily exercise, sleep, avoiding substance abuse, and other things that can help them develop healthy brain habits. Foster social awareness and support among your students for people who are different than they are, and make it clear that there is zero tolerance in your classroom for teasing, bullying, or other disrespectful behaviors.

Gender

How much of our sexuality matters? Is it determined entirely by our genetics? Around the world, scientists continue to debate. Here is the most current understanding we have about how gender impacts the uniqueness of the brain, including brand-new information on the transgender brain and those who experience same-gender attraction. The bottom line is this: Gender differences *do* show up in our brains.

Yes, it is still true that men have more total brain volume than women—by about 8% to 15% (Ruigrok et al., 2014). In the past, people have claimed that certain brain regions—especially regions of high interest to educators, such as the amygdala and the hippocampus—are larger (or smaller) in men than in women. Many of these claims still hold true—women have larger hippocampi, caudate nuclei, and anterior cingulate gyri. Men, on the other hand, have larger amygdalae. However, when overall brain size is controlled for, nearly all gender-specific influences become inconsequential (≤5% gender difference) or disappear altogether (Jäncke, Mérillat, Liem, & Hänggi, 2014).

Homosexual and Transgender

Generalizations within the field of gender get less concrete when we enter the subcultures of homosexuality and transsexuality. Here is why—the research on transgender brains is relatively new, inconclusive, and contradictory. Much of the disagreement is a result of small sample sizes, the significance of whether the study participants have already undergone hormone treatment, and the prevalence of homosexuality within the transgender community (Smith, Junger, Derntl, & Habel, 2015). Disentangling all these factors is a challenge for even the most skilled neuroscientists.

Here are some of the trends coming out of the research. Sexual orientation and gender identity both seem to be influenced by testosterone during the prenatal period. They appear to be masculinized by an exposure to testosterone or feminized by an absence of testosterone. This environmental factor, combined with studies showing that genes also play a role, provide further evidence for the proliferation of epigenetics (the ways that environmental experiences can influence both the functioning and structure of our genes) (Roselli, 2018).

But it is not just the prenatal environment that influences the brain of homosexual and transgender individuals. Evidence suggests that the more older brothers a person has, the more likely that person is to be homosexual (Roselli, 2018). This underlines the power of culture and the potential of the home environment to shape our sexuality. In addition, there is some evidence that during hormone treatment, the brain structures and systems of transgender individuals at least partly adjust to the characteristics of their desired sex (Smith et al., 2015). So hormones seem, to some degree, responsible for "sexualizing" the brain even into adulthood.

Another study, however, concluded that brain volume and gray-matter ratio among male-to-female transgenders were congruent with our understanding of a male brain. The researchers' conclusions suggest the male-to-female transgender brain is not "feminized" but rather looks more like the brain of a male (Savic & Arver, 2011).

While we wait for the neuroscientists to clarify the details of unique brain features based on gender, sexual orientation, and gender identity, there is plenty we can do as educators with what we already know. Clearly there are social and cultural factors that influence the brain functioning of individuals based on how safe and accepted they feel.

IN THE CLASSROOM

What matters more than the physical/scientific differences among your students? What matters is whether that student is surrounded by peers and teachers who respect her and treat her with compassion. Create a safe environment in your classroom for all students. Teach and model empathy, tolerance, and compassion.

Be aware of the gender identity and sexual orientation of the students in your classroom. Let them know they are safe and accepted in your classroom. Create and enforce a zero-tolerance policy for any form of bullying or teasing. Reflect on any gender-based biases you yourself might have, and work to eliminate them. A starting point might be this practical book for your students: *The Gender Quest Workbook: A Guide for Teens and Young Adults Exploring Gender Identity* by Deborah Coolhart, Rylan Jay Tesla, and Jayme Peta (Instant Help Books, 2015). Obviously, your staff would like a different resource. Check out *Why Gender Matters: What Parents and Teachers Need to Know About the Emerging Science of Sex Differences* by Leonard Sax (2nd edition, Harmony Books, 2017) .

Is there any part of you that believes girls can't be as good as boys at math? These types of bias in a teacher can impact students' efficacy, dreams, choices, and, ultimately, future achievement.

Luck

You might have been surprised to see luck on the list of major factors that make an impression on the brain. If so, hear us out. The student who wins the lottery to attend the prestigious charter school in his (or her) area is lucky.

Why? Because it was a lottery.

Some students "win" the "parent lottery" and are born to two loving, financially stable parents who provide enriching experiences for their child. Some students don't win the parent lottery, are born into circumstances steeped in instability, suffer chronic and acute stress, and are exposed to multiple traumatic events (divorce, eviction, loss of a family member, etc.). Some students live just a few miles from an imaginary line dividing the weakest from the best public schools. It is, unfortunately, bad luck.

The student who is randomly assigned to a class led by a passionate, caring, committed teacher who is well-informed on how to design and deliver her curriculum based on how students best learn will likely excel academically. Why? Because of his or her pure luck in being placed in a class with that teacher. (. . . Unless there has been some manipulation behind the scenes, perhaps by parents who are highly involved in organizing and leading school events. Then, it is not just pure luck.)

Sometimes luck is pure luck, and other times it can be influenced by choices that increase the probability of certain "lucky" experiences. You might say the person who is hit head-on by a drunk driver and sustains serious brain injuries experienced pure bad luck. You would probably be right. Add in the details that the person was driving at 3 a.m. on a dark two-lane winding country road, during poor weather, on New Year's Eve, and you can see how *even choices within our control* may partly affect our chances of being "lucky" versus "unlucky."

Acknowledge how luck has been distributed to the students in your classroom. Some of your students have no doubt been fortunate over their lives, while others have been less so. Be sure you are not unconsciously rewarding students who have been recipients of good luck, just as you should not be withholding from students who have experienced more than their fair share of bad luck.

IN THE CLASSROOM

Conclusion

The old paradigm of learning was, essentially, that the brain you were born with is the brain you get. You get either a good one or a bad one, or maybe one that's somewhere in between. For educators, the best news to come out of the new paradigm is not just that each brain is unique in so many ways but that our brains are changing every day. Your brain, and the brains of your students, can and do change. Unlike your actual fingerprints, your brain's "fingerprint" is different than it was last year, last month, and even yesterday. What is even more exciting is knowing how to purposefully influence these factors to help us better serve our students. That is what the rest of this book is about—how to use what we know about the brain to maximize learning.

So, the next time you feel exhausted, or the next time you're at a loss as to how to help a student, remember: There is hope. How a student showed up today does not define how he or she will show up tomorrow. Change is happening every day, both for your students and for you. The solution to poor behavior or a lack of focus could be as simple as (for you or your students) eating a well-balanced meal or (for your students) doing a quick learning activity that gets their body moving. This chapter began with five broad factors that alter the brain: age, genetics, environment, gender, and luck. Clearly, as a teacher you have the greatest influence over the school environment. Each of your daily choices, the habits you form, and the learning you orchestrate is either helping or hurting student learning capacity. The upcoming chapters will give you the tools to make more savvy choices, so stay with this. The best is on the way.

Laying the Foundation for Learning

How Our Senses Impact Learning 3

Let's begin with a few simple questions about senses.

- Do you ever have issues with pollen or asthma?

- Have you ever been carsick?

- Ever had one of those moments where you smelled something but could not identify it?

- Have you ever experienced a "gut feeling" about a situation?

- Have you ever had the sensation that someone was watching you?

- Have you ever stood near a waterfall and felt exhilarated?

In each of these instances your body is telling you that something is "wow," "different," or "off." Your body has sensory detectors that are designed to keep you informed about the world you live and learn in. This chapter is about not just the most popularly discussed senses, but *all* of them.

It is becoming more widely understood that we have more than the standard five senses: sight, sound, touch, taste, and smell. In fact, some experts suggest that we have up to 20 different senses. That may seem crazy to you, but for scientists a common mantra is, "If we can't measure it, maybe it does not exist." Yet of course, for centuries, no one had an empirical way to measure any emotions at all. Today, thanks to scientific technological advances, we know that when you feel a certain way, specific brain structures are far more active (electrical activity) and there are clear, measurable changes in chemical releases in your brain and body (e.g., more stress is correlated with higher cortisol). That's why our senses are so important; our bodies and brains are impacted by sensory stimuli, whether that impact is easily measured or not.

What we can reasonably measure (there are, of course, a dozen or more ways to do that), we will provide evidence of. That often comes from studies with a control group and an experimental group. Researchers can do a pre- and post-test and find out whether the intervention in the experimental group had any effect on student learning. That difference gets us closer to the *effect size*. Throughout this book, you will see an occasional reference to the "effect size" of a particular strategy or teaching principle. An effect size is simply a number that tells you the impact an intervention (or you) has on student learning. An effect size of approximately 0.4 to 0.5 has been equated to about one year of academic growth. Clearly, a higher effect size is better than a lower one, but an effect size is just one, of at least a half dozen, ways to measure the impact something or *someone* has on student learning. To learn more about the role of effect sizes in making informed pedagogical decisions, how they are calculated, and why they matter to teachers, get a complimentary deeper dive at www.lieslmcconchie.com/effectsize.

Okay, back to our senses! When it comes to multisensory input, you should know that our brains are wired to pay conscious attention *to only one input at a time* (e.g., when you watch a movie, you often don't usually notice the soundtrack . . . until you *do* notice it more than the scenes in the movie). This tells us that while we can be wildly attentive to any one sense, most of the incoming overall sensory information is being processed nonconsciously. In short, throughout the day, most of what students experience consciously is just the tip of the sensory iceberg. We simply don't have the brainpower to effectively "multitask" by focusing on two, three, or four senses at a time. The brain is not designed to do that. That's why most of the sensory input we receive is not registered consciously.

Senses Are Signals

A sense is any conduit through which your body can perceive itself or the outside world. Eat a substantial meal and you will experience satiation—the sense of feeling full. Walk outside early in the morning and your thermoception—sense of perceiving temperature—will process that cold air on your face (Sengupta & Garrity, 2013). Ever had that feeling that you were running late to an appointment, even though you hadn't looked at a clock? That was your chronoception, or sense and perception of time (Carstensen, 2006). Can you feel it acutely when the air is dry or humid? That sensation, hygrosensation, is even present in worms (Russell, Vidal-Gadea, Makay, Lanam, & Pierce-Shimomura, 2014).

Have you ever been carsick? You can attribute that unpleasant experience to your equilibrioception, your sense of balance. It comes from your vestibular system, in your inner ear. Have you ever known someone who seems to have a really good sense of direction? Humans possess proprioception, or awareness of the position and movement of the body. Then there is nociception, which detects the painful stimuli produced by physical events, such as stubbing your toe, or psychological events, such as the experience of social rejection. The "sense of internal pain" is as real as it gets (Woo et al., 2014). That's why even our mood is impacted by our senses. As an example of this, pleasurable sensory stimulations can protect us from mood disorders such as depression (Canbeyli, 2013).

Why is any of this significant to you as an educator? First, many of these sensory inputs have a direct impact on learning. If you don't have a high awareness of others around you, you'll likely get labeled as having low social intelligence. If you do have a good grasp of those around you, you'll likely do well in school (Meijs, Cillessen, Scholte, Segers, & Spijkerman, 2008).

And when it comes to awareness of the body's position and movement, or proprioception, students who have difficulty with proprioception often also have difficulty reading. Why? Because poor proprioception involves problems tracking one's body in relation to the ground (Han, Waddington, Adams, Anson, & Liu, 2015). This makes it hard for readers to similarly track the words on a page. There is strong support for the value of tracking-based activities in school, such as pointing and cross-crawls, especially with emerging readers (Anderson et al., 2013). Activities like balancing on a beam, walking along a drawn path, and pointing to various objects around the room improve both balance and reading skills.

In one study, participants were given two independent reading tests—one while *holding* the screen they were reading from (making use of proprioception), the other while only looking at the screen. They read significantly faster during the test in which they were physically connected to their reading material (holding the screen) (Mihelčič & Podlesek, 2017).

Other senses could influence learning as well. It is possible that chronoception, one's sense of time, is a factor in excessive student tardies. Students' levels of satiation (their sense of feeling full or empty—i.e., hungry) most likely have a large impact on student achievement. Here is why: Drinking provides less satiation than eating, and consumption of beverages is up 20% compared to the caloric intake through solid foods over the past 30 years (Martin, Hamill, Davies, Rogers, & Brunstrom, 2015).

Smell

Another sense that impacts learning is our sense of smell. One explanation as to why aromas have such a strong impact on the brain is the close proximity of the olfactory bulb (a protuberance of the brain near the nose, which processes smell) to the limbic system (which is linked to emotion and level of excitement) (Johnson, 2011). Some of the more stimulating aromas are lemon, peppermint, orange, and rosemary. Many of these have been shown to improve attention, cognition, and memory (Sellaro & Colzato, 2017). Peppermint, for example, contains menthol, which provides the brain with more oxygen (Meamarbashi & Rajabi, 2013). Conversely, lavender, chamomile, rose, and bergamot are some of the more calming aromas. Lavender has been shown to reduce stress, improve sleep, and build trust (Rhind, 2012; Sellaro, van Dijk, Paccani, Hommel, & Colzato, 2015). Even with small amounts of just the right aroma, you can prime the brain to respond a bit differently.

IN THE CLASSROOM

Are you striving to build relationships based on trust between you and your students? Place a few sprigs of lavender in a cup on your desk to foster a more trusting relationship when they sit down to discuss something with you. Want to help students feel comfortable on the first day of school? Want to calm their nerves on test day? Explore similar uses of scent. How you use aromas in your classroom will depend on school policy, student allergies, and other resources available. Consider your options, and choose what will work best for you and your students.

Air Quality

Perhaps even more than the scent of the air, the quality and purity of the air impact the brain and, consequently, learning. People inhale up to 15,000 liters of air each day (Wood, Burchett, Orwell, Tarran, & Torpy, 2002). Any contaminants present in the air can have an effect. As an example, carbon dioxide (CO_2) emissions can be very harmful—they can impair cognitive and behavioral development, increase the likelihood of developing a respiratory illness, and cause multiple chronic diseases (Perera, 2017). Poor air quality hurts learning and concentration in schools, plus they are a health hazard for kids and teachers (Daisey, Angell, & Apte, 2003).

Students who attend schools in areas with high vehicular traffic experience less cognitive development than students who attend schools in less trafficked areas (Sunyer et al., 2015). Why? Because more nearby traffic creates more air pollution—both on the playground and in the classroom—and air pollution is a developmental neurotoxicant. It negatively impacts working memory, attention, and general cognition.

Placing plants in your classroom can help filter (and even absorb) some of the pollutants present in the air. Some of the most effective plants for classroom air filtering are spider plants, snake plants, peace lilies, and bamboo palm (Wolverton & Wolverton, 1993). They contribute substantially to the microbial abundance and diversity in the built environment, and they absorb toxins at a high rate (Mahnert, Moissl-Eichinger, & Berg, 2015).

IN THE CLASSROOM

Negative Ionization

Have you ever heard of "negative air"? In spite of its label, negative air is a desirable thing. The air around us is electrically charged by many environmental factors, including cosmic rays, friction caused by air movement, radioactive dust, ultraviolet radiation, and atmospheric pressure changes. In densely populated areas, the atmosphere's healthy balance of positive to negative ions can be disrupted. "Ion" refers to any atom or molecule with a net positive or negative electrical charge. Human activity, it seems, destroys negative ions and ultimately reduces the amount of oxygen in the air. Smoke, dust, smog, pollutants, electrical emissions, heating systems, coolers, and traffic exhaust are all culprits. The air can become too highly electrified (i.e., contain too many positive ions), and the human reaction to it is counterproductive to learning.

The more negatively charged our air is, the better (Wallner, Kundi, Panny, Tappler, & Hutter, 2015). When the electrical charge in the air is too positive, it can cause you to feel groggy, lethargic, sleepy, or depressed. Have you ever noticed that when you stand in front of a waterfall, step outdoors just after a rain, stand atop a mountain, or just get out of a shower, you feel fresh and energized? In such cases, you may be enjoying the benefits of negative ionization.

Ion levels have been studied for their ability to speed recovery among burn victims and asthma sufferers, to stabilize alpha rhythms (brain-wave activity that is calm and restful), to positively impact reactions to sensory stimuli, and to reduce serotonin levels in the bloodstream (you may recall from Chapter 2 that serotonin is a stress hormone). Higher levels of alertness and an improved sense of well-being are definite learning enhancers. The primary message about aromas is this: Whether you "smell" it or not, what you are inhaling matters.

The three main sensory contributors to learning are sight, sound, and touch. There is evidence supporting these three factors as the main physical environmental factors that impact attention, problem-solving, and memory in the classroom (Xiong et al., 2018). Although a deep investigation into the effects of *all* sensory inputs would be beyond the scope of this book, a thorough discussion of the three main contributors in a school environment should help you derive some useful strategies. Figure 3.1 reminds us that there is the strongest evidence for the core physical environmental factors (sight, temperature, and acoustics), even though other senses play a part.

Sight

Approximately 80% of our sensory inputs are visual in nature. The main visual factors in a classroom are (1) physical environment and decorations, (2) lighting, and (3) seasonal impacts on learning. We open with a mention of the two mediums of sight: constant (ceiling/window lighting, teacher, and classroom walls) and intermittent (people and objects that move around). Our focus will be on the medium present for the greatest number of hours: the lighting.

The Physical Classroom Environment

Step into a classroom, and immediately your brain consciously and unconsciously begins to process the physical environment. It might

3.1   Core Physical Environmental Factors

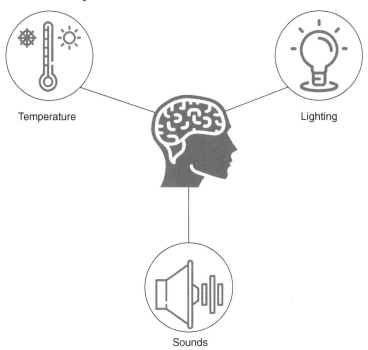

Temperature

Lighting

Sounds

conclude, *Wow! There is a lot going on in here*. Other classrooms communicate, *This feels more like a prison cell*. Or perhaps the feeling internalized is *It feels cozy in here*. There are many factors that contribute to the overall message a classroom sends to the brain—color, peripherals, decorations, and more.

Since the brain gives preference to novel stimuli, introducing more color into the environment can be a welcome change from the traditional black writing on white paper/board. Color has the ability to influence emotions, so it is important that you be purposeful in selecting the colors you use when decorating a classroom, designing a visual presentation, or creating handouts. Red is often subconsciously connected to negative emotions such as failure and anger. The colors most associated with positive emotions are yellow and white. In general, bright colors are associated with positive feelings, whereas dark colors are more commonly connected to inward or contemplative feelings (Sutton & Altarriba, 2016).

Peripherals are typically any sign, poster, or object placed on the wall or edge of the classroom. When used purposefully, peripherals can enhance student learning and recall (Lamb, Akmal, & Petrie, 2015).

For example, a poster or mind map summarizing the role of each punctuation symbol can reinforce new learning in language arts. Posting students' completed work on the walls can increase students' efficacy and sense of ownership of the classroom. A compelling question written on the side board that previews tomorrow's lesson can unconsciously pique students' curiosity and their motivation to be in class tomorrow. A poster that features a positive quote about perseverance may be unconsciously absorbed by all students and impact their choices for the better.

IN THE CLASSROOM

As you scan your classroom, can you verify the purposeful role of everything you see? Colorful and instructionally supportive environments are worth your time. Be aware that more is not always better when it comes to decorating your classroom. An overly decorated classroom can contribute to a condition called "cognitive load," or an overwhelmed working memory system that makes it difficult for the brain to process and store new information (Fisher, Godwin, & Seltman, 2014; Choi, Merriënboer, & Paas, 2014).

Lighting

Lighting strongly influences vision, which strongly influences learning. The right lighting helps make your students' eyes more comfortable in the classroom, which contributes to optimal learning. Even though we are rarely conscious of it, fluorescent lights have a flickering quality and a barely audible hum, which can have a very powerful impact on some of your students via the central nervous system.

Students who are exposed to fluorescent lights for extended periods of time (such as a full school day) are at greater risk of illness, dental cavities, poor academic performance, tardiness, and more. Lighting also impacts mood and can contribute to mental health challenges, including depression (Jean-Louis, Kripke, Cohen, Zizi, & Wolintz, 2005). The optimal light source for learning is natural light. Unfortunately, many school buildings were built before adequate research on lighting was widely available. Figure 3.2 illustrates what adequate natural lighting can do for learning.

3.2   Students in Classrooms With Longer Exposure to Daylight Show Greater Improvement in Math and Reading

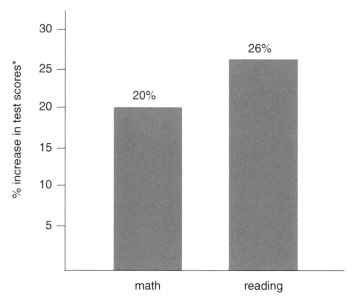

* as compared to students in class with the least exposure to daylight

Source: http://www.h-m-g.com.

The best-reviewed research on the impact of brighter daylight versus dimmer fluorescent lighting is quite compelling (Heschong, 2001). Researchers studied thousands of students in three states. Controlling for all other influences, they made the following findings:

1. Students with the most daylight in their classrooms progressed 20% faster on math tests.

2. Students with the most daylight in their classrooms progressed 26% on reading tests in one year compared to those with the least daylight.

3. Students in classrooms with the largest window areas progressed 15% faster in math and 23% faster in reading than those in classrooms with the smallest window areas.

4. In classrooms that had a well-designed skylight (one that diffused the daylight and allowed teachers to control the amount), students improved 19% to 20% faster than students in classrooms without a skylight.

3.3   Students in Classrooms With Larger Window Areas Show Greater Improvement in Math and Reading

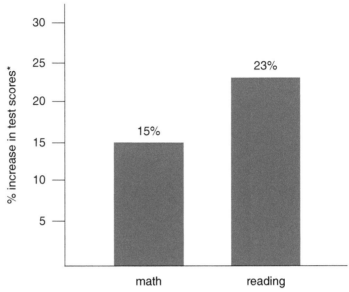

* as compared to students in class with the smallest window area

Source: http://www.h-m-g.com.

IN THE CLASSROOM

Regardless of classroom construction, there are many options available for schools and teachers to capitalize on these findings. First, find opportunities for students to be in natural light. Send them on a walk and talk around the building. Move their group assignment to a table in the school quad/courtyard area (if you do so, create clear expectations for students about not disrupting other classes and staying within certain boundaries). For inside the classroom, you might try requesting alternative forms of lighting, perhaps replacing the current lightbulbs or supplementing your classroom fixtures with lamps or other forms of overhead lighting.

Most students perform best with bright light, so limit long stretches of overhead projector use, movies, and other practices that require a darkened classroom (Xiong et al., 2018). If your dominant format of instruction involves the lights being turned off, it is time to collaborate with your colleagues to diversify your instruction. Yet, some students prefer less brightness and do better in a more light-neutral environment, so be sure to pay close attention to any head movement, squinting, and apparent stress among your students that would indicate bright light bothers them. Always ask, never assume, if they might prefer to sit away from the window. Their stress may go down and their learning may go up when the lighting is more comfortable to them, or they may have just wanted to move away from another student.

Seasonal Lighting

Seasonal affective disorder (SAD) is a pattern of reoccurring depressive episodes that commonly occurs during the winter months. It is estimated that the prevalence of SAD ranges from 1.5% to 9%, depending on one's geographic latitude (Nussbaumer et al., 2015). Those who suffer from SAD demonstrate impaired working memory, cognitive processing, and motor speed (Hjordt et al., 2017). Moreover, these challenges can remain prevalent during the bright summer months, when their depressive state is in remission.

Bright light therapy or infrared light treatment can reduce the risk of SAD by up to 50% (Nussbaumer et al., 2015).

Depending on your geographical location, it might be beneficial to acquire a light box or other form of natural light for the classroom. Encourage students to be outside in the winter months during daylight. Unless it is dangerous to their health due to extreme low temperatures, continue to hold recess, PE, lunch, and other activities outside during the winter. Be aware of any mood changes you notice in your students as the weather begins to turn late in autumn, and direct students who may have SAD to trained professionals for help.

IN THE CLASSROOM

Sound

It might sound obvious to state that being able to hear well in a classroom is important for learning. The acoustics of a classroom need to function in a way that allows for students to hear the teacher, for students to hear each other, and to minimize any extraneous and distracting sounds. A closer look at the variety of ways in which students' hearing is challenged in schools might have you wanting to make some adjustments.

Extraneous Sounds

The presence of extraneous sounds in a learning environment can significantly disrupt students' ability to process and store language. This effect has been repeatedly shown in studies of schools near airports, train stations, airports, and other sources of intermittent loud noises (Klatte, Meis, Sukowski, & Schick, 2007).

The presence of peripheral sounds can even be coming from inside the classroom. Loud air conditioning units, the humming from the fan of a computer, an overhead projector, or other electronics can also prove to be distracting. As one might suspect, the louder the sound, the greater the negative impact on students. This is likely due to the impact the volume has on students' central nervous systems—it provides too much stimulus, to the point of becoming a mild stressor that impairs cognition (Xiong et al., 2018).

Even those students having a side conversation in the back of the room are creating extraneous sounds that impair both the processing and storage of auditory information by other students. This is true even when students can still perfectly understand what the teacher is saying, amid the distracting side talk (Klatte et al., 2007).

IN THE CLASSROOM

If your school is adjacent to a loud source of extraneous noise (e.g., an airport or a highway), try to minimize the sound by keeping the windows and doors closed. Turn off any machine in your classroom that is not being used. Establish the expectation that students do not talk when others are speaking. If a student begins to talk while you are teaching, pause. Wait for him or her to stop talking (with a warm facial expression) and then proceed with your explanation. Be persistent in establishing this pattern early in the school year, and students will learn the life skill of respectful listening.

Music

Have you ever noticed how music can impact your mood, speed, efficiency, and even learning? If not, then see whether you press the gas pedal just a bit more heavily the next time your favorite upbeat song is played on the radio. Or consider the playlist you reach for when you are trying to fall asleep versus going for a workout. Music's impact can be felt on heart rate, as measured by the pulse, which tends to synchronize with the beat of the music we're hearing—the faster the music, the faster the pulse. A wise teacher can use this tool to help facilitate the ideal state for a learning activity.

Use calming music in your classroom to reduce anxiety or nervousness before a presentation, prior to exams, during a writing activity, or when students come back from recess with too much silly energy. Use energizing music to get students feeling alert and motivated for a challenging task. Consider how the lyrics of particular songs could emphasize important life skills and lessons you are teaching your students. Remember to be aware of students' preferences when it comes to style of music, and notice if any of your students seem to be stressed by the sensory stimulation the music provides. Seat those students away from the speaker, and possibly decrease the volume.

Keep in mind that lyrical music is best reserved for activities that do not involve memory formation (cleaning up; finding a partner; passing in papers; greeting at the door; celebrating mastery of a concept; moving into group seating arrangement, etc.). When students are engaged in an activity that requires more executive functioning (writing, reading, worked problems, group discussions, assessments, etc.) non-lyrical music is best, at a low volume. The lyrics of music, even in the background, can interfere with processing and contribute to cognitive load.

Another powerful way to use music in the classroom is to anchor specific songs to a particular behavior that supports student learning. This is especially helpful for tasks you ask your students to do regularly. Be purposeful in selecting the right lyrics and tempo for the particular task that students are expected to do: clean up, pass in papers, line up, move into groups, rearrange the desks, move to the reading rug, prepare their minds and bodies for yoga/mindfulness time, return to their seats, etc. Work with them to learn the cues, and present them with the challenge of completing the task before the song is over.

For an in-depth guide on how music can enhance your efforts in the classroom, see www.lieslmcconchie.com/music. The download contains more details on the science of music, when and how to use music to boost student learning and focus, as well as fabulous song lists, suggestions for speakers in your classroom, and more.

IN THE CLASSROOM

Who Does the Talking?

It's no secret that teachers do the majority of the talking in classrooms around the world. Considering the effect size of classroom discussion is 0.82, it is worth making efforts to balance the teacher/student talking time at around 50-50 (Hattie, 2017). Why is it so valuable to introduce more student voice into the classroom? Well, there is the initial value of simply having a different voice to listen to in the room. Variety and novelty are strong predictors of student achievement (Oudeyer, Gottlieb, & Lopes, 2016). It also encourages more student ownership of the learning experience. Has it ever happened in your classroom that the way a student explained something made more sense to the class than your explanation?

IN THE CLASSROOM

Here are some suggestions to encourage more student voice. To begin with, ensure that you have established a safe classroom environment where students feel safe to speak up and are completely aware of your zero-tolerance policy for any form of teasing or bullying. Be thoughtful in determining what questions or topics to discuss to facilitate more student voice. Allow for thinking time (three to five seconds) after you air a question before asking for responses or calling on volunteers.

Remember to diversify your approach for more introverted students, who might be challenged by speaking to the entire class. Use the think-pair-share strategy to provide them with a safe one-on-one place to share their thoughts. Jigsaws (effect size = 1.20) are a powerful strategy to empower students to be in the teacher role in smaller groups. Become more conscious of all the times you are talking in class, and consider whether that is something a student could do instead.

Touch

There are several ways in which the body is impacted through touch in a learning environment. The three most prevalent are (1) temperature, (2) tactile stimulation, and (3) overcrowded classrooms. We open with a mention of the two mediums of touch: constant (room temperature) and intermittent (people and objects we interact with). Our focus will be on the medium students have to deal with the most: the temperature.

Temperature

The ideal temperature for learning is no less than 68° and no more than 73° Fahrenheit (20°–23° Celsius) (Seppänen & Fisk, 2006). In general, being too hot is worse for learning than being too cold (despite some gender preferences), but both should be avoided. When our bodies are too hot, we experience a decline in both cognitive and physiological functions. Our attention time decreases, and our impulsivity increases; researchers have found this may lead us to perform

3.4   Heat Impacts Learning

1°F Warmer
Air Temps

=

1% Drop in
Learning

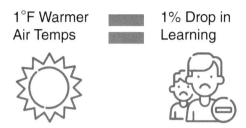

Based on 21 million PSAT scores over 12 years, with students from all
50 states, heat matters. Without air conditioning, each 1°F increase in
outside school-year temperature reduced the average amount learned
that year by 1% on student tests.

Source: Cedeño Laurent et al. (2018), Goodman et al. (2019)

more poorly in cognitive assessments (Gaoua, Racinais, Grantham,
& El Massioui, 2011). When our bodies are too cold, our concentra-
tion, vigilance, memory, and reasoning are affected (Taylor, Watkins,
Marshall, Dascombe, & Foster, 2016) and we make more blunders
(Pilcher, Nadler, & Busch, 2002).

The impact of heat on student learning and test performance has
been tested among more than 10 million students. The results are
as you might predict: When temperatures go up and there's no A/C,
test scores go down. In classrooms without air conditioning, for every
1° Fahrenheit higher the outside school-year temperature, students

**IN THE
CLASSROOM**

If your current classroom environment does not have a proper air
conditioning system, here are a few suggestions to get you started on
the path to a cooler room:

- Use social media and other communication channels to inform the
  community and school district of the poor learning conditions you
  are working to improve.

- Start a GoFundMe campaign (or other crowd-funding source) to
  raise enough money to purchase sufficient cooling equipment.

- Purchase a high-quality fan. If it doesn't provide enough cool air,
  place a tray of cold water or ice at the bottom of the fan. The air
  that it blows over the water and ice will be cooled. Some teachers
  report that even just tying ribbons to the fan so that everyone can
  see it's on makes students feel cooler.

learned an average of 1% less, as measured by PSAT scores (Goodman, Hurwitz, Park, & Smith, 2019). What's more, high indoor temperatures, such as during a heat wave, can have immediate effects on cognitive functioning among young adults (Cedeño Laurent et al., 2018).

Tactile Stimulation

Introducing a new sense to a learning experience often initiates the involvement of other senses too, thus increasing its impact. Each students' preference for tactile stimulation will fall somewhere on the spectrum between a sensory-seeker and a sensory-avoider. Students who are sensory-seekers will seek out more sensory input before information is best received and processed. Sensory-avoiders, on the other hand, can be overstimulated by tactile stimulation. A brain-based classroom would have options for all students.

Incorporating the sense of touch, or tactile stimulation, has more benefits than the ones directly related to touch. For example, it is well known that Braille is an effective method to teach people with visual impairments to read through touch. Those with visual impairments have heightened sensitivity to other senses. But what about those who are not visually impaired? When adults with normal vision were taught to read through Braille, they also demonstrated increased activity in visual and auditory areas of the brain, as well as the frontal lobe, known for its critical role in learning (Siuda-Krzywicka et al., 2016). Through the introduction of tactile stimulation, brain activity in other areas increased. We can see similar findings in fMRI brain scans of piano players watching a muted video of a piano being played—their auditory systems show activation, even though they cannot hear the music (Haslinger et al., 2005).

IN THE CLASSROOM

In the classroom, provide students with more opportunities for tactile stimulation. Do more experiments in science where students get to conduct the experiment rather than just watch the teacher demonstrate. In math, let students use manipulatives to learn their basic arithmetic, geometry properties, and even calculus-based rotations around axes. Have students work in groups to create story boards, dioramas, and so on based on the stories they are reading in language arts. In history, students can build models of ancient structures, 3D representations of their state and/or country, and places of historical or cultural significance. When students build, create, and work with manipulatives, they are creating an additional sensory experience; and they are also enhancing many other senses as well.

Overcrowded Classrooms

Overcrowding in classrooms impacts many of the sensory factors discussed in this chapter. It impacts the noise level, air quality, and limits mobility and opportunities for tactile stimulation and movement. Yet it is an unfortunate reality for too many teachers. The primary result in the brain from overcrowding (assuming all other variables are equal) is the stress of excessive closeness (Shah & Inamullah, 2012). In addition, or possibly as a result of stress, overcrowded classrooms are also associated with poorer academic achievement and behavioral problems at school, as well as the development of learned helplessness—a detrimental mindset that one's efforts do not produce worthwhile results (Evans, Lepore, Shejwal, & Palsane, 1998).

If you find yourself in an overcrowded classroom, consider strategies to create more space. Get creative with your seating arrangements and possibly even your seating furniture. Find the best arrangement given the space you have. Look around your school—is there another location that might be available for your use? An occasional stay-at-school field trip to the library, cafeteria, or auditorium could open up spacing for better movement. Consider your outdoor space also—being in a "green space" can help reduce stress—even if you stay indoors and can only see the green space through a window (Ekkel & de Vries, 2017).

The amount of sensory inputs that students are exposed to in a school environment has a tremendous impact on their learning capacity. A vast majority of these inputs are happening unconsciously; yet their impact may be greater than the ones students are more aware of. The exceptional teacher will give careful consideration to the variety of sensory inputs in his or her physical environment and teaching methods (both conscious and unconscious). He or she will make purposeful adjustments to eliminate any extraneous stressors in the classroom and incorporate elements (like those discussed in this chapter) that can enhance student learning.

Relationships in the Classroom 4

Several years ago, a student of mine was struggling. It was clear that something was wrong; he was simply not hooked into the seatwork. I had used buy-in and other hooks to energize and activate my other students, but this student seemed unmoved and unresponsive. Like an emergency first responder, I ran through my mental checklist of what to do ASAP. But the first thing that jumped into my brain was relationships! I had not done my usual "check-in" with him for several days. I had gotten busy and let that slip. We simply had not connected recently, and that was my first "reboot" step.

I went up to him and privately said, "I can tell something's not right. I am sorry that I haven't checked in lately. That's my fault. Can you tell me what's going on?"

That simple apology and invitation to share opened up the details of a heart-breaking traumatic event from just a few days ago. As I listened, my eyes moistened, and I fought back tears. Hearing his story brought me back to reality. I might be the only person in the world he has to share his trauma with, I realized. I asked him if he might have a moment after class so that we could finish up our interaction.

Perhaps you have wondered, "What do we really know about the brain's biology of relationships?" Or you might want to know, "How can positive relationships have anything to do with a student's behavior?" Or, "Do good relationships always help students do better, or are there exceptions?" On a personal note, "Why was it that when I was a student, I worked harder for teachers that I liked?" These and other "must know" answers will help you make better decisions in your work.

Sometimes a factor divulged in this book may be beneath the skin and more fitting for under the microscope. But this chapter is about the *overt, explicit social interactions that most of us have.* To be sure, there are students (e.g., those along the autistic spectrum) who find relationships quite difficult or foreign to their brain.

As a generalization, this chapter unpacks the validity (or not) of greeting students at the door, intentionally smiling at your students, asking them about their day, and giving a compliment. Relationships in this chapter also refer to having a pleasant conversation with students and offering genuine affirmations. These are the overt factors that impact your relationships with your students—the everyday things you can see, hear, and feel in a classroom. What are the effects in the brain of having a pleasant conversation, giving affirmations, or using any other overt strategies that impact your relationships with your students?

The Biology of Relationships

Understanding the significance of relationships in a learning environment begins with an understanding of how humans are biologically social in nature and seek connection. The absence of such connection is quite costly, as will be explained in this chapter. As the science of relationship is unfolded here, remember the value of modeling healthy relationships—it's one of the best ways we learn.

Humans Are Social Beings

In our distant past (e.g., the Stone Age), humans believed that "outside" tribe members were potential predators or thieves. But those *within your clan* depended on each other for survival. Today, our basic outlook hasn't changed. Humans are social creatures that still depend on each other for survival. While many animals can survive on their own at birth, humans depend on their parents and others for many years. We also need each other, even as we age, for mutual support and to advance our common welfare.

There are two main fields of study that offer valuable information regarding relationships and the brain: behavioral neuroscience and behavioral neuroendocrinology. This research allows us to focus on the actual science of social interactions, particularly as it relates to student learning.

Relationships can range from aggressive (or even predatory) to affiliative (positive contacts, friendships, and social play). Aggressive relationships are exemplified by bullying, entrapment, and abuse. Affiliative relationships are the essence of a quality classroom climate. They foster friendships, social skills, cultural norms, frequent communications, and even social play.

The relevance of this view is that the influencing biological factors—hormones (e.g., testosterone, estrogen, and progesterone)—are primarily genetic, produced in the testes, gonads, and ovaries. However, they can also be triggered by everyday experiences, as well as the biology that maintains our lives (Wärnmark, Treuter, Wright, & Gustafsson, 2003).

The hormone most relevant and important for relationships is oxytocin (Kendrick, 2004). Oxytocin, also known as the "cuddle chemical," can support closer human bonding. It is increased in the mother during pregnancy. Oxytocin is produced by the hypothalamus and secreted by the pituitary gland. In the classroom, it helps students trust each other and lowers the sense of threat (Domes, Heinrichs, Michel, Berger, & Herpertz, 2007). Oxytocin suppresses the activity of the brain region known as the amygdala, the area that processes fear and communicates it to the rest of the brain (Frijling et al., 2016).

Our desire for human connection goes beyond mere survival. The next time you are out in public and experience something funny that prompts you to laugh, notice what people do. You'll likely see people turn and look at the others around them. Whether they are strangers or close friends, humans have a desire to feel connected to each other in emotion-rich experiences.

You might notice a similar response when witnessing a surprising event like someone proposing to their girlfriend at a public event. Everyone looks to those around them, as if saying, "Are you here with me in this moment?" It also happens in times of tragedy and sorrow—"Am I alone here, or is there someone also experiencing this with me?" These experiences are nearly universal.

Our experience with relationships begins when we are babies, with implications that last far beyond those early years of dependency. In infancy, a healthy relationship is formed between parent and child when a parent is attentive and responds to the needs of the child. This healthy attachment that is, hopefully, formed has a long-term impact on the child. Children who experience a healthy attachment to a loving caretaker have significantly better social skills later in childhood, continuing into adolescence (Groh et al., 2014). Unfortunately, not all children are blessed with a healthy attachment in their early years of life.

Examples of Relationships Gone Bad

Foster Care

Children are placed in foster care most often because they have experienced serious abuse or neglect. Some reports indicate that nearly 6% of American children are placed in foster care at some point. These statistics are higher for certain demographics. Native American children (15%) and African American children (12%) are at higher risk of being placed in foster care (Wildeman & Emanuel, 2014). Their lack of consistent, loving caretakers has serious consequences. A caring teacher can help mitigate some of these effects.

RAD

Reactive attachment disorder (RAD) is a severe disorder relating to social functioning. There are two subtypes: inhibited and disinhibited. A child with inhibited RAD will be extremely cautious and wary around others. On the other hand, a child with disinhibited RAD will interact with others, including complete strangers, indiscriminately without the need to be near their primary caregiver. Both inhibited and disinhibited RAD are believed to be the result of stark maltreatment in early childhood (Pritchett, Pritchett, Marshall, Davidson, & Minnis, 2013). Again, notice that there are long-term implications of dysfunctional relationships in the childhood years.

Abuse

Children who are exposed to domestic violence or are abused themselves are at risk of several adverse consequences, both socially and emotionally. For starters, they feel more isolated, anxious, and depressed than their peers. They are more likely to drop out of school and engage in risky behaviors such as substance abuse and violence (Herrenkohl, Sousa, Tajima, Herrenkohl, & Moylan, 2008). The impact continues into adulthood and influences their attachment to romantic partners.

All of these examples paint a stark picture of the possible results of poor or destructive relationships in one's childhood. These youths need caring adults around them. In short, they need *you*. Why? Because you just might be the only caring adult in their lives. And that can mean the world to a student.

Relationship Costs and Benefits

How important are relationships to humans? First, the absence of a sense of connection can make people feel pain. Second, it can lead to losses in social, emotional, and cognitive skills. Finally, poor relationships can lead to bodily inflammation and even cell death. Let's look at each of those costs more closely before exploring the benefits.

Physical Costs

The feelings of *social* pain *and physical* pain are strongly interconnected. To begin with, they show almost identical mappings in the brain. When a person is feeling social pain (usually prompted by exclusion, rejection, teasing, etc.), the experience is similar to physical pain. It is therefore not surprising that physical connection (a hand on the shoulder, a hug, etc.) can ease the sting of social pain.

The reverse is also true: Social connection (feeling like you belong, feeling accepted, respected, etc.) can help heal physical pain (Eisenberger, 2012). In fact, the pain-relieving drug Tylenol, which acts to reduce physical pain, has been shown to also reduce hurt feelings and pain resulting from social exclusion (Dewall et al., 2010). Studies even link low social status to chronic physical and mental health conditions, such as heart disease and depression (Shively, Musselman, & Willard, 2009).

Emotional Costs

Social disconnection has been studied by scientists in relation to feelings of exclusion, isolation, or rejection. All of these experiences increase the levels of cortisol, the primary stress hormone, in the brain (Stanley & Adolphs, 2013). High levels of cortisol are very bad for our physical health as well as our learning potential. Excess cortisol, over time, can lead to anxiety and depression.

Cognitive Costs

It's not just our emotions and body that take a hit from a lack of social connection—it's our brains, too! There is a correlation between those who feel they lack social status and a reduction of gray matter (Gianaros et al., 2007). Social isolation also diminishes neurogenesis (the production of new brain cells) in the hippocampus—a brain region central to learning and memory storage (Hueston, Cryan, & Nolan, 2017).

An absence of healthy relationships has a detrimental impact on our physical, emotional, and cognitive well-being. The purpose of positive relationships extends beyond avoiding these potential consequences. There are significant additive benefits available to those who foster social relationships. Let's consider the same three categories of physical, emotional, and cognitive.

Physical Benefits

People with adequate social relationships (both in quantity and quality) live longer than those with little or poor social relationships (Holt-Lunstad, Smith, & Layton, 2010). The significance of forging strong relationships is equivalent to quitting smoking in reducing your chances of early death. Yes, having solid relationships may prolong your life. In fact, poor social connection is more detrimental to your longevity than obesity. So, if you're going to eat a donut . . . it's better to at least do it with a friend!

Emotional Benefits

Social connection is often defined as the perception of belonging and having the acceptance and respect of your peers (Mikami, Ruzek, Hafen, Gregory, & Allen, 2017). When someone feels socially connected to another, oxytocin is released (Stanley & Adolphs, 2013). This is the same chemical released when a baby is physically close to a parent or loved one. It creates a sense of social trust, leading to a shared feeling of safety. People with strong relationships are consistently happier and experience greater life satisfaction.

Cognitive Benefits

Social experiences activate portions of the brain that are also highly involved in learning, such as the medial prefrontal cortex (Hutcherson, Seppala, & Gross, 2014). In short, people learn better when they feel socially connected to those in their learning environment. These results have been shown across multiple settings, including in the workplace, in hospitals, and in schools.

Physical touch can stimulate the release of oxytocin, so greet your students at the door with a handshake, high-five, or other greeting that involves physical connection. Make eye contact with your students. Truly see them, and smile. Laugh with them. Laughter is one of the fastest ways to connect people together.

IN THE
CLASSROOM

Listen to them. Suppressing emotions lowers oxytocin levels. Withholding feelings and not dealing with them causes stress and other physical ailments. Create a safe atmosphere where students can share their worries and struggles.

Be empathic toward students. When they share about the challenges they are facing, respond by saying, "That sounds really tough. I've felt like that before." Even if you have never had the same *experience*, you likely have felt the same underlying *emotion*. Empathy is about connecting through common feelings, not exclusively through common experiences.

Give them words of encouragement. "I believe in you. I care about you. You can do this. I will be with you every step of the way. I am cheering you on. You have what it takes to be successful at this. I've seen you _____, so I know you have the ability to _____."

When students enter the room, or are transitioning to a new activity, play music with a positive message.

Engage your students in community outreach projects and other volunteer opportunities. Take 10 minutes a month to plan a class-wide random act of kindness for someone on campus (a custodian, security person, nurse, or cafeteria worker).

Meditate with your class for one to three minutes daily. Not sure how to do this with your class? Search the internet for guided meditations appropriate for the age of your students. Or ask other teachers on Twitter what they have successfully tried with class-wide meditation (Magon & Kalra, 2011).

The Value of Role Models

People with greater exposure to healthy relationships are more likely to engage in healthy relationships themselves. We unconsciously learn in our youth the behaviors and habits of relationships by those we interact with and observe. Whether they are positive or negative behaviors,

4.1 Relationships Communicate Answers to Students' Questions

✓ Do I have an adversary in this class?

✓ Will no one help me succeed?

✓ Will I be bullied or embarrassed?

✓ Do I have an ally in this class?

✓ Can someone (e.g., the teacher) help me succeed?

✓ Is it safe to learn here?

we tend to mimic these behaviors later in life within our own relationships. (The brain process used is the activation of mirror neurons, and is discussed further in Chapter 9 on the non-conscious learning climate. Our mirror neurons activate when we observe a person doing something that we ourselves might want to do also.) Of course, we can choose different behaviors than the ones that were modeled for us, but that requires conscious choice and significant effort.

As teachers, we are in a position to be role models to our students. In most cases, teachers are the adults children spend the most time with, from the time they are 6 years old to the time they are 18. This means that teachers have a tremendous opportunity to model—and, thus, teach students—healthy relationship habits.

IN THE CLASSROOM

These three overt and powerful relationship habits should be a part of every teacher's daily practice:

- **Greet students.** A teacher standing at the door, smiling, making eye contact, and offering a handshake (or other greeting) goes a long way in terms of building and modeling healthy relationships. Doing that can help build trust.

- **Use students' names.** Whenever possible, use a student's name and do so in a positive way. It strengthens the relationship, creates a positive classroom atmosphere, and shows that you care (Cooper, Haney, Krieg, & Brownell, 2017).

- **Get personal.** Of course, there are boundaries not to be crossed here, but it is generally a worthwhile strategy to share appropriate personal information with your students (your summer plans, your weekend highlights, etc.). When doing so, mention how important the people with whom you spend time are to you. Discuss what you look for in a friendship, and allow your students to reflect on the same. Remember to keep this a two-way conversation and allow students time to also share with you stories about their own lives outside the classroom.

Perceptions Matter

Words, body language, and tonality all impact a relationship. For most teachers, the early focus is on the students' patterns in these areas. When you feel like you have viable routines in play, increasing self-awareness is your next step.

Words

As someone who has spent decades working with couples, relationships expert John Gottman can predict with 90% accuracy whether a married couple will eventually divorce simply by listening to their conversation for several minutes. How does he do this? He simply tracks the ratio of positive comments to negative comments made in the exchange. If a couple has a 5:1 ratio of positive to negative comments, Gottman predicts they will remain together and have a healthy relationship (Gottman & Peluso, 2018).

Words have the power to build people up or break them down. When teachers use encouraging words and affirm the effort of their students, they are improving the learning experience. Upon hearing those positive words, students will have better self-confidence, they will put forth more effort, and thus they will perform better academically. On the other hand, among students who hear their teachers, parents, or peers speak negatively about them, self-confidence often plummets. This then decreases their motivation to do the hard work required for learning; thus, their ability to succeed is greatly diminished (Alcott, 2017).

Trust-Building

Focus on building trust. If you tell your students you'll have their papers graded by Friday, have them graded by Friday. If you promise five extra minutes of outside time, be true to your word. Broken promises erode your credibility as a teacher (Kidd, Palmeri, & Aslin, 2013). Trust is built slowly through continuous acts of being true to your word. It can, however, be broken in a single moment. So, model making mistakes. You don't have to intentionally mess up, but when you do . . . acknowledge it and share what you learned from it. Your students will appreciate the life lesson. Trust is built through predictable responses, not perfection. If you usually do what you say, and apologize if you forget, you'll still be thought of as a reliable teacher.

IN THE CLASSROOM

Give positive, specific affirmations to students daily. When students follow your directions, engage in an activity, stay focused on a task, ask valuable questions, and so on, be overt in acknowledging them for their positive attitude or behavior. "Wow! I saw you working really hard on that assignment." "Thank you for remembering to bring your signed permission slip." "I just wanted to let you know I appreciate looking out into the class and seeing your smiling face looking back at me."

Use positive verbal constructions when teaching students appropriate classroom conduct. In other words, frame your expectations in terms of desirable behaviors, rather than behaviors to be avoided. A firm but gentle direction to "Remember to walk as a class, with hands to your side, to the assembly" or "Please make sure your cell phone is put away for this next portion of our lesson" will create a better climate and better relationships with your students than saying "Don't . . .," "Do not . . .," or "Stop that!" Students will follow your rules more often if those rules help them visualize what they *should* be doing, not just what they *shouldn't* be doing.

Avoid making derogatory or conclusive comments to students. Statements like "You'll never graduate from high school if you keep this up" or even "Reading is not your strength, but you can do other things well" are never appropriate. It is not your right to label a student or make predictions about his or her future success or failures. Why? Because you have no idea what that student may be going through at home. You also don't know what's "inside" a student. For some, the greater the adversity, the stronger their determination.

To a student who is struggling in reading, you could say, "Let's keep working on this together. I promise, with time, you will continue to get better at reading." To a student who has been acting unmotivated, try to communicate, "I believe in you. I know you can master this and ultimately graduate. I'm going to help you every step of the way. Just continue to show up and try, and you'll be amazed at what you and I can do."

When a student exhibits undesirable behavior, get down on his or her level and say something like, "David, I want you to succeed in this class. I am concerned about your learning. It seems like you are getting distracted regularly by _____ (friends, technology, etc.) around you. I want to help. Let's spend a couple minutes after class today finding a solution to help protect your learning." Notice the focus on David's learning and on a collaborative approach to improvement.

Tonality

Imagine approaching a friend who has been going through a tough time and asking, "How are you doing today?" Depending on her tone of voice, her response of "I'm fine, thanks" could be an expression of gratitude or annoyance. Similarly, a teacher could say, "Listen up, class. I've got something very important to say" in a tone that communicates curiosity or criticism.

When it comes to relationships with your students, using the right tone of voice can be as important as making a physical connection. As mentioned earlier, release of the neurohormone oxytocin, which reduces stress and strengthens the bond between people, can be stimulated by physical touch. A recent study concluded that similar levels of oxytocin are present in children who simply hear their mother's voice (Seltzer, Ziegler, & Pollak, 2010). The implication is that hearing the pleasant tone of voice of a loved one, then—or, perhaps, a kind and trusted teacher—can reduce stress and foster greater connection.

On your smartphone, create a voice recording of yourself teaching. As you listen to it at a later time, pay close attention to your tone of voice. Do you sound happy and excited to be teaching? Do you sound warm and approachable? Do you ever have a harsh tone or perhaps an annoying vocal pattern that would be unpleasant to listen to all day? Work to improve your tone of voice, if needed, and then record yourself again a couple weeks later to check on your improvements. Teachers can cultivate good relationships with their students in many ways. This illustration highlights just a few of those ways.

IN THE CLASSROOM

4.2   Factors That Contribute to Good Teacher-Student Relationships

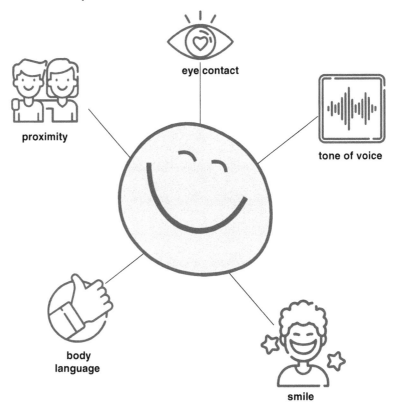

Body Language

It is not just the words that are spoken, and how they are said, that carry our message. Our nonverbal cues often speak louder than our words. Perhaps you have memories from your childhood of a parent standing with hands on hips, eyebrows raised, and lips pursed. No words needed to be spoken (although they often followed)—you knew you were in trouble. A lot can be said through a facial expression, an eye movement, a head movement, or a gesture such as folding your arms.

Body language, especially facial expressions, is a way to express emotions to others. It is a form of feedback to the other person. Based on someone's facial expression, we naturally make inferences about their personality and intentions (Liu, Zhu, & Yuan, 2018). Is this person kind, approachable, and trustworthy? Or does he or she appear rough, distant, and of questionable integrity?

When a teacher gives a scolding look to a student, that student can feel the teacher's disapproval. When a student sees a teacher smiling, the student feels more trusting of him or her (Ueda, Nagoya, Yoshikawa, & Nomura, 2017). And when student trusts their teacher, they are more likely to feel it's safe to ask for help. Not surprisingly, there is a strong connection between students who ask for help and high achievement (Ryan & Shin, 2011).

In addition, people are more likely to comply with a request made by someone who they can see has a positive facial expression, and they are more likely to avoid requests made by someone whose expression conveys anger or another negative emotion (Ruggiero et al., 2017). So, if you'd like to get better results next time you ask your students to read the text quietly to themselves, try saying it with a smile.

IN THE CLASSROOM

Smile. Smile as you greet students at the door, to communicate your pleasure at their being in school today. Smile as you explain the learning goals/plan for the day. Smile as you help students solve a challenging problem.

Make a video recording of yourself teaching. Notice your body language and facial expressions. It is likely you are unaware of what your "resting face" or posture looks like and the message it sends to your students.

Avoid pointing to students with a single finger. Instead, gesture with your entire hand, open palm facing up. This signals a welcoming invitation, rather than a way of picking a student out for criticism or scrutiny.

Recognize and Act on Equity

The uniqueness of every student has been established in earlier chapters. This important reminder comes into play when building relationships with students. There is no "cookie-cutter" recipe for this process. The critical role of equity comes into play as you learn what is needed by each individual student. Continue to ask yourself, "What does this student need to succeed?" Some students need more one-on-one time, while others will thrive in group settings.

Equity Is Not Equality

We all recognize the importance of students getting an "equal education." But equal makes no sense when our students have unique brains, experiences, and needs. All students benefit from positive, healthy relationships with their teachers, but some students simply need it more than others. Some students have less than ideal home circumstances and relationships with family members. There is strong evidence indicating positive relationships with a teacher can compensate for the negative effects of the student's relationships at home (Benner & Mistry, 2007).

Ideally, a child will experience positive relationships both at home and at school. This dynamic creates the optimal setting for academic success. As you consider how to invest your time in fostering relationships with students, keep this in mind: The students with the worst relationships at home have the greatest need for relationships at school.

Students Have Unique Needs

Some might argue that the best approach would be to ensure a teacher spends equal time investing in a relationship with each individual student. That would be true if all students had equal needs. Every child is different and possesses a unique combination of strengths and needs, both as an individual and as a result of their home environment. Teachers must invest the time with students, school counselors, and parents to properly identify the needs of each student.

Some students might need a caring adult to constantly communicate care and concern for their well-being. Teachers can provide that. A coach can provide that. A music director can provide that. These are the students who need to hear their teacher saying every day: "Good morning. I am so glad to see you here today. How was your soccer game yesterday?"

It's smart to invest time in the students you don't connect with as naturally as you do with others. Make an effort to learn about their lives. Listen. Ask questions. Then listen some more. The better you understand your students, the more you will connect with them and expand the boundaries of your perspective. There is evidence that spending just a few minutes a day with individual at-risk students can improve the teacher's view of that student (Driscoll & Pianta, 2010).

While some students might need steady bonding with their teacher, others might benefit from more social connection with their peers. It is not just the student-teacher relationship that predicts school success; students also benefit from strong relationships with their classmates (Mikami et al., 2017). Pay attention during transition times in your classroom—are there students who aren't socially connecting to others? At lunch, are there students of yours who eat alone? These are red flags telling you that a student needs a friend. Identify a student who you think might connect with one who displays a need, and give them a special project to do together to help spark a friendship. Having them help you organize supplies for 5 to 10 minutes might be all it takes.

Promote the social aspects of school. Capitalize on the many opportunities within your class and your school to help students create friendships.

IN THE CLASSROOM

- **Build systems in your own class** that promote social connection: reading buddies, student spotlight, daily social traditions (Monday: share the highlight of your weekend with a neighbor; Thankful Thursday: share one thing you are feeling grateful for this week; Friday: share one thing you are looking forward to over the weekend; etc.).

- **Encourage your school to embrace traditions** that build social connection: assemblies, class names/colors/teams that create a unified identity for each class.

- **Encourage students to participate in small groups** that better meet their needs: tutoring, small learning groups, extracurricular activities at your school or within the community (sports, music, drama, robotics clubs, etc.).

Encourage students to work together. There are very few professions that out there in which people work in complete isolation. You can begin to prepare your students for occupational success right now by allowing them and teaching them how to work together. Cooperative learning strategies are a great place to start (Gillies, 2016). Challenge yourself every day—is it really important that students do an activity independently (and not just because that's how you imagined it), or is this something they could work on with each other?

Are You Using Social Shaming?

Some students lack connection to a caring adult. Others lack connection to their peers. Both of these circumstances can create a feeling of social exclusion for the student. Some of the social exclusion students feel is initiated by other students. And, yes, there are even things good-intentioned teachers do that contribute to feelings of social exclusion and isolation. There are strategies you can implement to eliminate both.

Student-Led Social Shaming

Be serious about eliminating bullying (in class, on the playground, in the halls, and online) among your students. Create a zero-tolerance policy in your classroom for any teasing, bullying, or demeaning sarcasm in a learning environment. Keep at it until disrespectful behaviors are gone! Create a classroom culture where respect is paramount—not just among students, but as modeled by you, the teacher.

Teacher-Led Social Shaming

Unfortunately, a lot of outdated behavior-management strategies, strategies that evoke social shaming, have been passed down to us from earlier generations of teachers. If you have adopted any of the following strategies from the "old school," we urge you to stop.

- Writing students' names on the board
- "Behavior walls" with students' names divided into categories of good/bad students
- Posting grades with students' names
- Green/yellow/red card boards for student behavior
- Using a reward-based "point system" for classroom behaviors (Goodman, 2017)

You might have also been taught to use "proximity" as a discipline tool. Another way to describe proximity is "spatial bullying." It involves using your size and authority in a student's "personal space" to remind the student to stop the misbehavior. There are better options, and we'll get to them in a moment.

Social shaming is a poor way of achieving behavioral change in your students. Instead of motivating students to change, it's more likely to get students to dislike the class or to dislike you personally. Some "hand-me-down" strategies might get you the immediate result you are looking for in a compliant student, but the academic and long-term impact of these strategies can be catastrophic. All of these are counterproductive to your goal of creating a learning environment built on respect, acceptance, and belonging. You can elicit a better response from your students by focusing on classroom relationships as discussed in this chapter, promoting greater engagement, and ensuring the relevance of the work.

The Power of Neuroplasticity 5

It may seem like every time you use the internet, links to articles lure you with headlines trumpeting "Top 10" lists. If we were to give you a "Top 10 list" of brain-based learning "miracles," near the top would be this particular brain event. Your life is better because of this event every single day. You are who you are because this is a big part of your life. Because your students have it, every one of them can grow and improve. So, what is the big "it" for this chapter?

It's arguably one of the most mind-bending discoveries in neuroscience in the last 100 years and, perhaps, the one that is most relevant to educators. This discovery, **neuroplasticity**, is an inherent property of the human brain. It is the capacity of our brains *to change* based on either external or internal influences. Neuroplasticity has unfolded in detail through a wide range of research over five decades, has changed every textbook that delves into human nature, and *should change every educator's thinking worldwide*.

Here's how it works, in a nutshell. Any time a motion, thought, or activity is generated or even a memory is accessed, your brain strengthens or changes the neural networks associated with that activity or memory (Schaefer et al., 2017). How? This happens when electrical impulses are passed from neuron to neuron along the synaptic gap. In other words, the brain's capacity to change (based on external inputs or internal reflections) is what generates our capacity for learning.

The discovery of neuroplasticity may be one of the most hopeful discoveries in the entire field of education. Brains can and do change. Learning can change us. Daily experiences literally change the structure of the brain. Attitudes can change. Beliefs can change. In fact, a clean summary might be: Neuroplasticity is the brain's ability to change (temporarily or permanently) based on influences in the environment or other brains (Tovar-Moll & Lent, 2016).

Why is this important for educators?

For starters, if you want to change a student's negative thinking pattern (e.g., *I'm not good at math!*), it is possible. If you want to prepare students for a challenge that will require consistent focus and effort, it is possible. This chapter will outline the rules of plasticity that guide these changes in the brain and explain why it is critical that you foster these changes in your students. In short, you're about to learn the answer to the question, "In what ways are the brains of your students most receptive to change?" In addition, we will discuss several powerful teaching habits that you can use to bring about rapid brain-based changes.

This chapter features several ways to understand and act upon this paradigm shift in science. We will unpack some of the properties of neuroplasticity, the crucial need for it, and how you can promote it in your classroom.

The Properties of Neuroplasticity

Before you or anyone on your staff starts thinking students can't (or don't want to) learn, let's dig deeper into the rules that guide how the brain makes changes.

Here's what neuroplasticity is and how it varies dramatically based on the person, circumstance, and whether it is creating a better brain (or not).

Neuroplasticity Is Inherent

Plasticity is an inherent (hardwired) property of the brain (Del Giudice, 2015). Inherent property? It might be easy to believe otherwise. Many teachers complain about how hard they work, and yet, "My students still don't learn!" This, of course, is faulty reasoning, because effort (in terms of calories expended), while valuable, has never been a guarantee of desired outcomes in *any* field, much less teaching.

Many other factors besides hard work also determine success in learning, You may recall from an earlier chapter that context begins the whole process. Next up, we include the students' prior knowledge, schema, and brain health; the strategies used (priming, behavioral relevance, chunking, quality feedback, etc.); the teacher's attitude (his or her self-confidence, expectations of students, and beliefs about the value of the learning); and, of course, the quality of the instructor's skill sets.

Neuroplasticity Is Subject to Variability

Just as individual differences contribute to variability in our brain structure and function (Gu & Kanai, 2014), neuroplasticity emerges in different ways in different individuals. Indeed, a growing number of studies suggest that the rules and mechanisms that govern cortical plasticity are more variable than was previously thought.

Why is there such broad variability?

Because neurological change can be initiated by a variety of sources and with varying degrees of intensity. It can be a result of learning something new, practicing a skill, nutrition, exercise, environmental enrichment, or neurofeedback. It occurs when an individual acts on the thought *I want to do this* and then proceeds to engage in guitar lessons, an exercise routine, or a search for a lasagna recipe (Sampaio-Baptista & Johansen-Berg, 2017).

Alternatively, neurological change can occur through internal input. We can influence our brains through self-talk rehearsal—whether negative, such as looking in the mirror every day and telling yourself, "I'm so fat!" or positive, such as announcing to your reflection, "I am going to make this a great day!" (Walter, Nikoleizig, & Alfermann, 2019).

It can also be imposed by positive external factors, such as having a teacher who is exuberantly passionate about teaching his or her class. Finally, it can be imposed by negative external factors. A student might notice a subtle unfriendly nonverbal cue from a teacher, or that same student might witness the teacher shouting at another student in front of the class—each of these negative events literally rewires the student's brain, but to different degrees. Recent research has also uncovered the importance of critical periods, plasticity inhibitors, and neuromodulator systems in determining neuroplasticity (Patton, Blundon, & Zakharenko, 2019).

Of course, age, gender, disease, and genes apply as well (Voss, Thomas, Cisneros-Franco, & de Villers-Sidani, 2017).

To put it all together: Neuroplasticity is always happening, but rarely in the exact same way for every student in your class. There are simply too many factors that make each brain unique at any given point.

Changes Can Be Good or Bad

As hinted at in the previous section, there are two primary drivers of neurological change: Change, whether it is internally generated or externally generated, is either (1) *chosen* by us, through our own volition (or through autonomous habit-like actions), or (2) *imposed upon* us. Either way, the results might end up being healthy (i.e., good for your mind/ brain/body) or unhealthy (Sasmita, Kuruvilla, & Ling, 2018).

Your brain can learn how to heal or hurt itself, as well as be healed or hurt by outside influences. Figure 5.1 helps us make sense of this topic, by breaking down the possibilities and giving some examples.

Neurological change can be a good thing, whether it is imposed or chosen. For example, your students are likely too young to make choices about where they live.

Yet, positive outcomes more predictably result when we make our own choices. When a student chooses a positive friend group, forgives the friend that embarrassed him or her at lunch, or raises his or her hand and asks for support, these (and many other) conscious choices may change the brain because of neuroplasticity.

5.1 Neurological Changes

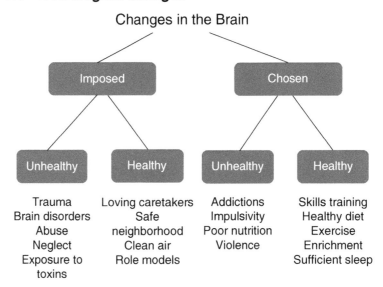

On the negative side, neuroplasticity is largely responsible for the damaging impact of growing up stressed, with constant changes in family members and even the crises of eviction notices. When a 7-year-old student cannot get a good night's sleep because of household or neighborhood noise, lack of heating in winter, or lack of cooling in summer, it affects the way that student's brain works (Klatte, Meis, Sukowski, & Schick, 2007).

Other examples of undesirable causes of neurological change are trauma (childhood neglect, abuse), brain disorders, poor air quality, and exposure to toxins (e.g., lead in the water supply).

Not all negative changes in the brain are imposed from outside. Some are the result of conscious decisions. For example, you could choose to start a bad habit or make unsafe choices. Poor outcomes (negative changes in your brain) might be the result of not maintaining healthy friendships, drinking too much alcohol, developing a gambling habit, using dangerous drugs, and (potentially) battling symptoms of depression. Yes, you can choose to do things that will change your brain for the worse.

By now, you can see that neuroplasticity is critical to our lives. Changes in our brains can be chosen (or not), and they can be good or bad. With that in mind, there are plenty of strategies that can help you get good changes to happen by choice.

Why the Brain Needs Plasticity

Knowing that the brain *can* change leads us to the next question: Why would we want to change anything? The short answer is because we don't learn everything perfectly the first time. In fact, we get a lot of it wrong. Memories, for example, are not as static as you might wish. They are, by nature, dynamic, flexible, and thus prone to distortion (Schacter, Guerin, & Jacques, 2011).

However, we don't always want to change what the brain has learned. Sometimes, it has already learned something quite well, as in the case of the hand on the hot stove. Some types of learning are fairly accurate the first time around; this is more typical of episodic (location-based) or sensory learning. When it comes to declarative (words, pictures, and sounds) or procedural (using hands or body when making, building, or demonstrating) learning, however, we often have some correcting to do. Let's begin with a better understanding of why our initial learning or memories are often wrong.

We Get a Lot Wrong

Most of the time, we go through life only gathering a quick overview, or "rough sketch," of the inputs our brains are processing, subconsciously searching for anything that threatens our survival. Why? We briefly assess the information and environment, seeking answers to important questions like "Is this dangerous?" "Am I safe here?" "Do I need to remember this information to keep me alive?" "What do I need to do to fit in with this group?" Taking a long time to process everything may put your survival at risk.

Much of the time, our brains only need to capture the "gist" of the new inputs to have enough information to keep us alive. As a result, we have developed two distinct cognitive systems: one fast and largely automatic, and the other slower and more deliberate. Nobel Prize–winning psychologist and behavioral economist Daniel Kahneman referred to the fast-acting system (rather straightforwardly) as System 1 (Morewedge & Kahneman, 2010), because it's the one we use first.

If the brain needs more information, however, it will seek out more. In other words, our brains make a quick sketch based on inputs (using System 1) and hold it until we decide to either try to resolve the picture in fine detail (using System 2) or delete it.

As it turns out, we tend to rely quite a bit on "just enough" knowledge to get us through the day. Thus, we continue to get a lot of things wrong. Sure, we keep on living—we avoid life-threatening mistakes—but our individual and societal learning, based on prejudices and false assumptions, sometimes takes a toll. Misperceptions hold on, and often, a wrongly accused person spends years behind bars (Lacy & Stark, 2013). Or, less tragically, a student in English class gets her *there*, *their*, and *they're* uses all mixed up. All of this is a result of the rough draft or "sketch" the brain initially creates.

Surprisingly, even when retrieving information regarding an emotionally charged event like 9/11 or the *Challenger* space shuttle disaster, our brains depend on only a rough sketch of our experience of it (Sharot, Delgado, & Phelps, 2004). In a study by Talarico and Rubin (2003), students wrote detailed descriptions of the experience within a week after it occurred. From three months to three years later, many of the students' retrieval attempts proved inaccurate. Regarding certain details, their recall was only slightly better than a random guess. Even though an emotional experience creates the illusion that you are remembering better, the influence of strong emotions doesn't seem to improve the factual accuracy of our memory (Rimmele, Davachi,

Petrov, Dougal, & Phelps, 2011). In short, your brain remembers *that* the event happened, and the rest is pretty blurry.

The process of forming long-term memories also seems to entail a protection against "information overload," which, over time, leads people to only remember the general gist of what they experienced. The details get lost, forgotten, or just omitted in the memory reconsolidation process (Schacter, et al., 2011). As an example, your students might remember that you learned about plant cells last week, but the details and distinctions between "nucleoplasm" and "cytoplasm" might not survive into a solid memory.

Rough Drafts and Sketches Need Refinement

All learning should be considered temporary;—it is all susceptible to change. This makes sense, because what you believe to be true today might turn out to be not true next week. Your students might learn that Santa Claus is actually their parents. You might learn that your friendly neighborhood isn't so "safe" after all. You might even learn that your political leanings, religious beliefs, or other cultural influences no longer align with your parents'.

We are exposed to new information all the time. Whether this information comes externally (from others, from our surroundings, or from something we read) or internally (from a change in our perspective), when it comes to complex declarative or procedural learning, our rough sketches often need refinement for accuracy.

A quick look at history offers stunning evidence that learning can, and often should, change as more information becomes available. People used to believe the world was flat, it was safe to use cocaine as a numbing agent for children's toothache, and slavery was acceptable. It was once believed (not too long ago) that neurogenesis was impossible, genetics determined everything about a person, and placing a student in a corner with a dunce cap on was an effective behavior-management tool. Neuroplasticity will continue to be the impetus for learning and progress at both the individual and the societal level.

Whatever Students Need, It Can Be Learned

Perhaps the most hopeful implication of the discovery of neuroplasticity is this: In whatever way a person needs to learn, grow, or heal, it is possible. Whether it be a skill, a content area, or a self-regulation toolkit, it can be learned.

If a student needs to learn to read, he or she *can*. Regardless of whether that student is dyslexic, ELL, or below grade level, the skill of reading can, with the right approach, be successfully learned. If a student needs to learn the process of photosynthesis, how to graph a parabola, or how to shoot a layup in basketball, he or she *can*. That is what neuroplasticity is all about—the brain's ability to create new or modify existing neural networks.

The brain's ability to change is not limited to declarative or procedural learning. Neuroplasticity extends to all forms of inputs, to meet an individual's needs to learn *anything*. Students who need to learn how to manage their anger and peacefully resolve conflict *can*. Students who are inclined to be pessimistic, shrug off responsibility for their choices, or be unkind toward others can learn to take a better approach.

How can teachers help this happen? First, modeling positive behaviors goes a long way. From there, direct instruction, deliberate practice, and reinforcing feedback all support the neuroplastic process of learning new life skills.

How to Foster Neuroplasticity

Now that neuroplasticity makes a bit more sense to you, the next question is, "Can we accelerate it?" Yes! There are three key factors that can strengthen or weaken neuroplasticity, as well as influences that can speed the process up or slow it down. Indeed, there are certain conditions that allow for much greater plasticity.

Before we get into those, be aware there are exceptions. A child who places his or her hand on a hot stove typically creates permanent neurological change and is forever wired to believe a hot stove will burn him or her. These and other traumatic experiences, such as child abuse, have the potential to create lifelong change. Even so, research is discovering remarkable interventions that can foster greater neuroplasticity in those circumstances.

Figure 5.2 gives you an overview of the process of fostering neuroplasticity.

The length of this process will vary. Some forms of neurological change happen in an instant, such as with trauma or an epiphany. In the case of learning a new language or being exposed to toxins, it will take much longer for changes in the brain to become apparent. The three most relevant factors that foster neuroplasticity are as follows:

- Readiness
- Coherent construction
- Consolidation

5.2 Guidelines for Fostering Neuroplasticity

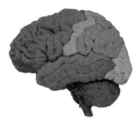

❖ **Readiness**
   (Buy-in/relevance; energizers; meaningful, inspiring goals; clear starting point for learning and progress)

❖ **Coherent Construction**
   (Fast initial learning curve, interdependency [partners or digital], increasing challenge and complexity, pauses to integrate learning and daily focused practice of 10–15 minutes 3–5 times per week, and 8–12 weeks with feedback)

❖ **Consolidation**
   (Ensure quick, clear feedback for error correction after learning, use breaks or sleep, no reviewing; use retrieval practice for 3–5 times over 4–8 weeks.)

Ensure Readiness

In the big picture, we begin with the context for learning. In the micro picture, we know our students' brains need to be "in the right state" and open and willing for modification. Plasticity is a neural process which is highly state-dependent. State-dependency entails a positive energized (or stimulated) receptiveness for input on a cellular and whole-body level (Olcese, Oude Lohuis, & Pennartz, 2018).

A heated argument over politics with a family member rarely leads to changed opinions. Why? Because, in such circumstances, our brains are typically not "in the mood" or not open to the possibility of modifying our cognitive circuitry. Generally speaking, the more alert and motivated to learn a person is, the greater the potential for change in that person's brain. The effect is similar to the well-known "critical periods" and "sensitive periods" in early childhood that allow for higher receptivity to learning (Knudsen, 2004).

Naturally, this rule does not hold true in cases of trauma or serious accident. In those circumstances, plasticity is "forced" into play by the extreme state of the individual. It doesn't matter what state someone is in when hit by a drunk driver—the body and brain will be changed.

With the myriad of inputs our brains are exposed to every minute, only the most *relevant* ones (those with perceived importance) will have a significant neurological impact. Lasting brain change occurs when new inputs are perceived as highly relevant or compelling. As a brief example of how you can use relevance to prompt behavioral change: Want to encourage your students to participate in an active learning activity? Show them how critical physical activity is for their physical and mental health, in addition to enhancing their learning potential.

Relevance actually happens on a cellular level. An existing neuron simply connects with a nearby neuron to make a connection. If the content is irrelevant (lacks understanding or emotional valence), it's unlikely that a connection will be made. While neurons are constantly firing, much of the time it's an inaudible chatter. The meaning we experience happens when a multitude of connections or the activation of a neural field takes place. In the brain, a nearby connection is often less than a centimeter away. The brain's nerve cells rarely move; they simply extend their axons to connect with other dendrites. If they can't make the connection, it's going to be harder to establish relevance.

Neuromodulators also play a key role in the process of neuroplasticity. The three most influential of these naturally produced chemicals are dopamine, norepinephrine, and acetylcholine. Dopamine is associated with the anticipation and acquisition of reward (Lloyd & Dayan, 2015). Norepinephrine creates heightened receptivity to long-term memory formation (Mather, Clewett, Sakaki, & Harley, 2016). Acetylcholine is released when we experience heightened levels of surprise or novelty (Rangel-Gomez & Meeter, 2016). These neurotransmitters enhance synaptic plasticity. When *any* of these neurotransmitters is blocked, synaptic plasticity is weakened.

Cortisol also has a role in impacting plasticity. A high level of cortisol has been shown to interfere with the strengthening of synaptic connections. It is now well known that chronic stress has a negative impact on learning and memory. Exposure to prolonged, intense stress can even cause certain brain structures to shrink (Conrad, 2010). Luckily, thanks to neuroplasticity, these changes can be reversed. In fact, all learning, including the painful lessons of trauma and the insidious effects of prejudice, can be modified. As you might suppose, getting the brain "ready" for new learning can be a bit tricky. But it is *very* doable.

In your classroom, foster high levels of curiosity and anticipation to help create readiness among your students. ("Are you feeling it? Are you ready for change?"). A thought-provoking question written on the board for students to see as they enter, an object hidden under a blanket at the front of the room, or statements like "In five minutes you'll learn the secret to . . ." all enhance readiness and thus increase the possibility of change in students' brains.

IN THE CLASSROOM

For learning to best occur, the brain must also feel like there is a reason for accepting the input (i.e., there must be behavioral relevance). Your students must agree that "This is important for me right now." If you yourself are not sure why it is important for students to learn what you have planned for tomorrow, do some research. Type your learning goal and the words "real world application" into an internet search engine. If you don't get any good hits, and your colleagues are also baffled, maybe it is time to evaluate the importance of that lesson.

Every student has their own "learning triggers." For some students, activating prior learning works best. You might also precede the lesson with an energizer to raise all students' levels of dopamine, cortisol, and norepinephrine. Or start with focused, deep breathing to oxygenate the brain as you lead your students through a mindfulness exercise to clear their heads for learning.

Support Coherent Construction

The phrase "coherent construction" is a bit of a mouthful. Our brains are "constructing" our new learning. That suggests we are active and mindful in the process. But unless what we piece together makes sense and has some meaning, it is not likely to make sense, be valuable, or be recalled. In short, not all new learning is useful.

The changes in our brains that we are referring to when we talk about neuroplasticity are carried out based on the type of input. The input types are as varied as (you might recall from Chapter 2) sensory, associative, non-conscious, emotional, mindfulness, explicit (declarative), episodic (location-based), and procedural (using your body).

If the input is too chaotic, irrelevant, or overwhelming, the cellular response is instability.

The optimal signal-to-noise ratio is critical; too much noise (environmental distractions or input that is off-target) and the "input signal" for learning becomes degraded and hard to decipher. For example, if you go to a crowded party where you don't know the other guests, you'll find lots of "noise" but not enough quality "signals" (e.g., hearing your name, making new connections) (Gourévitch, Edeline, Occelli, & Eggermont, 2014).

In the brain, coherence rules! In a classroom setting, you can influence and even orchestrate input in any of the following ways to support the coherence of what your students are learning. While these are broad categories, it gives you a way to think about what is going into a student's brain:

- **Self-directed** (this is the most flexible way of doing things, since some students prefer to start at the end and work backward, while others jump in the middle or start at square one.)
- **Schema-based** (go step by step, start with what you know, add vocabulary, build layers over time, always be using sense-making)
- **Complex immersion** (massive content embedded within a relevant context, like learning a new language)
- **Deliberate practice** (perfect for skill-building)

IN THE CLASSROOM

The overarching guideline is this: Start small and build. Begin with prior knowledge and then pause. Start with a simple mental model or surface learning. As you begin to introduce new inputs, ensure that the first step ends with a simple success for all students. Chunk the learning into small content or skill parts and, allow for practice time.

Use a multisensory approach to learning as you introduce new inputs: facilitate conversations (via pair shares, table talks, trio reviews), employ visuals (sketch notes, mind maps, short videos), and encourage hands-on experiences (with manipulatives, in role-plays, with gestures).

Consolidation, Error-Correction, and Transfer

Although neuroplasticity is powerful, its transient nature doesn't guarantee accurate memory formation. The initial stage, known as the consolidation stage, depends on a process known as *activation—latency—reinforcement* in order to commit the new knowledge to long-term memory (Sehgal, Song, Ehlers, & Moyer, 2013). In short, if you have the option, taking a "brain break" right after the activated learning is very smart for the brain. Too much content overloads the brain's mid-range "layover" depot, the hippocampus. In some ways, the hippocampus acts like a surge protector for your long-term memory storage areas. It holds new explicit learning until it's reinforced or it has had time to evaluate for relevance (Eichenbaum, 2017).

Part of the consolidation stage requires the brain to get feedback during or at the end of the task. Otherwise you may be forming memories of something that has not been error-corrected. Ultimately, when it comes to providing your students with feedback, you have to assess the long-term goal. For those learners who just want to get it right, just telling them the right answer (vs. details on how and why) helps them remember the correct answer better (Fazio, Huelser, Johnson, & Marsh, 2010). The simple chart in Figure 5.3 is a reminder of some of the keys to better feedback.

Research has shown that *repeated stimuli separated by timed spaces without stimuli can initiate neuroplasticity*. This happens via long-term potentiation (LTP) that enhances long-term memory (LTM) encoding. These processes occur in time scales of minutes and have been successfully demonstrated in real classrooms. If the learning is well-orchestrated, and spaced right, students can learn in a matter of hours what typically takes days or weeks (Kelley & Whatson, 2013).

For most declarative types of learning (talking, listening, reading, etc.), the hippocampus acts as a decision-maker to either conserve and enhance the memory being formed or allow it to degrade without any further processing. The original input is held "hostage" for further evaluation until the brain is convinced it is worth saving. This consolidation of "working memory" (which is transient) to short-term or long-term memory moves that information from the hippocampus to

5.3 Feedback Specifics

1. **Feedback** is information provided by any agent (e.g., a teacher, a checklist, a peer, a book, a parent, a video, a reflection, or an experience) regarding one's understanding or performance.
2. **Feedback** may be positive, neutral, or negative.
3. **Feedback** may be timely (or not), personal (or task- or process-directed), and effective (or not).
4. **Ideal Feedback** is specific, is actionable, and includes an attribution (the "why").
5. **Feedback** done well answers, "Where am I now? Where am I going? How do I get there?"

Source: Hattie & Timperley (2007).

higher cortical structures, such as the prefrontal cortex (Wierzynski, Lubenov, Gu, & Siapas, 2009).

It usually works like this:

1. A network of knowledge is initially formed as a result of an experience or internal reflection—for example, someone learns how to play a new card game on family night.

2. Time passes (e.g., a week goes by, and family night comes around again).

3. The new network associated with the knowledge is reactivated (e.g., the person plays or simply thinks about playing the card game).

If the latent period is too long (based on the perceived degree of relevance), the new network will be lost. In education, we traditionally call this "forgetting." In actuality, it is simply that the newly established network did not receive enough "attention" or reinforcement to survive the brain's natural pruning process.

Such a system-level consolidation process requires relevant reactivation and replay of memories (Girardeau, Benchenane, Wiener, Buzsáki, & Zugaro, 2009). To create lasting change, new pathways typically need to be reinforced multiple times. You might recall the modern-day adage known as Hebb's Postulate: "Neurons that fire together wire together." It's a catchy summary of a basic learning process, reminding us of the importance of reviewing new information—making those same neurons fire again and again—to wire it into our existing knowledge.

Time should be a significant consideration in the process of fostering memories. Essentially, our brains need some time (free of external input) to decide "keep this" or "trash that." For much of school-based (declarative) learning, the hippocampus works on a timed schedule, usually just days, when the new experiences are undergoing memory consolidation.

These post-conditioning LTM processes are also enhanced as long-term memories are consolidated during sleep. This has been demonstrated in a number of ways, including studies showing that task performance can be increased without further training following a night's sleep (Walker & Stickgold, 2010). Your brain strengthens its new connections while you slumber! To borrow from an old saying, "You snooze, you gain."

Follow this formula: Learn, then do error correction, then pause. Do error correction again. Get the learning, do error correction (feedback), then let it rest. Reactivate it to turn it into a long-term memory. This is the *active-latent-reactivate* phase. ("Have I got this? I've got a question first. Now I'll take a break, then review it later"). Teach students why sleep is so important for memory consolidation.

In a formalized school setting, one of the best ways to "edit" the rough drafts of new knowledge in your students' brains is through retrieval practices. Much different (and better) than reviewing or studying, *retrieval* is any exercise that challenges the learner to retrieve information from memory. With proper support from the teacher (i.e., you), retrieval practices can function almost as an "auto-correct" tool to help modify any incorrectly constructed networks.

Here are a handful of retrieval strategies.

- **Practice tests.** As Butler (2010) showed, for students, these are a much better use of time than repeatedly studying.

- **Flash cards.** If you or your students make your own cards, ensure that the correct answers appear on the back, to support accurate memory formation.

- **Partner quizzing.** Remember to establish a system to "error-correct" to prevent students from reinforcing incorrect information.

- **Learning stations.** Have students travel around the room to different stations completing practice test–style questions. Again, be sure the correct answers are readily available.

Students should typically not need their book, their notes, or their digital device during these activities. An occasional prompt may be useful to jump-start the retrieval process. Consider retrieval a way for students to "test" their memory. Be careful to not use every retrieval exercise to count toward a grade—the purpose can simply be to improve their learning (Karpicke, 2012; Barber, Rajaram, & Marsh, 2008). As far as timing, retrieval practices work best when done the same day new information is learned and then at intervals for two weeks afterward (Roediger & Butler, 2011).

IN THE CLASSROOM

Conclusion

Neuroplasticity is at the root of our learning. At the most basic neuro-logic level, learning is the process in which new connections are made in the brain. Although most teachers already do most things fairly well, we hope you now recognize there are *many* small adjustments that you can make that will propel your students to new, higher levels of learning.

Whenever one of your students appears to be stuck in a rut and simply not changing, step back for a moment. If a student has been "the same" for years, ask yourself, *What has actually changed (for the better) in this student's life? What habits are new, what teachers have been amazing, and how have others around this student shifted to methods that* do *work?* After all, neuroplasticity encourages us to believe that students with ADHD can, in fact, improve their attentional capacity and behavior. It assures us that students who have consistently read below grade level need not be destined to struggle.

The influence of neuroplasticity is not contained to the classroom. It extends beyond our learners and beyond us as teachers, into our social interactions and society as a whole. It is neuroplasticity that reminds us that the bad relationship habits we picked up from our parents can be unlearned, and new, healthier behaviors can be learned. Looking forward to the day when people no longer have racist, sexist, or homophobic beliefs? At the most basic structural level—our brain's biology—it is neuroplasticity that will get us there as a society.

The Brain's Learning Strengths

How Emotions Impact Learning 6

A teacher is standing excitedly at the front of the class, waiting for the starting bell to ring. She has been looking forward to this lesson for days and can't wait to see the impact of all her hard work.

Her beaming grin dims a bit as she sees a student shuffling into class looking as if his dog had just died. *Hmm*, the teacher thinks. *He's not in the best mood for today's lesson.*

As the teacher begins her lesson, she notices a group of girls learning over one of the girls' smartphones, apparently looking at something shocking. "Girls, let's focus on the lesson," the teacher says, ignoring any thought of what might be causing the distraction.

Later in the class, the teacher outlines the homework assignment. A student sighs. Frustrated, the teacher snaps at him: "Seriously? You know we have homework every night. Get over it." The student wrinkles his face in disgust. The teacher sees this reaction and tells him, "Hey, don't give me an attitude!"

It could be argued that it is not your job to deal with a student who is depressed, the emotions that accompany students watching mass shootings streamed live on their phones, or their feelings of being overwhelmed by all the demands and pressures being placed on them. It might even seem like you could do your "job" of teaching better if students didn't drag all this emotional baggage into class with them. Yes, today's world is different.

The challenges that come when your students bring all of their emotions into your classroom *never end*. And still, you are expected to teach them about punctuation, tectonic plates, a math theorem, or irregular verbs in Spanish. Yet, some days, being a teacher may feel more like an arcade game of "whack-a-mole," where it's all you can do to respond to the behavioral issues that keep popping up among your students. That's no fun. That's also why this chapter will be so valuable to you.

In this chapter, you'll learn how to anticipate problems, read the emotional climate of the classroom, and then take action to keep your students engaged. You will learn how to facilitate new emotional states among your students and, in the process, teach them how to regulate their own emotions.

Our Basic Emotions

The backstory of emotions reveals two "origin" theories you should know about. The first theory is the "conceptual act" theory of emotion. This theory posits that we have a constructionist brain that uses the interactions of brain structures-to-function connections to create emotions "on the spot," spontaneously, moment after moment (Touroutoglou, Lindquist, Dickerson, & Barrett, 2015).

The other, competing theory argues that we have about only six or seven "hardwired" emotions (Ekman, 2016). The rest of our emotions would have to be taught in a geographic-specific culture (home, school, malls, etc.).

In short, we are not yet 100% certain of the origins of emotions. So what *do we know* that's relevant in our classrooms and school? We likely have at least six or seven of these "primary" emotions—joy, fear, contempt, surprise, disgust, anger, and sadness—regardless of *how* they are sourced. If you include shame and guilt, then there are nine. How important are these core emotions? Well, every one of them is a reason why we're alive today (Shariff & Tracy, 2011).

Emotions are essential at all times, because they aid our individual and group survival. For starters, **joy** causes us to relax and make better decisions essential for our survival. It helps people create and reinforce supportive social bonds, and joyful people live longer and are healthier. **Fear** makes us aware that we're in danger. It stimulates the release of adrenaline and triggers our "fight, flight, or freeze" response. **Surprise** awakens our autonomic nervous system to prompt us to take

6.1 Seven Hardwired Emotions

Hardwired Emotions
(Additional Emotions Must Be Learned as if Learning New Keys on a Piano)

✓ Sadness
✓ Joy
✓ Disgust
✓ Anger
✓ Fear
✓ Surprise
✓ Contempt

Source: Ekman (2016).

the next necessary step, whatever that may be. The survival benefit of **disgust** is that it may be a warning for others around you that something (or someone) is potentially toxic or otherwise dangerous and to be avoided. **Anger** is a sign that one of our needs (e.g., love, security, resources, acceptance) is not being met, and it pushes us to assess and rectify the situation. **Sadness** is a signal about loss. It tells that there is something that has soured, disappointed us, or been taken away. This unpleasant feeling of sadness generates signals to people we associate with and motivates us to do something about it in order for it to go away.

This list of emotions is the same across all cultures. That's why we shouldn't ignore or dismiss emotions—they're an important part of what makes us human, and they help us navigate our lives. Why should it be any different in the classroom? As teachers, we must acknowledge learners' emotions and channel them into the learning process. Whereas previous generations of educators saw their students as passive recipients of knowledge or skills, the prevailing academic model recognizes the active role of the learner. The more we understand what is happening for learners, the better we can support them in their learning. And emotions are a huge part of what is driving your learners. The more you recognize and work with your students' emotional states, the more effective you'll be as an educator.

IN THE CLASSROOM

What does the fact that we have only seven hardwired emotions mean to you, as an educator? In the classroom, when a teacher gets a response from a student that she or he was not expecting (as in the introduction above), there's an insight for you as the teacher. Some students only know how to respond with one of their seven basic emotions. Many have not learned the language of other emotions (empathy, optimism, kindness, gratitude, etc.) and thus struggle to express them—not only in words, but also through behaviors and even expressions. Thus, the emotion a student seems to display may not be an accurate reflection of what he or she is feeling. Let's go back to the scenario at the beginning of the chapter . . .

The teacher outlines the homework assignment. A student sighs. Frustrated, the teacher snaps at him: "Seriously? You know we have homework every night. Get over it." The student wrinkles his face in disgust. The teacher takes offense and tells him, "Hey, don't give me an attitude!"

The student's "display" emotion was disgust (one of his seven basic emotions). The teacher is then in a position to make one of two assumptions:

1. This student *should know how to behave* and is purposefully withholding a more appropriate emotion, such as remorse or empathy. This assumption is based on a belief that the student already has a high level of "emotional intelligence," or skill in both communicating the way he feels and empathizing with others (reading their signals, inferring their emotions, and deducing why they might feel that way).

2. No one has taught this student emotions outside of his core seven. Thus, the student doesn't know a more appropriate response than disgust.

The brain-based teacher will make the second assumption and see this as an opportunity to teach the young man a new emotional skill. She is invested in fostering emotional intelligence because it helps her students mature, and it will make her life as the teacher easier. She might say: "Hmmm . . . you don't seem too happy with having homework. Tell me, what's going on for you?" She will listen and try to empathize and then help the student label and learn a new emotion. "It sounds like you are feeling *overwhelmed* with all your homework, practice, chores, and other responsibilities. I get it now. Thanks for explaining."

Subsequently, if the teacher notices similar responses in other students, this is a sign that she should do some teaching about specific emotions to the entire class. At the primary school level, it would be appropriate to do so perhaps once a month for seven months: Each month, a new emotion is taught, then reinforced, labeled, and fleshed out until proper and acceptable expression of that emotion becomes automatic for students. At the secondary school level (where the school year is split into semesters), the teacher could discuss a new emotion every two weeks. By the end of the semester or school year, her students will have a richer life ahead of them.

The majority of classroom-behavior problems are rooted in students' knowing only the emotions they were born with. Emotions such as gratitude, compassion, empathy, and kindness aren't hardwired; they're learned through interactions with others. Instead of blaming parents for not teaching these skills to their children, teachers can instead use that frustrated energy to teach students the social emotional skills they need to know. This approach works better than dismissing or attempting to ignore displays of emotion, as you might be tempted to do. A teacher who chooses to ignore the emotional state of a learner will be faced with new challenges when the student doesn't sufficiently learn or engages in disruptive behaviors to satisfy an emotional craving. Try to keep in mind that emotions are a two-sided coin. Even if we could magically eliminate all the anxiety, frustration, and anger that students experience on a day-to-day basis, we would also be erasing comparable moments of joy, excitement, and confidence. While emotions have the potential to impede learning, they can also improve and accelerate learning (Tyng, Amin, Saad, & Malik, 2017). More on this later.

Emotions vs. Moods vs. States

Emotions are hardwired and typically last no longer than a few minutes (Trampe, Quoidbach, & Taquet, 2015). But emotions are so omnipresent that 90% of your waking hours you are likely to experience emotions (Trampe et al., 2015). A state, on the other hand, is a mind-body response that has been learned or taught as an indicator of attitudes, perceptions, sensations, and beliefs (Oosterwijk et al., 2012). Some examples of states are worry, anticipation, frustration, cynicism, and optimism. A state may involve a sudden but brief change in posture, breathing rate, and chemical balance in the body.

It can dramatically alter a person's frame of mind and body. Yet the same emotional state may look different for each student in your class.

A mood could be described as an extended state. Whereas a state will last for only moments (or possibly a couple minutes), moods can last for hours or even days (Kragel, Knodt, Hariri, & LaBar, 2016). Emotions can be more difficult to regulate when they're part of a particular mood. Perhaps you have experienced how much angrier you get when someone cuts you off on the freeway when you are already in a bad mood. Both states and moods are self-reinforcing, meaning the longer you are in them the more "comfortable" they become (Hudson, Lucas, & Donnellan, 2017). The body and brain are more apt to slip into familiar states because they have been practiced so frequently.

Whether someone is experiencing a hardwired emotion like sadness or joy, or a state they have learned like being frustrated or confident, or a mood like grumpy—each one impacts all areas of life in significant ways. Emotions trigger chemical changes that affect our moods, our behaviors, and eventually our lives (Scarantino & Griffiths, 2011).

It can be hard to loosen the grip of a negative emotion. Changing your state is easier than changing your mood, yet both are possible. Changing your state can be accomplished by changing your posture or facial expression, breathing deeply, or doing a different task. Whatever helps you relax and move on from the input that bothered you in the moment. Changing a mood usually takes a bit more effort—such as a change in diet, a different sleep pattern, environmental changes, or changes in social support.

The wide impact of emotions on almost every system in our bodies (Pessoa & McMenamin, 2017) and their contribution to states and moods that can either help or hinder learning is due to the way they are generated and processed in the brain.

Emotions in the Brain

Our bodies generate sensory data, feed it to our brains, and then integrate it with emotions and intellect to form a *thinking triumvirate* for optimal performance and decision-making. Emotions are, in effect, a critical frame of reference for our subjective reality. See Figure 6.2.

The critical networks that process emotions link the limbic system, the prefrontal cortex, and perhaps most important, the brain areas that map and integrate signals from the body (Pessoa & McMenamin,

6.2   The Overlap of Cognition and Emotions

Emotive Bodily Responses

Most of our cognitive processing is informed and influenced by emotions

High Reason, Rational Thinking

Source: Immordino-Yang & Damasio (2007).

2017). The limbic system (primarily the amygdala and anterior cingulate) is the seat of our primary emotions (e.g., innate fear, surprise) (Frühholz et al., 2015). The prefrontal cortex is responsible for our secondary emotions—that is, our feelings about our thoughts (Immordino-Yang & Damasio, 2007).

The Role of the Amygdala

The amygdala—an almond-shaped mass of nuclei within the limbic system (see Figure 6.3)—is highly involved in emotions. It is "online" (already working) when we are born, and it matures when we are teens. It stores intense emotions, both negative and positive (Janak & Tye, 2015). We have two amygdalae (one in each hemisphere).

The amygdala exerts a tremendous influence over the cortex, which generates our thoughts. By far, the amygdala is more reactive, while the frontal lobes (cerebral cortex) are reflective (Sakaki, Nga, & Mather, 2013). The cortex has more inputs from the amygdala than is true in the other direction, yet information flows both ways. What this means is that while our emotions are designed to sway our thinking and decision-making, our thoughts can, to an extent, either excite or calm our emotions. One way to understand the potency of the amygdala in a learning environment is that it is situated right next to one of our primary learning structures, the hippocampus. See Figure 6.3.

6.3   The Location of the Amygdala

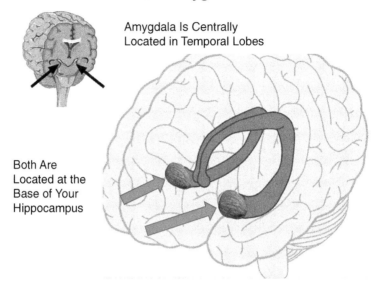

Amygdala Is Centrally
Located in Temporal Lobes

Both Are
Located at the
Base of Your
Hippocampus

The amygdala's primary task is to ensure our survival (Fox, Oler, Tromp, Fudge, & Kalin, 2015). To do that, it operates as our *uncertainty* detector. Any time we don't know what's going on and the likelihood is that it's not good, the amygdala becomes activated. It is activated not only by fear but also by an overall sense that something isn't right at the moment. Have you ever had that feeling walking down a street that maybe you shouldn't be there? It's not a guarantee that something is wrong, but your amygdala is detecting the possibility (uncertainty).

Emotions Can Impede Learning

When the amygdala senses uncertainty in any form—physical, emotional, or even social—it harnesses all the brain's energy to focus on the potential threat. This means any cognitive functioning will be at best impaired, if not temporarily halted (McGarry & Carter, 2016). This is happening among your students all day, every day. Some have developed self-regulation skills to quickly manage these experiences. Others get lost in the emotional processing and lose focus on learning.

This can happen when a below-grade-level student is asked to read in front of the class without any warning or support. It can happen when a student is afraid to raise her hand and ask a question, because the last time someone did that the class bully teased her and the teacher did not react. It can happen when a student is sitting in class worried about his sick grandmother in the hospital. It can happen when during a spelling test a student is ruminating on the words she heard from her mother this morning: "If you don't get at least 80% correct on your spelling test today . . ."

You might notice, some of these examples relate to things going on outside of the classroom. Yet any of them may activate the amygdala (the "uncertainty detector" in the temporal lobes). That action can potentially overwhelm students' cognition, impacting their ability to engage, to learn, and to meet classroom expectations. Your students' brains will naturally prioritize emotional processes over academic content. Students who are preoccupied with something emotional, not related to the learning, will struggle. This "lack of attention" is actually the diversion of their attention to something more relevant.

Teachers' behavior and the classroom culture they create can directly contribute to the frequency of such occurrences. Thus, teachers should give every effort to avoid triggering not only negative emotions, but also negative states or moods in their students. A student in a state of frustration or discouragement will not learn as well as a student in a state of curiosity or self-confidence. The same is true for a student in an anxious, a sad, or a depressed mood.

Be perceptive and aware of emotional states among your students. Foster trusting relationships with your students, so that you have a better sense of what they might be going through emotionally at certain times. Then quickly notice any adverse emotional displays in class and mitigate them with redirects, state changes, and activity changes (more on this to come). You'll find yourself enjoying teaching much, much more, and your students will love being in your class.

IN THE CLASSROOM

Emotions Can Accelerate Learning

Not all emotions in the classroom have a negative impact. In fact, getting students emotionally invested in classroom activities can be a powerful teaching tool. Because the amygdala connects to the hippocampus, it plays a significant role in coding memory (Madan, Fujiwara, Caplan, & Sommer, 2017). As the source of emotions, the amygdala supports other brain structures by embedding memory with meaning. And meaningful input is what gets remembered (Oudiette, Antony, Creery, & Paller, 2013). Many emotional states improve focus, learning, and achievement (Tyng et al., 2017). Emotions also drive success. Our frontal lobes allow us to elaborate on the details of our goals and plans, but it's our emotions that drive the execution of these goals (Hallam et al., 2015). That's why when we ask students to set their goals, it's just as important to ask them *why they want to reach them* as it is to ask what their goals are. You might say, "Write down three good reasons why reaching your goals is important to you." Then have students share their answers with others. It is the emotions behind the goals that will provide the energy to accomplish them.

IN THE CLASSROOM

Be proactive; orchestrate the kinds of emotions you want to have in class. Take advantage of an often-untapped resource by accelerating student learning through more emotion integration. These four simple but highly effective strategies can help maintain positive states for learning.

Role Model

Exhibit a love of learning. Bring something to class that you're in the process of learning about—something that really excites you. Build suspense, smile, tell a true emotional story. You might bring in a favorite book or discuss one you recently read, bring a pet to school, or get involved in community work. But most important, show enthusiasm. Your positivity will be contagious.

Celebrate

Provide acknowledgments. Incorporate high-fives, team cheers, food, music, decorations, and costumes in the classroom. Show off student work. For example, when students are finished doing a group mind map, have them share it with at least two other groups. Tell the groups to find at least two things they like about each other's mind maps. Do this in an atmosphere of celebration, and provide positive words for a job well done.

Create Controversy

Set up a debate, a dialogue, an academic decathlon, a game show, or a panel discussion. Any time you vest two groups in competing interests, you'll get action! Theater and drama can create strong emotions as well. The bigger the production and the higher the stakes, the more emotions will be engaged in the learning. Event planning on this scale evokes stress, fun, anxiety, anticipation, suspense, excitement, and relief. What better way to engage a wide range of emotions?

Promote Introspection

Incorporate assignments that require journaling, small-group discussions, story swapping, surveys, interviews, and other reflection tasks. Use people and issues to engage students personally. Ask students to write or talk about a current event that has drawn wide attention. Help them make personal connections between current events, your curriculum, and their own everyday lives.

Teachers who help their students feel good about themselves through learning success, quality friendships, and celebrations are doing the very things the learning brain craves.

Creating a Positive Environment With Classroom Traditions

Whatever emotion, mood, or state your students are experiencing when they walk in your classroom, it *can* change. Positive emotions can be prompted by the physical environment, the teacher's facial expressions, sounds, smells, and a variety of other sensory factors. Be purposeful in infusing as many positive emotions into your learning environment as possible.

In addition to a positive environment, small, purposeful teacher actions can shift students' emotional states. Exceptional teachers create habits/ traditions that foster valuable states. The goal is not to have a variety of strategies you randomly incorporate, but rather to instill **habits** in your classroom culture that promote positive emotions. Habits free up mental space for you to focus on other important things.

Between the beginning and end of class, there are many opportunities to facilitate positive emotions, states, and moods.

Be sure the first three minutes of your class involves something that intentionally sparks positive emotions. It could be a class motto everyone repeats, upbeat music with a positive message playing as they enter the classroom, your smiling face greeting them at the door, a special handshake or high-five, a quick stretching routine they do every morning, two-minutes of mindfulness, a positive quote written on the board, etc.

(Continued)

IN THE CLASSROOM

(Continued)

The same goes for the last few minutes of your class time. Be sure students are leaving your classroom feeling positive, confident, and successful. End-of-class habits that promote positive emotional states include celebration songs, affirmations, self-assessment, journaling, and class/team cheers.

Students are not usually "stuck" in the emotional state they walk in with. But the more time they spend in any particular state, the more that state feels "normal" to them. Consistently positive emotional classrooms can and do alter the "set point" for a student's baseline.

Developing the skill set of influencing students' state should be near the top of every teacher's list of priorities. With focus and practice, educators can become masters at artfully orchestrating positive states. Here is how:

Four Steps to Becoming Masterful at Influencing States

1. **Develop emotional acuity.** Exceptional teachers can "read" the state of a classroom or an individual student. Be present with your students, so that you can really "see" them. This requires being fully prepared with your lesson, so that your thoughts are not preoccupied with lesson preparations. Watch for the nonverbal cues of posture, direction of gaze, body movement, and even small details like eyebrows (raised = excited/surprised; furrowed = confused/mad) to help you understand your students' current emotional state.

   Having strong, positive relationships with students will accelerate your skill building in this area. Build relationships founded on trust. Get to know your students—learn about their family life, hobbies, worries, and passions. Take advantage of every "down" moment in class to strengthen a relationship. Students will then be more likely to tell you about their grandma in the hospital. This will alleviate the pressure of playing a guessing game relating to their emotional state.

2. **Reengage and reset the student entry states.** Be intentional with your opening minutes to invite students into a positive state from the moment they walk into your classroom. Put on

pleasant background music, meet students at the door with a smile, and give them an affirmation. That may instantly change a student's state.

As you go through your lesson, if you notice students are in a positive state, congratulations! Make note of what influenced their state, and use that strategy again.

Reinforce positive states when you see them. Acknowledge students for their curiosity, excitement, and joy. Remember, states are self-reinforcing—the longer students stay in a positive state, the easier it will be for them to return to this state. As you enjoy a room full of students in a positive state for learning, don't get too comfortable. States typically don't last for longer than a couple minutes. You'll want to be prepared.

3. **Foster emotional agility: influence/change states.** When you notice a student is in a negative emotional state, evaluate what prompted such a state. Was it something you did or said, or was it an outside influence? If it was something you did or said, take action and commit to not do that again. A teacher who is humble enough to admit an error and apologize can build a lot of credibility with students. If the state was initiated by an outside influence, acknowledge the situation (e.g., "I'm so sorry your grandma is in the hospital again") and try to redirect the student's attention to something positive ("I hope your time here today can give you a small break from that worry.")

   Shift either students' bodies (have them sit up, stand up, take a deep breath, or follow a clapping pattern) or their thoughts (interject, "Hey—I almost forgot"; "Let's do something crazy for a minute"; "That reminds me of . . .")

4. **Be prepared—recognize students' state will change again . . . soon!** Realizing your students are in a negative state for learning can become paralyzing for an unprepared teacher. Develop a collection of strategies, and keep them readily available to influence students' state at any time. Plan them into your lesson, and then have some "backups" for the unexpected moments. You can change students' state in a variety of ways, some of which can even reinforce content.

   An instructional state change is one that is directly related to content and supports learning. Strategies in this category include standing review, walk and talk, practice problems in between lecture points, and station learning.

A non-instructional state change does not directly relate to content but still supports student learning because it fosters a positive emotional state. Try "brain breaks," having students stand up/stretch, playing Simon says, having students touch three walls, or taking a one-song break.

Summary

Emotions are at the core of what makes us human. From an evolutionary psychology perspective, they help us survive.

Emotions are often fleeting, but they generate distinct emotional states. Each emotional state is activated by an internal or external trigger—a reaction to an event, a cue, a person, or a thought. It is a "snapshot" of a person's bodily reaction and frame of mind. States are the minute-by-minute report on how your day is going.

When a person is in an extended emotion (sadness, anger, etc.), we refer to it as a mood. Each emotion that is associated with a particular mood causes events or thoughts to be more easily associated with that emotion. An irritable mood causes a person to interpret events or thoughts more angrily. Our brains' natural inclination is to assign too much importance to the way we're feeling, letting it dominate our thoughts and direct our attention. This may have helped us survive 25,000 years ago, but not today. Why? Because our brains get fooled by "false signals." We won't die if our friend is upset with us; but our concern may lead to ensuring we look after those in our "tribe" a bit better. Our self-preservation instincts can interfere with learning. It can impair our quality of thinking and lead to lost learning opportunities and poor decisions.

Your learners' emotional state is at least as important as the intellectual-cognitive content of your presentation. Never avoid emotions; deal with them gently and personally. Allow negative ones to be processed and positive ones to be celebrated. Elicit positive emotional states from learners with enjoyable activities, games, humor, personal attention, and acts of caring. Modeling these states will not only foster more positive emotions and infuse emotions into content but teach learners indirectly how to better manage their own optimal states for learning. A great deal of our success and joy in life comes about from the power to run our own brains, your thoughts, feelings, and actions you take. You can do this, and you can teach your students to do the same. Remember, the more time we (or your students) spend in any individual state, the more that state feels like "normal" to us. This means you have the capacity to influence your students' lives—not merely in class, but for their future. They will spend less time in negative states and find more happiness and success if you're willing to make a few changes.

Reflect on your priorities as a teacher. Do you put learners' emotions and feelings on par with the mastery of content and skill learning? Remember, the two are directly biologically linked. There are plenty of takeaways from this chapter, but the bottom line is that you have much greater influence over how your class turns out than you ever thought possible. Embrace your superpowers!

Physical Movement and the Brain 7

At one public high school, an unusual experiment was done. The timing of each class's schedule was used as a variable in an attempt to discover what (if anything) could improve learning. Students were enrolled in a physical education class directly before their most challenging subject (one in which they had, up to that point, done poorly). As a result of this one simple change, so many students at this school did better *than they ever* did, that the entire school's scores are well above the national average. In fact, the school's scores placed their students **among the top five countries in the world!** (Ratey, 2008, p. 12). It is no longer a subject of dispute; the mind, body, and emotions are *so* well-connected that playing any sport (e.g., baseball, jogging, swimming, running) *will change the brain.*

Decades ago, physical education at both the elementary and secondary levels were a "given." Everyone took some form of physical activity (unless you had a doctor's note). Today, the majority of American schools have eliminated recess or physical education because of excuses like "We must focus on the academics." Or, worse yet, "Some students don't like it." That's a silly reason; you might as well have a vote on *every subject* taught in school and see what the students "like."

One of the main barriers to implementing physical education in schools is that many educators believe it will take time away from other subjects without offering a compensatory benefit (Nathan et al., 2018). Yet, in addition to the proven impact on student learning we just gave an example of, exercise benefits students' emotional self-regulation and health. It may be no coincidence that with the decline in physical activity in school curricula over the last three decades, teen suicides are up, school shootings are up, and teenage depression rates are the highest ever (Ivey-Stephenson, Crosby, Jack, Haileyesus, & Kresnow-Sedacca, 2017; Lowe & Galea, 2017; Vos et al., 2017). Remember the countless outdoor games kids used to play in decades past? Games like hide-and-seek, hopscotch, dodgeball, whiffle ball, and others all teach structured behaviors, which lead to better self-regulation. Remember the countless coaches who turned talented athletes into well-behaved adults? Athletes learn to follow directions; stay on schedule; help, not hurt, their teammates; and be supportive.

For these reasons, our remaining PE teachers play a critical role in enhancing the learning happening in all classrooms at a school. Ideally, physical education will soon return to every school, at every grade level. Students need a minimum of 20 to 30 minutes of moderate to vigorous exercise every day.

However, the responsibility to keep students active does not rest solely on PE teachers. Regular classroom teachers share the responsibility of keeping students active to maximize their cognitive, emotional, and physical health. Bearing in mind that students might not be getting enough exercise in PE, at recess, or outside of school, teachers have a whole seven hours of classroom instruction in which to incorporate physical activity totaling only 30 minutes.

7.1 How Movement Impacts Learning

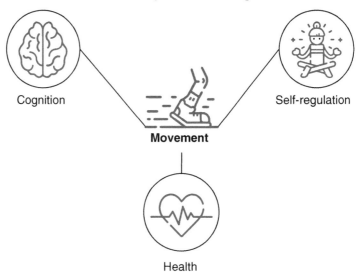

Cognition

Movement

Self-regulation

Health

Yes, it is just as important for students to move around in content classes as it is for them to be active in physical education classes or extracurricular athletics. In this chapter, we examine the compelling reasons why every teacher should be incorporating more physical movement in their teaching.

Movement and Cognition

Studies link low levels of physical activity with reduced academic performance (Esteban-Cornejo, Tejero-Gonzalez, Sallis, & Veiga, 2015). By contrast, students who are physically active perform better academically (Michael, Merlo, Basch, Wentzel, & Wechsler, 2015).

The goal for every teacher is to help students succeed by using every tool available. Biologically speaking, that mission includes the quest to find and manage the right balance of the brain's primary baseline chemicals. Physical exertion, along with its counterpart of physical relaxation, is a powerful way of moderating neurotransmitters that excite us (dopamine, norepinephrine, glutamine, etc.) and those that calm us (serotonin, oxytocin, GABA, etc.), all of which contribute to a significant response rate in both brain areas and student testing (Donnelly et al., 2016). Add the increased oxygen flow that comes with activities as simple as focused breathing or energizers, and you get the recipe for a high-performing brain. Let's dig into three specifics that highlight the impact: attention, memory, and fostering new brain cells.

Attention

Has this ever happened to you? After hours of working on a task, your brain seems to be a bit slow, and you're struggling to stay focused. You decide to stand up, stretch, and grab a glass of water and—perhaps after a quick walk around the block—are ready to get back to work.

The benefits of physical activity on student attention are both immediate and prolonged. It is true that doing some form of physical activity before a task will improve your attention (with an effect size of 0.43); however, it is the sustained habit of physical activity that shows the most impressive impact—an effect size of 0.90 (de Greeff, Bosker, Oosterlaan, Visscher, & Hartman, 2018). That is nearly two years' worth of improvement of attention due to regular physical activity.

How does this work? Physical activity enhances circulation so that the cellular mitochrondria and even individual neurons can get more oxygen and nutrients (Nyberg, Gliemann, & Hellsten, 2015).

Exercise also regulates norepinephrine and heart rate, which is significant in terms of increasing blood flow to the brain and improving attention (Yang et al., 2016).

IN THE CLASSROOM

If you have students who are struggling to pay attention, stay focused on a task, or perhaps even stay awake, it is time to get them up and moving their bodies. Here are some ideas to get you started.

- Take two minutes when you start your class to activate your learners. A short stretching session, a brisk walk, or breathing exercise can increase circulation and oxygen flow to the brain.

- During a transition, play an upbeat song and have a one-song dance party.

- Give learners permission to get up without asking to move around, stretch, or change postures so that they can monitor and manage their own energy levels.

Memory

From preschoolers to elderly with Alzheimer's disease, physical activity is a key ingredient to improving memory. Both working memory and short-term memory are enhanced by physical activity (Chen, Zhu, Yan, & Yin, 2016). In addition, exercise releases dopamine in the brain. A little surge of dopamine is good for our working memory (Knecht et al., 2004). In addition, long-term memory is enhanced by norepinephrine, which is produced from physical activity. Students who participate in some form of physical activity within an hour before learning demonstrate better long-term memory retrieval than those who did not exercise (Pontifex, Gwizdala, Parks, Pfeiffer, & Fenn, 2016).

Perhaps the most dramatic effects of physical activity on working memory as it relates to the classroom were shown in a longitudinal study involving more than 1,000 children. In this study, children who at age 6 were reported (by their parents) to have low physical activity levels performed worse on working memory tasks at age 14—that is, eight years later. The researchers concluded that those 14-year-olds' working memory skills had dropped by more than 5% (López-Vicente et al., 2017). All the more reason, it seems, to get your students as active as possible as early as possible.

Exercise enhances memory ability by triggering the release of brain-derived neurotrophic factor (BDNF), a natural substance that boosts the ability of neurons to communicate with each other (Griesbach, Hovda, Molteni, Wu, & Gomez-Pinilla, 2004). Daily exercise contributes to elevated BDNF levels in various areas of the brain, including the hippocampus, which is critical for memory processing. But there are immediate results as well. Increased BDNF levels can be detected after just one session of physical exercise (Venezia, Quinlan, & Roth, 2017). Clearly, every little bit of activity helps! BDNF has also been shown to accelerate the development of long-term potentiation (LTP), or memory formation (Vignoli et al., 2016). By contrast, low levels of BDNF have been correlated with major depressive disorder (Phillips, 2017)—a topic discussed further in this chapter.

Neurogenesis

We now know that on average, the brain produces from 700 to 1,000 new brain cells every day (Spalding et al., 2013). In a ground-breaking study done by the team at Salk Institute of Biological Studies in La Jolla, California, even elderly patients with terminal cancer were producing new brain cells before their death (Eriksson et al., 1998). Yet, our brains are also losing cells every day. The key to maximizing the brain's capacity is to produce more brain cells than is lost and keep more of those you generate. The research indicates that daily, high-intensity physical activity (running, swimming, cycling, etc.) for 20 minutes yields the massive benefits of neurogenesis (Jeon & Ha, 2017).

These new brain cells, however, will only survive if there is reason for them to do so. Your ideal pairing is both physical activity (to produce the cells) and challenging, relevant learning to ensure their survival (Yau, Li, & So, 2015). How do you keep new brain cells alive? Use them! Engage students in challenging tasks, tough problem-solving questions, and group challenges to maximize those new brain cells they worked hard to create. The cognitive gains will far outweigh the exercise time invested.

In addition to exercise, there are a variety of enrichment activities that significantly impact the growth (and preservation) of new brain cells: diet, lifestyle, social interactions, and emotional state (Poulose, Miller, Scott, & Shukitt-Hale, 2017). By cultivating the right conditions, we can literally double the daily production of new cells!

IN THE CLASSROOM

Your goal is to facilitate student movement at least every 20 minutes. Incorporating more physical activity into your classroom might require you to acquire new strategies. What follows are several ideas to help you keep those students moving.

- "Follow the leader" activities are always fun and valuable for students. The leader can even incorporate content review into the activity by slapping a content poster on their way or saying key learning phrases out loud.

- When doing station learning, give them instructions on how to move in between each station. For example, "do 10 jumping jacks on your way to the next station."

- Engage learners in cooperative activities and group work where they are moving, building something, or going on a treasure hunt around the school.

- After accomplishing a difficult task, have students celebrate by taking a running victory lap around the building.

- Set up relay races where teams line up 20 to 50 yards from you and race to you to spell a vocabulary word, solve a math problem, or conjugate a Spanish verb.

Neurogenesis has been shown to occur in several areas of the brain, including the hippocampus—a region highly involved with learning and memory (Voss, Bridge, Cohen, & Walker, 2017). Students who engage in regular physical activity will produce more brain cells in their hippocampus, resulting in better and stronger memories. Educators who work with teenagers may notice the biggest gains, because during adolescence neurogenesis is heightened in the hippocampus (Hueston, Cryan, & Nolan, 2017). As you probably remember from your own time in middle school and high school, however, adolescence is a stressful phase of development, and stress negatively impacts neurogenesis. Thus, students engaged in physical activity, particularly during adolescence, can reap two critical benefits: (1) increased production of new brain cells, to improve cognition, and (2) an improved ability to manage stress. This brings us to our next topic: the impact of exercise on stress and our ability to control our emotions and behaviors.

Movement and Emotional Self-Regulation

The correlations between movement and better behaviors are strong. When students get less physical activity throughout the school day, classroom behavior issues increase (Carlson et al., 2015). Students who are physically active, on the other hand, exhibit better classroom behavior (Michael et al., 2015).

Earlier, we mentioned that exercise can help you manage your stress. How? It's a bit complicated. In the short term (while you're exerting yourself), exercise ramps up your body's stress. But over time, that constant "ramping up" builds a resiliency to daily stressors. Movement also supports better mood, improvements in classroom behaviors and a higher, functional stress regulation. Let's begin with mood.

Mood

Physical activity might make you smarter—it likely will make you happier, and boost your self-worth, too (Reddon, Meyre, & Cairney, 2017). Have you noticed that going for a brisk walk or workout in the morning can help you feel good all day? People report being in a better mood after engaging in moderate to vigorous physical activity. The opposite is also true: People report being in a poorer mood after long stretches of inactivity (Wen et al., 2018). Exercise releases dopamine in the brain, and a little surge of dopamine is good for our mood (Knecht et al., 2004). Therefore, it is not surprising that exercise is one of the most effective researched interventions for depression. In fact, there is evidence that exercise is a better intervention for depression than antidepressant medication or psychological treatments (Kvam, Kleppe, Nordhus, & Hovland, 2016).

Classroom Behavior

To your brain, physical activity is all about learning to "run yourself" while moving. With all the ups and downs that come with life, exercise is literally a training program in self-regulation—keeping your emotions, thoughts, and behaviors in check. This may be why students' behavior dramatically improves when students engage in regular physical activity (Álvarez-Bueno et al., 2017).

In one study, involving nearly 1,500 students from three low-income schools, students' classroom behavior was monitored (to determine the percentage of on-task versus off-task behavior) *prior* to initiating a long-term physical activity program. Researchers later compared

7.2   PE Impacts Academics

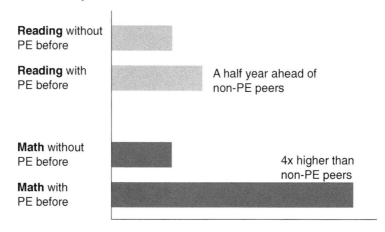

their initial observations to observations made after 6 weeks of the program and after 12 weeks of the program. The results were almost miraculous. After 6 weeks of regular physical activity, the chance of a classroom reaching 80% on-task behavior was *seven times as much as prior to the exercise program.* After 12 weeks, the likelihood of on-task behavior jumped to *28 times as much as* before the exercise program (Burns, Brusseau, Fu, Myrer, & Hannon, 2016). There is no school behavior program (especially one that's nearly free) that can produce results like that!

Remember, a proper balance of stimulation (increased physical activity) and relaxation (reduced activity) helps us maintain optimal levels of differing categories of neurotransmitters. This is a biological need. Consider that students who consistently make poor behavioral choices may currently not be getting sufficient doses of the neurotransmitters that are generated by exercise; thus, they are driven to seek out similarly stimulating experiences, in the form of behaviors that can be disruptive. Make physical activity a priority and witness for yourself the reduction it leads to in classroom disruptions.

Stress

The relationship between stress and exercise is not as simple as exercise reduces stress. In fact, that isn't always the case. Think back to the last time you exercised so hard that your muscles were sore the next day. Those sore muscles were likely a result of your putting a significant amount of stress on your body. Physical activity often introduces short-term high levels of stress to your body, and that is good.

Exercise is one form of *acute* stress. Acute stress is stress that does not last for long and has a definable ending time or conclusion in sight. For example, the stress of your workout ends when you decide to leave the gym. Why can acute stress be beneficial in the classroom? Because in low doses, cortisol (the neurotransmitter associated with stress) can help a student focus, stay sharp, and jump into action on a task (Sapolsky, 2015). Giving your students a pop quiz, or an engaging timed task, can trigger this "good" stress just like a challenging workout. (Too much of it, though—e.g., if you tell your students the pop quiz will contribute greatly toward their grade—and they might get overwhelmed.) But in addition to that, there's a core biological difference between stressing *yourself* (on purpose, as with exercising) and *being* stressed (by circumstances outside your control) (Zoladz, Park, & Diamond, 2011).

Stressing *yourself* temporarily increases your cortisol, but afterward it drops to a low level, which helps you rest and recharge. *Being* stressed increases your cortisol level and keeps it there. After all, if you have little to no control of the situation, how are you supposed to know when you can relax? You end up in a state of almost constant tension and anxiety. This effectively reduces your ability to tackle new issues as they arise, or even to function on a day-to-day basis, because it drains your physical and mental resources. Meanwhile, your stress may keep climbing. If you don't take matters into your own hands by flooding yourself with cortisol through exercise or other time-limited activity so that the level will then recede, you will remain "up to your neck" in it. This is the picture of *chronic* stress.

Chronic stress can be caused by toxic environments, intolerable home life, trauma, poverty, anxiety, racism, social isolation, sexism, and many other factors (Raffington et al., 2018). It is this type of stress that has damaging effects on learning, as well as on students' physical and mental health. In fact, chronic stress is one of the biggest brain-cell killers (McEwen, 2017).

The good news is that physical activity can help students with chronic stress. Although teachers cannot remove every source of stress for their students, physical activity can really take the edge off and make a difference to students' lives. Students who have regular exercise habits will make healthier choices when faced with stressful circumstances. Also, their exercise routines will build stress resilience to help them better cope with future stressors. Figure 7.3 enumerates several of the long-term advantages of people who exercise.

7.3   Life-Changing Benefits of Physical Activity

✓ **Your Stress Response to Reduce Illness**

✓ **Brain Chemistry for Enjoyment and Thinking**

✓ **Oxygen Utilization and Production for Longevity**

✓ **Glucose Regulation to Reduce Inflammation**

✓ **Cellular Health for Healing**

✓ **Growth Factors to Heal and Grow New Cells**

Source: Phillips & Fahimi, 2018.

Movement and Health

Physical activity boosts your immune system and provides protection from illness and disease (Bermon et al., 2015). Thanks to epigenetics, the ability to influence gene expression through lifestyle choices, a regular exercise routine can extend your "health span"—not just your longevity, but the length of time in which you remain healthy into old age.

The long-term implications of exercise for your students might not be your highest priority (although we commend you if you are concerned). Surprisingly, there are *immediate* consequences that impact their ability to be at school, and the health of others in the classroom (including you).

Classroom Attendance

Students who are physically active have better attendance (Michael et al., 2015). Students with higher fitness levels are less absent from schools (De Groot, Van Dijk, Savelberg, Van Acker, & Kirschner, 2017). One study followed students for three years to track their physical activity and school absence. Some students increased their physical activity by 20%; other students decreased their physical activity by 20%. How did this impact their school attendance? The students who decreased their physical activity were absent 12% more than the other students (D'Agostino et al., 2018). That equates to approximately 22 extra days of missed instruction as a result of poor physical activity. That evidence is another reason why less-active students struggle in school.

Classroom Health

Missing 22 extra days of school can put a tremendous strain on families to care for sick children when many of them need to be at work. Hence, some students attend school when they are sick, increasing the spread of colds, flu, and other viruses. Perhaps you have also dragged yourself to school to teach when you were sick.

Overall health in your classroom and school can be improved by all students and staff engaging in consistent physical exercise.

Disease Prevention

Recent science has been making connections between exercise and disease prevention. If you want to increase your chances of avoiding heart disease, cancer, diabetes, dementia, Alzheimer's disease, and dozens of other chronic diseases then regular exercise is critical (Grazioli et al., 2017). Exercise doesn't just protect you from these diseases—it can also reverse the effects they might already be having on you, your students, or other loved ones (Varga, Kyselovič, Galfiova, & Danisovic, 2017).

A sedentary lifestyle is one the top 10 risk factors for all disease, and it is responsible for 9% of all deaths worldwide (Lee et al., 2012).

IN THE CLASSROOM

When implementing the suggestions in this chapter, remember to look for the nonverbal cues your students' bodies are sending you afterward—is it greater attentional focus or a more diffused energized state? Once you find the right balance, you'll reap the benefits of improved attention, memory, and even new brain cells.

Here is more evidence for how movement helps students learn—the dopamine released when you exercise helps regulate your mood and hormone levels. Dopamine is one of the brain's and body's main motivators—it is willing to do whatever it was that initiated the dopamine release (Lloyd & Dayan, 2015). So, if you're searching for more ways to motivate your students, add more physical activity to your repertoire of motivational tools.

You can further contribute to your students' well-being by modeling, supporting, and reinforcing healthy habits that relate to physical activity. Be a role model to your students of optimal health and gratitude for your body by exercising. Teach your students the value of physical activity, join them for an occasional game of kickball at recess, or challenge them to a race against you every Friday afternoon. Take your pick of strategies like the following:

- Facilitate hand movements each day with clapping games, dancing, puzzles, and manipulatives. Invent new ways to shake hands or greet each other.

- When students need to move to gather supplies or find a partner, invite them to lunge, moonwalk, leap, or squat on their way. "You next partner is 17 lunges from where you are standing now."

- Have students paste a chart inside their notebook to track their physical activity. "Did you move your body for 30 minutes straight today?" Check the box. Guide them to set personal and class-wide goals that they check in with daily or weekly.

- Set up a competition between classrooms for the greatest total number of steps taken per class per month. Winners receive a random act of kindness from the other class.

- Schools can compete with neighbor schools for the most laps per month, steps per day, or minutes of exercise per day.

Conclusion

The mind-body link is long past any speculation. It's real. Physical activity can supercharge the brain. The data clearly tell us that cognition, health, and self-regulation skills are all boosted by physical activity. Students who are physically active have better attendance, exhibit better classroom behavior, and perform better academically (Michael et al., 2015). Getting frequent exercise gives students almost every advantage in school. It enhances their attention, memory, and brain-cell production. It improves their mood, decreases their overall stress, and reduces their likelihood of illness.

Unfortunately, most school leaders have decided that their students can manage to scrape by without regular PE classes. That means it is up to you and your commitment to a more "brain-friendly" approach to remind others of the incredible value of physical activity. The options are endless; the benefits are profound.

Remember all those classic childhood games mentioned earlier? So many elementary-school teachers are getting caught up in the race for better scores that these common activities are being forgotten. Yet active games like "red light, green light" are proven to improve student attention and self-control (McClelland et al., 2019). And variations of the game "Simon says" have been used to measure students' behavioral regulation, which includes inhibitory control, working memory, and attention (Ponitz et al., 2008). Given that how well students perform on these types of games is a clear indicator of future academic achievement and behavioral regulation, let's make more time for them in school.

Teach your students the joy of physical activity. Model a healthy lifestyle, and get active with them. Be an advocate for daily physical education in schools. Encourage your students to participate in extracurricular activities such as sports, drama, and dance. Get them to start thinking about their lives over time, not just tomorrow. Finally, ensure that when they are in your classroom, they are immersed in an active learning environment where movement is encouraged, purposeful, and celebrated.

Motivation That Works 8

Some days teaching feels more like pulling teeth. You push, pull, twist, bend, and nearly do a cartwheel—and your students still don't budge. Whether it is trying to get them to do an assignment, participate in an activity, or contribute to a class discussion, some days you are doing all the work. It can feel exhausting and perhaps even frustrating when your efforts to motivate students fall short. Perhaps you have even experienced how your students' level of motivation impacts your own motivation? To keep everyone's motivation levels at their peak, this chapter will unpack the neurobiology of motivation, explore what might be demotivating your students, and give you the most powerful (and practical) motivational strategies.

Let's begin with this question: Where do motivational urges and surges come from? The short answer is genes, environment, and the combination of the two (epigenetics). Some of what motivates kids in school in Algeria or Zimbabwe, Alaska or Wyoming, will also motivate kids in your own home town. The secret is to know what motivates your own students (as well as yourself) and then make it a habit to implement the strategies often.

Our short-term, in the moment, motivators are actually state management tools. You might use camaraderie and enthusiasm: "All right, now team; let's get this done!" The longer term motivators are what are often called "drivers." Those are biologically driven and either internal (e.g., to gain mastery) or external (e.g., to boost social status). As an educator, you'll want to use tools from both groups.

Understanding Motivation

In every stage of life, we are motivated to learn who is an ally and who is an adversary. We learn to do things that ensure our survival (e.g., eat, look both ways before crossing, and avoid objects moving fast toward our head). What might change as we age is how we interpret the term "survive." For some kids, going to and from school each day is about survival (daily fear—you might die if you go down *that* street).

For others, trying to survive the social structures of a playground full of peers can be a bit similar to weaving in and out of stampeding animals. What we refer to as "behaviorally relevant" means that which will help you reach your current goals. In one moment, a student's goal might be to stay alive; in another moment, it might be to gain social status.

Developmental Motivations

While it is easy to say the brain's primary motivator is **survival**, some motivators change as we age. Certain drivers become more dominant, while others "fade away" to some degree, based on a variety of factors. As a result, what matters most to an infant is different than what

8.1   Examples of Developmental Drivers

Many Exceptions and Variations Among Your Students

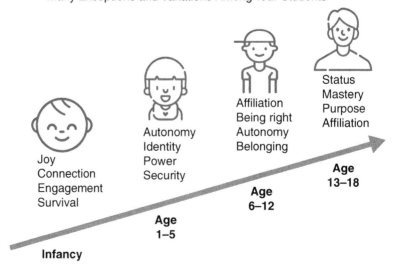

matters most to a tween, which in turn is different than what matters most to an emerging adult. Here is an overview of some of the developmental stages.

Early Childhood: Ages 1 to 5

While infants' primary motivation is survival, children ages 1 to 5 are also driven by a need for **security** (Kim, Chow, Bray, & Teti, 2017). This is why it can upset them to be separated from their primary caregiver or when their normal routine changes. They are also motivated by a desire for **autonomy**, like the determined toddler who declares, "I can do it myself." Their sense of identity is developing as they begin to recognize their role within a community (son, friend, sister, etc.). Their sense of autonomy, security, and quest to be in charge is front and center daily.

Childhood: Ages 6 to 12

If you want to see how significant **a sense of belonging** (Cillessen & Rose, 2005) is to children in this age group, watch the catastrophic impact it has on a child to be told by a peer, "You can't come to my birthday party." **Being affiliated with a group** is a high motivator for pre-adolescents. In addition to a desire for autonomy, they are also driven by **a need to be right** ("I told you so!").

Adolescence: Ages 13 to 18

In the adolescent years, new motivating factors begin to emerge as students mature and begin to see the world outside of themselves. It is during this phase of development that some begin to be motivated by **a mission or sense of purpose** to contribute to a cause (environmental issues, gender equality, suicide prevention, etc.). They are motivated by more than their affiliation with a group ("Our team rocks!" is no longer enough) (Burrow & Hill, 2011). After all, belonging is good, but it is not enough just to be in a group. Teens are motivated by **wanting to differentiate themselves from others**. That means this age group begins to pursue social status (Ojanen, Grönroos, & Salmivalli, 2005).

By adolescence, students want status *within their group* (e.g., as someone who's the best at fixing a smartphone, who has seen the latest shows, who plays a sport, who's up on music trends, or who knows the funniest YouTube channels) or want others to recognize their individual accomplishments (e.g., "Everyone says I am so smart!"). Their desire for status among their peers grows to new, sometimes reckless levels of wanting to show off their digital "likes" to their friends. They still love being right ("I knew I was right about *that one*"), which now also involves **a sense of mastery** ("I am pretty good at _____") (Brechwald & Prinstein, 2011).

We'll describe some ways of tapping into most of these motivations later in the chapter.

Three "Hardwired" Motivations

Although it is true that our motivations shift as we age, there are some highly reliable ways to elicit immediate motivation. There are three consistent factors that are always driving us, regardless of age, gender, or ethnicity. Figure 8.2 highlights these universal motivations. It should be fairly easy to imagine how each one might be important to our survival at any given time.

Curiosity

Want to see natural human curiosity at its peak? Spend time with infants as they investigate and explore the world around them. Or toddlers who incessantly ask the question, "Why?" for every new wonder they discover. We are naturally curious—our brains are wired to learn and discover the meaning of things (Kidd & Hayden, 2015). Maintaining and encouraging this level of curiosity can be challenging in an educational environment that is purely driven by

8.2   The Brain's Three Hardwired Motivations

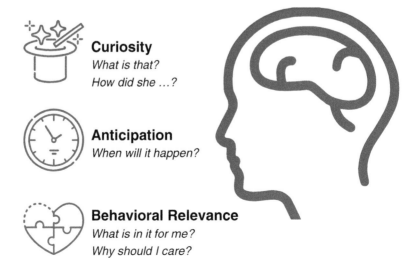

Curiosity
What is that?
How did she …?

Anticipation
When will it happen?

Behavioral Relevance
What is in it for me?
Why should I care?

standards and assessments, but it can be done. It is often as simple as framing a "standard" through questions or experiments that spark students' natural curiosity—for example, "Why do people do risky things for love or money?" Just asking the question can invite curiosity, causing students to think, *Maybe there's something I am missing out on.*

Anticipation

Being able to predict what is going to happen next (or at least possible outcomes) provides a tremendous survival advantage to any species. The anticipation of threat creates immediate motivation (Nelson & Hajcak, 2017).

Teachers should never use threats to motivate a student to learn, but they can strive to replicate this anticipatory state in other ways. The tension and excitement it engenders increases attention, a key ingredient for motivation. Students may perk up and be on the lookout for clues or start piecing together existing bits of knowledge to be able to guess what's coming around the corner. Although structure and routines are valuable in that they provide certainty for learners, if students know exactly what is going to happen, there is nothing to anticipate. In other words, there is nothing to be motivated to discover. Anticipation can also engage our desire to be right, as it feels satisfying to have made a pretty accurate prediction.

Behavioral Relevance

Have you ever noticed how you sometimes listen in on conversations happening at tables near you at a restaurant? But not all conversations are interesting to you. You might be interested in a discussion about how to remove a wine stain from your carpet, but not a conversation about stroller brands. Why? Well, perhaps you spilled wine on your carpet recently (or anticipate it happening someday), and your days of pushing a stroller are long past. The brain naturally pays attention to things that are of greater relevance (Oudiette, Antony, Creery, & Paller, 2013). From a survival perspective, this only makes sense.

These motivations apply to students who are learning math as well as those who are learning a foreign language. They exist equally among students in Copenhagen and those in Chicago. You can use them to influence the behavior of a 5-year-old or a 95-year-old, because each one of these motivations is strongly connected to three important neurotransmitters:

1. **Dopamine** is released when there is perceived or anticipated success or reward. It is also released when success is ultimately achieved (Lloyd & Dayan, 2015).

2. **Norepinephrine** is the neurotransmitter of urgency, excitement, and risk (Unsworth & Robison, 2017).

3. **Cortisol**, in moderate levels, gives the body and brain a boost of energy to meet a challenge (Corbett, Weinberg, & Duarte, 2017).

IN THE CLASSROOM

Is your content naturally interesting to your students? Do they find it relevant to their lives? Are they curious to learn the algorithm for polynomial long division? Or, are they almost holding their breath till tomorrow when you discuss the main themes of the Federalist Papers? If not, hook your learners by creating curiosity, anticipation, and relevance. Here are some suggestions to get you started:

1. Keep students curious throughout the classtime. Start with a "what if" question—for example, "What if we reversed our learning and tried this out?'" Ask students to help look up fascinating or colorful facets of the topic that other students would not likely know. In addition, keep them looking ahead with teasers and mysteries to dig into that will motivate them to do their homework. For example, announce at the end of class, "The next chapter holds the secret to obliterating racism. Be sure you read it before next time."

2. To foster greater anticipation, dedicate a special corner of a bulletin board or wall space for a "Coming Soon" spotlight area to preview topics with a phrase or picture hinting at an upcoming lesson.

3. To create greater relevance, connect new learning to a current event, pop culture, a popular video game, or anything meaningful to your student population. "Borrow" meaning from something your students care about, and use it to improve the quality of their memory.

Understanding Demotivation

The human brain loves to learn. So why, by the time they reach school age, do some students frequently seem not so inclined? In this section, we'll explore what may be going on for your students under certain conditions, at certain times, or in their lives in general. We'll start with the demotivating factors that teachers are best positioned to try to address before moving on to those that more stubbornly stymie our efforts at motivation because they follow students around. The toughest demotivators are those we hope never show up in students' lives—but when they do, we can seek to recognize them, comprehend the situation, and refer to outside intervention.

Adverse Environmental Demotivators (Triggers)

Our brains store many types of learning in our memories. When any student walks into your classroom, a switch flips in his or her brain, and certain memories are activated. Some of these memories are associative (*This reminds me of that*), some are emotional (*That makes me feel . . .*), and others are episodic (*This reminds me of that situation*). What triggers the switch can be the shift from outdoors to indoors, from open space to confined space, or from being around friends to being around lesser-known students (or the reverse.) The bottom line is our environments constantly trigger responses. Here we introduce three common activations that can be adverse.

Physical Demotivators

For some students with enough bad memories of school, simply walking onto a school campus can trigger feelings of being demotivated. So could entering a particular classroom, hallway, or recess area. If walking into the science lab triggers a student's memory of the last experiment and the upsetting chemical smells that accompanied it, the student's motivation may be mostly to get the experience over with fast, not to learn the material (Clayton, Salwiczek, & Dickinson, 2007; Schacter, Gilbert, & Wegner, 2009).

Instructional Demotivators

Instructional demotivators can relate to the content or the way the teacher conducts the class. Each student is unique and motivated by different subjects, class activities, and teaching styles and personalities. A student might be highly motivated in her art class, but as soon as the bell rings and she begins walking toward her math class her motivation could plummet. Some students are motivated by group work, while others prefer to get down to business on their own. What can teachers do about such quirks and peculiarities? Our suggestion is that they try to pay attention to the cues their students give them, ask for feedback, and listen as they modify their instruction to maximize student motivation.

In addition, day after day monotony of routine with no novelty can be demotivating. For example, if a teacher continually uses the overhead projector—never varying the method of presentation—students may feel demotivated as soon as that teacher turns off the lights and takes a position next to the projector yet again. A teacher's apparent lack of enthusiasm for the content, or for teaching as a profession, also impacts student motivation (Mahler, Großschedl, & Harms, 2018).

Social Demotivators

Students who lack social connections with their classmates are less motivated than those who do have friendships within their class (Mikami, Ruzek, Hafen, Gregory, & Allen, 2017). How safe (emotionally and physically) students feel in the class directly impacts their motivation. It is understandable how a student who was teased endlessly after he embarrassingly missed the soccer ball when he attempted a kick is now fearful of participating in PE class, especially during the soccer unit. It can also be demotivating for a student to be directed to join a group project with a classmate she does not like or believes will not be a contributing team member.

The giveaway signs for most of these factors include students rolling their eyes, being hesitant to start a task, and engaging in little dialogue

IN THE CLASSROOM

Reflect on the multitude of actions (and non-actions) you take every day, to determine what is improving students' motivation and what is not. Ask yourself, "What am I accidentally doing that is demotivating my students?" Or "How can I undo the damage that was done to this student in his or her past?" Here are some suggestions for reducing the incidence of *social* demotivators.

- Build systems in your class that promote social connection: reading buddies, student spotlight, daily social traditions (share the highlight of your day so far; share one thing you are looking forward to this week.)

- When doing long-term group work (longer than one day), encourage students to create a team name, mascot, or cheer.

- Incorporate positive peer praise into your classroom culture—for example, invite students to "Tell your neighbor what you liked most about their essay."

in group work. It can also be a sign of demotivation if there is little to no side talk (an indicator of social connection) happening before or after class or during transitions.

Three Temporary Demotivators

There are three temporary types of demotivators that may have little to do with what goes on in your clasroom. Each of these usually lasts for more than a day or two but hopefully not much longer than that. Once you start noticing the signs, you'll be far more empowered to open up a dialogue with each affected student and start working on the long-term solutions.

Fatigue

Daily fatigue is commonly the result of illness, lack of sleep, or poor diet (Shan et al., 2016). Fatigue, for example, may be present in a high school student who rarely gets enough sleep because she or he works 25 hours a week (and looks after a younger brother). Lack of sleep is a common problem, particularly among students at the secondary level. Most teens need seven to nine hours of sleep nightly to avoid compromising their immune system, their cognitive capacity, and their physical energy levels.

A student who is acting demotivated might be ill with a common virus, minor bacterial infection, or other temporary illness. When the body is using a lot of energy to stay healthy, it has less energy for activities that are not as crucial to survival, such as multiplying mixed numbers. Students who have missed school due to illness probably won't be quite up to snuff on their first day back, as their energy level hasn't yet returned to normal.

A lack of energy may also be a consequence of eating poorly. A poor diet may consist of foods that lack nutritional value, foods that don't help learning (like too many sugars and starches), or foods with additives, colorings, or flavorings that can trigger adverse reactions in the body. High intake of sugary snacks and caffeinated drinks can lead to nosedives in energy when the jolt they provide wears off, making it hard to stay motivated. (The role of nutrition in student academic performance has been well-studied and is better detailed in Chapter 11.)

Signs

- Students are slumped in their chairs or dozing off in the middle of your lesson.

- Students are snacking on candy and energy drinks throughout the day.
- Students seem congested, have flushed cheeks, or look a bit pale.

Distractions

Distractions are most likely due to unrelated but pressing issues. In class, a student may be distracted by the emotional residue of an interaction with the teacher or another student. Perhaps a friendship has quickly gone awry and the student is ruminating about the discord, worrying over what people may say, or thinking about how unfair life is. Some of the more pressing issues shift students' attention inward as they wrestle with negative emotions, serious challenges, or upcoming decisions. These might relate to something disturbing they saw on the way to school, a big fight at home, a breakup, a parent being in trouble with the law or simply not coming home as soon as hoped, or a suspicion that a parent is having an affair (Guyer, Silk, & Nelson, 2016).

Signs

- Students seem to be daydreaming, often either staring off into space or looking down toward the ground.
- Students who are caught up in distractions sometimes miss the instructions for a task, so they look around at what others are doing to follow their lead.
- Older students who are distracted might be seen checking their device frequently, looking for an update on a situation or a response from someone.

Hopelessness

Hopelessness usually means a student has given up on either learning the subject or the social climate. Sometimes a student gives up on himself or herself. Maybe the student quits caring about school or a particular subject because it has gotten too hard, or there seems no reasonable way to pay for college so why bother doing well in high school? Students who have had only boring teachers for a couple years in a row might also struggle to maintain a positive outlook toward school. Others go into hopeless states because their hopes have been dashed too often and it simply is easier to expect nothing (Marques, Lopez, Fontaine, Coimbra, & Mitchell, 2015).

Signs

- When you issue an engaging challenge to the class, students will not buy into the challenge. Look for a lack of excitement about or enthusiasm for things the rest of the class is pumped up for.

- As you track your students' progress, keep a close eye on students who are in a phase of consistent struggle or poor achievement. They are most at risk of losing hope.

There are some cases where these temporary demotivators are longer-lasting and become chronic. They may also indicate more serious issues.

Three Chronic Demotivators

For the moment, let's focus on the three most common (and lasting) long-term demotivators in our schools today:

1. Drugs (marijuana and opioids)

2. Abuse (emotional shutdown)

3. Learned helplessness (cognitive shutdown)

Drugs

Marijuana and opioids are both highly demotivating drugs that limit the cognitive side of learning. Marijuana use is associated with decreased hippocampus volume and poorer memory compared to non-marijuana users (Filbey, McQueeny, Kadamangudi, Bice, & Ketcherside, 2015). But there are far greater risks than just a bad memory, and students should learn about them in your class. Marijuana use is associated with an increased risk of mental health problems, particularly psychotic disorders and likely depression and anxiety. It is also related to respiratory and heart problems (Bechtold, Simpson, White, & Pardini, 2015). Students should know that marijuana use during adolescence has a more severe and lasting impact on the brain than it does for adult users (Lubman, Cheetham, & Yücel, 2015).

Opioids have their own unique way of damaging cognitive processes and other areas of one's health. Opioid addiction can block long-term potentiation, the process of long-term memory formation and storage (Nugent, Penick, & Kauer, 2007). Abuse of this drug is also linked to a decrease in neurogenesis, the production of new brain cells (Zhang, Loh, & Law, 2016). As with any drug abuse, the brain craves more of the substance until it gets the next "hit." This desire may be so powerful it cripples your motivation for anything else, hurting your ability to do what was once important to you and to act in your own best interest.

Abuse

Abuse of any kind can be a chronic demotivator. Victims of abuse are often consumed by feelings of anger, shame, contempt, and depression. They might feel small, unimportant, "dirty," or even guilty. These intense emotions take over the cognitive side of learning, in what could be called an emotional shutdown. A student will not be motivated by your attempts to teach him about the Battle of Bunker Hill if he is grappling with internal questions like "Should I tell anyone? Have I done anything to deserve this? When will it happen next? Would anyone believe me if I told them?" (Lim et al., 2016).

Learned Helplessness

Learned helplessness is a belief that one's behavior does not influence the outcome; therefore, one makes little effort to improve their situation (Maier & Seligman, 2016). It is a symptom of a stress disorder. Genuine learned helplessness is a serious and chronic condition. It is not treated by a few compliments and a smile. Teachers who have students who fit the description should know that they are in for a challenging test of their patience and skill. The good news is that there are steps you can take to facilitate hope and contribute to healing. See the "Student Empowerment" strategies later in the chapter.

IN THE CLASSROOM

Most of these chronic demotivators will require the help of trained professionals. Seek out your school counselor and other professionals with the necessary expertise.

The teacher's main role in these circumstances is to provide a supportive, positive atmosphere for each student to learn. If you deem it appropriate, consider teaching students about the dangers of drug abuse through your specific content area. Build positive relationships with all your students, so that they feel they have a caring adult they can confide in. Provide students with autonomy to increase their sense of control and influence in their life.

Short-Term Motivational Strategies

There's nothing phony or irreverent about short-term motivation. In some ways, it is no different than healthy fast food (hard to find, but it does exist). The salient feature is that it works (again and again and again). With some novelty, thoughtful framing of the activity, and a smile, you *could go for an entire school year* using short-term motivation boosters. *But it would be exhausting.*

Remember that our brains prefer a balance of habit and novelty (predictability and change). Just about everyone is different in their preferred ratio of those two factors. From those who prefer extremely consistent habits (e.g., students with autism spectrum disorder) to those who favor extreme novelty (e.g., students with attention deficit disorder), every teacher has to continuously monitor the class and decide, "What do I need to do next?"

The bottom line is that you will want to develop a strong "toolbox for motivation" that is both internal and extrinsic, and both short-term and long-term. There is no perfect motivator. Why? Even if you think you found "it," the likelihood is that students would soon habituate to it and its effectiveness would plummet.

In the short term, you will engage two types of short-term motivators: overt *state changes* and covert *nudges*. Each of these is incredibly easy to do and highly effective. You might be thinking, *If they are that good, why doesn't every educator use them?* Actually, most do use them. But they have never been thoughtful about them, strengthened them, and looked for ways to broaden their use.

State Changes

A state change is any action that shifts the current physical, emotional, or psychological state of a student (Oosterwijk et al., 2012). (We introduced this concept in Chapter 6, on emotions.) Having students stand and review a topic with a partner could change a student's state. Stretching can be a state change, and so can a one-minute dance party. Writing a thought-provoking question or quote on the board as students enter the room can get them curious before the bell even rings. A state change can be directly connected to instruction and often reinforce learning (as with transitioning to review activities, discussions, or learning stations). Although not all state changes reinforce learning, all state changes *support* learning. Breaking off instruction to play a quick game of Simon says, to lead the class in a clapping pattern, or to crack a clean joke can also change a student's state.

Nudges

A nudge is a prompt to change behavior. But it is done in a particular way. The most public proponent of the nudge is Nobel laureate Dr. Richard Thaler. He describes the nudge as "any aspect of the choice architecture that alters people's behavior in a predictable way without forbidding any options or significantly changing their economic incentives. To count as a nudge, the intervention must be easy and cheap to avoid. Nudges are not mandates" (Thaler & Sunstein, 2009, p. 6).

The food-service manager at your school can "nudge" student choices with a dozen tiny alterations. They might include what time food is offered, the sequence in which each of the components of the meal is offered, the type of display used, the information provided about the food, the surrounding foods on each side, the speed of the food line, the options for portion sizes, portion containers, and on and on. Even the simplest modifications, such as color-coding foods with green (for healthy), yellow (for acceptable), or red (for unhealthy) labels have changed employees' food choices (Levy, Riis, Sonnenberg, Barraclough, & Thorndike, 2012).

In your classroom, you might use nudges all the time. Having upbeat music playing as students enter the room, or during transitions, is a type of nudge that can shift students' attitude or attention. Sharing a brief, compelling story can nudge a class toward increased motivation. The key to a nudge is to keep it subtle and under-the-radar. For example, don't let on that when you've asked students to open their books and you say: "Look over at your neighbor's book. Raise your hand if they are on the same page as you," you're using the tactic of peer influence.

Long-Term Motivational Strategies

Short-term motivators work, but typically for only a few minutes. To motivate students for extended stretches of time, teachers should tap into students' long-term drivers. Here are nine (of many) long-term motivators that can be incorporated into a teacher's daily practice.

Autonomy

Students are motivated by choice. Their perception of autonomy is, indeed, a strong motivator (Lazowski & Hulleman, 2016; Cheon & Reeve, 2015).

- Let students choose which book from a provided list they read.

- Provide flexible seating arrangements with choice (and reminders of responsible behavior).

- Allow students to choose how they present their learning to the class (video creation, PowerPoint, oral presentation, etc.).

Student Empowerment

Empowerment is closely related to autonomy. Participation and motivation are boosted by inclusion, ownership, and choice. They are impaired by autocratic insistence and tight control. As you provide more learner control, you will find that participation and motivation increase quite naturally.

- Schools and staff have to ask themselves hard questions, such as "What are we doing that makes learners feel powerless?" and "In what ways might our behavior create helplessness, and how can we change this?"

- Make a list of choices you provide to learners. Do they have control of their environment? For example, who maintains the temperature, volume, lights, and other physical elements in your room? Do students feel free to get up and walk around when they need to move? Can they get water when they are thirsty? Can they take a break from one type of learning if they feel the need to do so?

- Increase students' perception of their ability to control the outcome of an event.

Success

When students *know* they have actually learned something, or done something right, the natural reward system of the brain releases dopamine.

- Use rubrics and success criteria to help students know what is needed to master a concept or assignment.

- Facilitate the perception or anticipation of success or reward. Set your students up for a boost of dopamine by allowing them to self-assess, predict their grades, or check their answers at learning stations.

Belonging

Students consistently show higher levels of motivation when they believe their teacher cares about them personally (Urhahne, 2015).

- Begin by having one-on-one conversations with students about topics not related to school.

- Notice a student who seems to be listening to music on his device? Ask about what he is listening to.

- Overhear a student talking about her plans for recess? Join that activity for five to seven minutes during recess.

- Keep your focus on building your relationship with each student. The motivation will naturally follow.

Social Status

A friendly competition works well in the classroom for a few reasons. Remember the power of dopamine with success? Well, people like to win. It feels good. Young people are driven by social status. In other words, they like to look good to their peers. A healthy level of competition releases testosterone and cortisol in the brain in doses that boost motivation (Casto & Edwards, 2016). If the competition is too intense or the stakes are too high, cortisol levels could create stress levels too high for learning, so keep the competition friendly.

- Create a simple, homemade "award" or trophy for the group that demonstrates the greatest teamwork, trust, or responsibility on an assignment. Let those students show off their trophy by having it on display at their table for the entire day/week.

- Designate a "student of the day" with specific responsibilities and privileges (e.g., line leader, DJ, or greeter). Allow that student to wear a special accessory (e.g., a hat, sash, or vest) if they'd like.

- Create a competition between classes for who can increase their class average of homework completion for the month. Winners get bragging rights.

Challenge

With some researchers citing students already know 50% of what is being taught, it's no wonder many students have low levels of energy and motivation (Nuthall, 2005). Students need more challenge, and a challenge-seeking mindset is a hallmark of highly successful learners (Hochanadel & Finamore, 2015).

- Give students less time to complete a task, or provide them with fewer resources to support them in the challenge.

- Remember, norepinephrine is the neurotransmitter of urgency, excitement, and risk. A simple exclamation, such as "Oh no! I forgot about something. We only have five minutes to finish this up, and then I've got something else for you" will jump-start students' motors (Unsworth & Robison, 2017).

- Want your fourth-graders to be motivated for a challenge? Try something like "Most students don't learn this till fifth grade. Are you kids ready to show those fifth-graders what we're made of?" Cortisol gives the body and brain a boost of energy to meet the challenge (Corbett, Weinberg, & Duarte, 2017).

Validation/Worthiness

Students are more motivated when they can interact and feel connected to their peers (Ryan & Deci, 2013). When students feel socially connected to the students in their class, it creates a culture of safety where students are willing to take learning risks (ask a classmate for help, admit they are struggling, etc.). Students who feel socially connected to their classmates are more intrinsically motivated, have higher levels of cognitive attention (because they aren't consumed with worry about whether their peers like them/will tease them), and ultimately demonstrate higher levels of achievement (Mikami et al., 2017).

- Allow time for students to get to know each other and build relationships. "Before you start this assignment with your group, share with your team which store you would love a $100 gift card to and why."

- Have students write an interesting fact about themselves on a piece of paper, and place it in the class "We are family" jar. When you have a spare moment, read one of the facts and then reveal who the student is.

Risk-Taking

The adolescent years are a time of self-exploration and risky decision making (Reyna & Farley, 2006). Most of teens' risky decisions can be explained by the delayed maturation that happens in the pre-frontal cortex—an area of the brain known to manage critical thinking, responsible decision making, and anticipating consequences of choices. This part of the brain is not fully developed in teens *and* can be impaired even further by the high emotions that dominate the life of a teen.

Capitalize on students' craving for high-risk activities by peppering your preliminary remarks with phrases like these:

- "I'm not exactly sure if this is safe, or even school approved . . . but we are going to try it anyway."

- "Please don't try this at home."

- "This could totally backfire on us, but who here is feeling risky today?"

- "I'm not sure if we should try this . . ."

Deeper Meaning/Purpose

People first begin to explore their sense of purpose in the world during their adolescent years. It is a time of exploration and your students are beginning to notice the world outside of themselves. When they are engaged in a task that is both meaningful to themselves and contributes to the world, their sense of purpose becomes the driving force behind their motivation (Damon, Menon, & Cotton Bronk, 2003).

- Listen to your students to decipher what social issues are important to them. It might be an environmental issue, homelessness, youth depression, or any other social issue. Then design the lesson/activity around solving that issue. What do they believe an adolescent struggling with depression needs to hear? Use that as a writing prompt in language arts. Or have students put their math skills to work and calculate the lengths, angles, or cost of supplies needed to build a shelter for a homeless person.

The Power of Habit-Building

Teachers can quickly reach burnout when they are running around all day nudging, state-changing, and tapping into student drivers amid all their other responsibilities. They key to keeping your students motivated and maintaining your sanity is to transform these motivational tools into habits. The formula to successful habit formation is simple: **Cue—Behavior—Reward**.

- Connect to students' desire to belong and feel worthy every day with a morning affirmation ritual. As soon as the bell rings, lead your students in saying: "Today is a great day for learning. I am a scholar who pays attention, works hard, and supports my classmates. I am an important member of my class. I can choose to have a great day, and I choose to have a great day today!" Positive self-talk is a powerful life habit that improves performance, motivation, and attention (Geurts, 2018; Hatzigeorgiadis & Galanis, 2017).

In the example above, the cue is the bell ringing; the habit is the self-talk; the reward is the motivation that follows. You can follow the same formula to increase student motivation to complete an assignment.

- Ten minutes before the end of class, announce that it is time to "Start your engines." Students get out paper and then write their name and the homework assignment at the top of the paper. Then they write out their plan to get it done: an estimate of how long it will take, and what time they will start. Then they write down a contact for help in case they need it (a Plan B). Finally, they write a one-sentence affirmation and a strong reason *why* finishing the homework is important—for example, "It makes parents happy," "I can show what I'm made of," "I can impress someone who did not believe in me," or "I can get closer to college."

You can also build habits around your students' desire for mastery, which comes into play during adolescence. Students find mastery goals motivating because of the challenge and interest inherent in the task (Meece, Anderman, & Anderman, 2006).

- Before beginning a new unit, project, or exam, have students set an ambitious goal that connects to their drive for mastery. Guide your students to set goals that are challenging. If their goal is too easy, they won't be motivated, because the goal won't seem very important.

The key to embedding your classroom with motivation-based habits is to neurologically connect the cue to the reward. The brain craves the reward and will thus be driven back to the behavior that gave the reward last time.

Conclusion

You can come up with ways of connecting with most students' developmental motivations and hardwired motivations. You can minimize environmental demotivators, investigate temporary demotivators, and keep a watchful eye out for chronic demotivators. Your efforts will pay off and your students might learn better than ever before. Still, at some point one of them is bound to ask that age-old question again: "Is this going to be on the test?" After all, that question speaks to the behavioral relevance of the learning and subsequent evidence procedure.

When this happens, just roll with the question. Say to the student, "I love your kinds of questions. What your question tells me is I failed to make our learning as relevant as I should have. That is important feedback for me; thank you. By the way, yes, this will be on the test." Be honest; just take in the feedback and grow. The long-term goal of brain-based teaching is to help your students learn to foster brain rewards for its own growth, just as it is naturally equipped to do. If you believe your job is to be a learning catalyst (one who lights a fire for learning), rather than someone who simply delivers information once you have students' attention, you will naturally be driven to focus in on students' levels of motivation.

Putting This Together in Your Classroom

The Non-Conscious
Learning Climate ⑨

Take a look at a tree. It might appear healthy, green, and full of life. But that's of course, not always the full story of the tree. As you know, what is happening underground with the roots, water source, and soil has a tremendous impact on the well-being of the tree. Both "sides" (above and below ground) of the tree's "story" matter. It's just that one side of the story is easier to see, whereas the other is "beneath the surface."

If ever things aren't going as planned in your work with a particular student, and you just can't "put your finger on" a reason why, it is possible there is something happening beneath the surface: at the non-conscious level. These "invisible" factors in education can easily be forgotten by learners and teachers who are busily managing all that is happening "above ground." But there is a structure that is acutely aware of, and immensely influenced by, the non-conscious elements surrounding it—your brain.

Implicit, or non-conscious, learning can be described as inputs received and processed by our brains outside of our own conscious awareness. But how much of our learning is non-conscious? Since we are unaware of it (by definition), it is tough to calculate. However, even early researchers agree that the vast majority of input (over 90%) is taken in at the non-conscious level (Dehaene, Changeux, Naccache, Sackur, & Sergent, 2006; Smythies, 2003).

Why is this so relevant to educators? Because, if most of what's being communicated to our learners' brains is "under the radar," there may be much for *us* to learn! Let's dive into three factors that operate at the non-conscious level that are needed for optimal brain performance and learning:

1. Safety
2. Belonging
3. Hope and support

Safety

When our brains perceive any sort of uncertainty, it is registered by our amygdala as a "concern," since it could potentially become a threat (Mobbs et al., 2009).

Our brains are constantly registering information gathered from the physical environment, the emotional climate, and even the people around us to determine our level of safety at any given moment. If there are no potential threats, brain function continues "business as usual" (Fox, Oler, Tromp, Fudge, & Kalin, 2015).

If there are concerns, brain function is altered as resources divert to the potential threat. When the amygdala is agitated (in other words, dealing with potentially *dangerous* stimuli), the frontal lobe functions can become compromised. Why? Because survival always trumps doing homework (or any other second-order task). The three main areas of our brains' concern for our safety are our physical environment, our emotional environment, and our social environment. Figure 9.1 previews the key attributes of safety to the brain.

Physical Safety

The brain's primary function is to keep you safe and ensure your survival from moment to moment. It therefore has structures and systems designed to detect any potential physical danger *first* before processing other details of your surroundings. For example, when you look at a person's face, your brain quickly perceives whether the expression on that face seems to be one of pain or anger, before it even perceives whether that face is male or female (i.e., before it judges the person's gender) (Czekala, Mauguière, Mazza, Jackson, & Frot, 2015). Why? Because being able to quickly evaluate any potential dangers or threats—as indicated by someone who looks to be on the attack or, alternatively, injured (because perhaps whatever injured that person might also injure *you*)—is far more critical to your survival than knowing *the gender* of the person you're looking at.

9.1 Safety

✓ Am I safe from any physical harm or threats?

✓ Do I enjoy being in this learning environment, and do I feel happiness, calm, hope, and excitement here?

✓ Do I have friends in this class?

✓ Is it socially safe for me to ask for help?

Have you ever walked down a dark alley alone and had an uncomfortable feeling in your stomach? Whether there is an actual threat to your safety or not, your brain is exercising its ability to detect or predict a potentially dangerous situation. Many animal species can, in fact, sense an impending attack by a predator (Casas & Steinmann, 2014).

What does any of this have to do with learning? In order for students to be in an optimal state for learning, the brain should be free from any non-conscious stimuli that could possibly be interpreted as a threat. Such stimuli could range from the non-conscious threat of being seated near a bully to having a teacher who looks intimidating or doesn't smile very often. By the way, students won't tell you that they feel threatened; they just won't be successful learners.

Emotional Safety

Every time we hear about another teen suicide, it shatters our soul. On the surface, a student may seem just fine. She attends classes and gets decent grades. Maybe she has friends, even *likes her classes*, and has caring parents. Then, the gut-wrenching news breaks: She has been found dead from an overdose. Another family is in shock, more friends are in mourning, and the whole school shares the grief. What happened? The big discussion going on is "Why?"

Students' brains are constantly registering information they gather from interactions with those around them—tone of voice, facial expressions, proximity, gestures, volume, positive language patterns, negative language patterns, and so much more (Adolphs, 2010). This is especially true of interactions with their peers and their teachers. The amygdala filters through all that information to make a neurological decision as to whether a teacher will be a source of **negative academic emotions** (anxiety, stress, threat, shame, anger, fear, hopelessness) or **positive academic emotions** (enjoyment, pride, relief, hope, excitement, happiness, calmness) (Lei, Cui, & Chiu, 2018). Students can detect, quite accurately, the emotional climate and warmth of a teacher—and they can do it in a matter of seconds, based on the teacher's nonverbal cues (Babad, Avni-Babad, & Rosenthal, 2003).

In other words, students are constantly assessing and updating their feelings about you as their teacher. One positive interaction with a student in September, at the beginning of the year, will not have the lasting effects one might hope for. The brain's salient-sensing center, the amygdala, is constantly evaluating the stimuli it receives in a highly dynamic and context-sensitive manner.

This is great news when you consider the opportunity to "correct" an interaction with a student in which you didn't show up as your best self. This also means, though, that teachers must be vigilant in regularly providing positive emotional stimuli to students.

Each teacher's relationship with his or her students is producing emotions somewhere on the scale between joy, enjoyment and anxiety, even fear. Students with positive teacher relationships experience more enjoyment (and thus learning). Students who report negative teacher relationships experience anxiety (and thus little to no learning) (Ahmed, Minnaert, Werf, & Kuyper, 2008).

Social Safety

As discussed in depth in Chapter 5 on relationships, humans are social creatures who depend on each other for survival. Social exclusion can make us feel physical pain (Eisenberger, 2012), lead to anxiety and depression (Stanley & Adolphs, 2013), and impair our cognitive abilities (Gianaros et al., 2007). Having strong, healthy social connections helps us live longer (Holt-Lunstad & Smith, 2010), be happier (Stanley & Adolphs, 2013), and learn better (Hutcherson, Seppala, & Gross, 2014). At the non-conscious level, we want to feel socially accepted and respected by those around us. How does this affect the brain and its capacity to learn?

When students feel safe, socially, with the students in their class, it creates a culture where students are willing to take learning risks (ask a classmate for help, admit they are struggling, etc.) (Mikami, Ruzek, Hafen, Gregory, & Allen, 2017). The social connection breeds respect, which creates an environment where students feel safe to ask for help without fear of being shamed. These help-seeking habits are a hallmark of high-achieving students (Ryan & Shin, 2011), especially in secondary schools where this learning skill is less common (Ryan & Shim, 2012).

Students who feel safe in the social structures in their classroom are also more intrinsically motivated, have higher levels of cognitive attention (because they aren't consumed with worry about whether their peers like them/will tease them), and ultimately demonstrate higher levels of achievement (Mikami et al., 2017).

What if students have friends, but they are not in the same class? In that case, they are reaping the health and social benefits, but to gain the cognitive benefits, *the social connection must exist with peers within their own classroom* (Mikami et al., 2017). This level of social safety can be built, and the teacher plays a critical role in making it happen (Farmer, Lines, & Hamm, 2011).

IN THE CLASSROOM

- Establish rules in your classroom that foster safety and trust. Help students know that bullying will not be tolerated.

- Invest time in building strong relationships with students—greet them at the door, ask about their family life, hobbies, goals, and dreams. Open up your classroom to be a safe place for students to hang out before school, after school, or during lunch.

- Foster strong social connections between students in your class. Set a goal to learn all your students' names within the first week of school. It is equally worthwhile for students to learn each other's names.

- Utilize as many social learning activities as appropriate—pair shares, partner reviews, and team projects.

- Create traditions that are unique to your class. It can be a special class handshake on Amazing Mondays, pass-around affirmations on Thankful Thursdays, joke-telling time the last five minutes of every Wild Wednesday, and celebrations on Fabulous Fridays.

Sense of Belonging

Wired into the human brain is a sense of "tribe." Either we belong and we feel safe and valued in a sustainable tribe, or we do not (Jensen, Vaish, & Schmidt, 2014). It is therefore important that every learner feel as though he or she *belongs* in the community of learners. There is strong evidence that this sense of belonging is strongly connected to students' academic performance (Farrington et al., 2012).

Students who have a sense of belonging to a school or classroom community are more likely to engage in positive academic behaviors that produce higher levels of engagement and performance (Osterman, 2000). They see themselves as more competent and show higher levels of intrinsic motivation than their peers who lack a sense of belonging. In addition, they have a more positive attitude toward school, classwork, teachers, and peers.

For some students, their classroom community at school is the only community they feel a sense of belonging to. When familial stability or connection is low, the teacher-student relationship can mitigate the effects of a poor home environment (Benner & Mistry, 2007). Teachers don't have to be substitute parents—but they can offer the same safety and warmth that every child *should* feel at home.

9.2   Belonging

    ✓ Is who I am valued in this environment?

    ✓ Is who I am (in relation to others) seen and valued in this environment?

    ✓ Am I good enough? Do I fit in?

    ✓ Do people care about me?

    ✓ Do I belong in this environment?

What drives a sense of belonging? In other words, how can this sense of belonging be cultivated? We'll focus on three main drivers that lead to a greater sense of belonging (see Figure 9.2).

Identity

"Who am I?" is the central question to describing one's personal identity. When learners feel their identity is seen and valued they, in turn, feel as though they belong in that environment. This is very different from feeling as if they are just another body in the room.

The answer to the question of self-identity often includes elements of one's race, gender, beliefs, sexual orientation, personality, and looks. For example, your identity might include being an African American female. Maybe you are Asian, and your grades are poor. What identity will help you cope? Perhaps your identity includes being a homosexual, tall, Hispanic male. Whatever students' identity is, the question they seek to answer is this: "Is my identity valued in *this* environment?"

Status

While all of your students have a need to belong in your "tribe" at school, a new need emerges at the secondary level. It's not enough to simply belong; the students want to feel special and uniquely valued. The question the brain seeks answers to relates to the pending level of status the learner feels in the community. *Is who I am (in relation to others) noticed in this environment?* (Utevsky & Platt, 2014).

This slight variation on the question above about identity focuses more on the social aspects prevalent in a learning community. *If I belong, in what ways am I any different (or better than) the students sitting on either side of me?* Status is about the social position within a group.

Students can find status in a classroom community in many ways. Some find status as the "smart kid." Others gain status as the "funny kid." Some can find status as the "athletic one." Essentially any valued quality can be a source of status. Think back to your favorite teen movie, and you'll likely recall the variety of "status roles" that adolescents often take on. Attaining a positive status affirms social value. It also increases the likelihood of survival (in a social sense). Perceiving that you have a negative status among peers, on the other hand, feels dreadful.

The adolescent brain is highly susceptible to the influence of words indicative of social status. There is a network of brain regions that compose the "social brain network." These regions include the medial prefrontal cortex (MPFC). The MPFC is of interest to educators because it is highly involved with processing new learning and memory formation. When a depressed adolescent is exposed to socially negative words, such as "loser," the brain regions in the "social brain network" are negatively activated (Silk et al., 2017).

Status can also be gained by being the best at something or winning a competition (as discussed in Chapter 8, on motivation). This is why students are often motivated by a friendly competition. Adolescents like to look good to their peers, because it feeds their status. There is also important brain chemistry happening with a competition. A healthy level of competition releases testosterone and cortisol in the brain in doses that boost motivation (Casto & Edwards, 2016). If the competition is too intense or the stakes are too high, cortisol levels could create stress levels too high for learning, so it is important that teachers keep competitions fun and friendly.

Affiliation

A large number of students—particularly those who come from low economic status, English language learners, or those whose parents lack a high school or college degree—may wonder whether they "belong" in an academic classroom. This is an important question!

Dr. Camille Farrington discovered that students who struggle with content at school are, first and foremost, struggling with a bigger barrier to their academic performance—feeling like they belong (Farrington et al., 2012). Before they are willing to buckle down and do the work required to learn, students first want to answer the question, "Do I belong here, in *this* academic culture?"

Unless students can answer yes to that question, they will put forth little effort, and, as a result, teachers will perceive them to be unmotivated. If they feel like the culture you are providing *will work only for white, middle-class kids*, your students who don't fit that category will pull back. The sad part is that they really *do* want to care about learning and really do want to work hard. How do we know this? Because schools with students who answered yes to the question above consistently performed higher than other schools (Farrington et al., 2012).

Teachers who make student learning (rather than teacher's teaching) the central focus of their teacher planning help students (a) feel like they belong, (b) see how their efforts will directly improve their ability levels, and (c) believe that success is possible for them (Farrington et al., 2012). They motivate students to be learners (Cheon & Reeve,

2015) and provide positive feedback to build students' confidence (Jenkins, Floress, & Reinke, 2015). All of these habits improve student learning and are common traits of exceptional teachers.

IN THE CLASSROOM

- Tell students directly, "I am so glad you are a part of our class."

- Give students responsibilities that help them feel like they are needed and belong in your learning community. Have a student be the greeter for the week that welcomes each student into class. Another student can be the DJ for the week with the responsibility of playing music at appropriate times. A student can collect or distribute supplies, erase the board, post the assignment on the class website, or send out a digital reminder of an upcoming deadline.

- Give students personalized attention so that each student feels valued and sees himself or herself as an important member of the learning community. Create classroom traditions for celebrating birthdays. Get to know each student as an individual. One easy way of accomplishing this is to insert requests into classwork. For example: "At the bottom of your paper, write one sentence about your weekend that you'd like to share with me"; "Tell me something about your family that you'd like me to know." Then use that new knowledge to strengthen your relationship with them.

Feeling Hopeful and Supported

School-aged kids (both younger children and adolescents) show greater emotionality (in frequency, intensity, and volatility) compared with adults (Casey et al., 2010). When researchers sampled both adolescents' and adults' emotional states over a one-week time frame—you guessed it!—adolescents were both more euphoric and more depressed in response to the events of those days. This simple insight may help you understand why students have difficulty maintaining optimism and hope.

Have you ever witnessed the slow decline of a student's level of hope? Day after day, their discouragement grows as their hope sinks. Have you noticed how as their hope plummets, so does their effort? Perhaps you have observed the opposite as well—when hope is prevalent, a learner performs better (Stoddard & Pierce, 2015).

Why does hope (from within or from outside support) lead to better academic performance?

The best way to understand hope is to understand the opposite of hope—learned helplessness (which is the same as hopelessness). Learned helplessness is a belief that one's behavior does not influence the outcome; therefore, one makes little effort to improve their situation (Maier & Seligman, 2016). Without hope, effort drops and learning requires effort. This makes hope is an essential component of learning.

Hope includes three important beliefs: (1) *There are pathways to my goals, and I know what they are*, (2) *Success is possible*, and (3) *It is possible **for me** to use those pathways to reach my goals and succeed* (Snyder, Rand, & Sigmon, 2005). A learning environment filled with hopeful students and teachers creates a climate poised for high achievement, because, as studies have shown, people with high levels of hope:

- **perform better academically** at all levels (Marques, Gallagher, & Lopez, 2017);

- tend to be **healthier** (Kok et al., 2013);

- are **happier**, **more confident,** and have **better relationships** (Satici & Uysal, 2017; Alarcon, Bowling, & Khazon, 2013);

- **handle stressors** better—they see it as a challenge (Rand, 2017);

- use **feedback** to improve their future efforts (Reichard, Avey, Lopez, & Dollwet, 2013); and

- report higher levels of **self-worth**, **life satisfaction**, and **lower levels of depression** (Marques, Lopez, Fontaine, Coimbra, & Mitchell, 2015).

Fostering high levels of hope for your students is a steady job. It requires always having high expectations, being culturally responsive (understand what your students need in their situation, in your classroom, based on the culture they know best), and, finally, ensuring all students have access to allies. The three areas of hope-building are shown in Figure 9.3.

Having High Expectations

Teachers with high expectations will boost student learning. Teachers with low expectations, by contrast, may have little to no effect on their students' growth over the course of the year. Those were the general findings of the well-known Rosenthal and Jacobson research study done in 1968. That was the study in which students were pretested and then, *supposedly based on how well they had scored*, some

9.3 Hopefulness

- ✓ Do my efforts even matter?
- ✓ Does my teacher believe I can succeed?
- ✓ Is my culture seen, respected, and celebrated?
- ✓ Do I have an ally in a teacher, mentor, or coach I can turn to for help?

of them were identified to teachers as high performers, "ready to bloom." The students themselves were not aware of any such distinction. In fact, there was no basis for it; they had been identified at random.

The results spoke of the power of teacher expectations. The students who teachers had been led to believe were high achievers significantly outperformed the other students (Rosenthal & Jacobson, 1969). The Rosenthal Effect, sometimes called the Pygmalion Effect (after the sculptor in Greek legend), made waves in the world of education because of the following two conclusions of the study, which were revelations at the time:

1. Teachers' expectations of students can be manipulated. (Remember, the "high-performing" label was random; yet the teachers believed, as they had been told by the researchers, that it was based on students' performance on the pre-test.)

2. Teachers' expectations can affect students' academic performance.

The effect size of "teacher estimates of achievement" is 1.29 (Hattie, 2017). This is only slightly smaller than the effect size of something that is obviously *directly* related to students' performance, which is their expectations *of themselves* (effect size: 1.33). Teachers' expectations of students, then, clearly have a tremendous influence on their achievement level.

Teacher bias may be unheard and unseen, although perhaps sometimes felt by students at the unconscious level. It is more common for teachers to quite simply give less attention to a student they expect less of than to tell that student outright, "You are not going anywhere in life." Unfortunately, experiences of the latter sort still happen for far too many students. However, it is those of the former sort—non-conscious low expectations from a teacher—that are negatively impacting more students.

The foundation of teachers with high expectations is a core belief in the opportunity to learn. Teachers with high expectations believe that *all* students can and *will* succeed. Hence, they have high expectations of *all* students.

Most teachers want to be high-expecting teachers. But many are held back by preconceived beliefs or mindsets about learning or about certain types of students. Consider whether you share any of the following beliefs that lead to low expectations:

- Math comes more naturally to boys than girls.
- Students can't learn much after lunch on a Friday afternoon because they've already "checked out" for the weekend.
- Students who speak English as their second language won't do as well in school as those who speak English as their first language.
- These character concepts are too advanced for elementary-aged students.
- Students diagnosed with ADD/ADHD will always struggle to focus in class.
- Students living in poverty simply won't become as successful as middle- and upper-class students.

Teachers with these kinds of beliefs can negatively influence their students' achievement. Remember, your beliefs influence your actions, so, for the benefit of your students and their learning, it is critical to confront any negative beliefs you have about teaching, learning, and your students.

In contrast, here are some habits of high-expecting teachers. Teachers with high expectations:

- provide all students with **high-level thought-provoking activities;**
- set **challenging goals** for all students;
- closely **monitor student progress** and provide **frequent feedback;**
- **celebrate successes** with their students;
- create a **positive climate** in the classroom;
- expect **high standards of behavior;**
- implement **positive, preventive classroom management** techniques;
- let their **students know they care about them** and their learning; and
- are **personally motivated by their students'** learning success (Rubie-Davies & Rosenthal, 2016).

Those practices consistently obtain impressive results from students.

A 2016 study (similar to the classic Rosenthal study) has shown, again, the tremendous impact of high teacher expectations on student learning. Students in this study scored on average **28% higher** in mathematics than students in the control group did. The only difference was that the researchers had trained the teachers of the experimental group in three crucial areas related to expectations: grouping and learning activities, class climate, and goal-setting.

Grouping and learning activities. The teachers were taught to create flexible student groups rather than groupings by ability level. This leads to greater levels of self-efficacy. Ability-level groupings are detrimental to students' self-belief (Dumont, Protsch, Jansen, & Becker, 2017).

The teachers were also taught to provide students with greater levels of autonomy by offering choices in learning activities. Autonomy increases student motivation. Self-efficacy and motivation both contribute to student achievement (Ryan & Deci, 2013).

The teachers were trained in how to create appropriately challenging learning activities. Challenging activities increase student motivation and thus improve learning (McDonald et al., 2014).

Class climate. The teachers learned specific tools to create a positive climate within the classroom. Positive teacher-student relationships, along with positive student-student relationships, have been shown to improve academic achievement (Pianta, Hamre, & Allen, 2012).

Goal-setting. The teachers were taught how to set clear, specific, and challenging goals with their students. Goal-setting can enhance student achievement (Travers, Morisano, & Locke, 2015). This is especially true when teachers monitor students' progress toward the goals and provide feedback on their progress.

IN THE CLASSROOM

Here are some specific suggestions to help any teacher become a high-expecting teacher.

Grouping and Learning Activities

- *Eliminate ability-level grouping.* It doesn't help students academically, and it sure doesn't improve students' belief in themselves (self-efficacy) to know that they have been officially placed in a group with other "low" kids. Social groups are a powerful way of communicating expectations to students. Students learn from the teacher by which group they are in. Just as important, they learn from their peers how to be more competent when they are not in a lower group.

- *Allow students to make choices regarding which learning activity they complete* (all related to the same learning goal). If you are doing a unit on clouds, for example, you might tell them, "To demonstrate mastery of your knowledge of clouds, you can either choose to write a creative story outlining the differences between cloud types or create a short skit to perform for the class." Student autonomy is a huge predictor of student motivation.

- *Provide opportunities for students to work with a variety of their peers.* Switch groups weekly, at the end of a unit, or even with each assignment. Make it random but interesting: "Today you'll be working with people born in the same month as you (or neighboring month, if there are not enough matches)" or "Your partner for this next activity is exactly 17 steps away from where you are standing now."

- *Assign challenging tasks.* How challenging is too challenging? Well, the answer you probably don't want to hear (but is true) is *it depends on the student.* You wouldn't take all your students out to the track and expect them all to run a mile in seven minutes or less. But I hope you would expect them all to improve their time on subsequent attempts. The same is true for their academic performance. Each student is unique. Look for signs of boredom, and then increase the challenge for that student. When you see signs of frustration or anxiety, decrease the level of challenge.

Class Climate

- Remember the brain's need for physical, emotional, and social safety. Create expectations that support these needs. Work to create a positive relationship with each student.

- Use positive language patterns when communicating expectations or when calling on students to mind their behavior. Negative commands—such as those beginning with "Stop" or "Don't"—bring down the climate and relationships in the classroom. Instead of telling a student, "*Stop* leaning back in your chair," say, "Please keep all four legs of your chair on the ground." Instead of "*Don't* forget your permission slip," say, "Remember to bring your signed permission slip back tomorrow." Substitute "Please focus your attention right over here" for "Stop looking at the class walking past the window."

Goal-Setting

- Teach your students the basics of goal-setting. Show them how to create a goal that is specific and may be achievable. Walk them through the process of creating progress-based goals for their academic achievement. At the start of the year, to set a strong, gutsy goal for math or reading, encourage students to take their current level and add two grade levels of growth to it by the end of the school year. This makes the goal achievable and challenging.

- Guide your students to set goals that are challenging for them *personally*. If a goal is too easy for a particular student, he or she won't be motivated because the goal won't seem very important. Goals can rarely be too hard; they *can* lack the "why," lack support, or lack a clear, doable path.

- For all students, staying energized about big goals is a challenge. So, ask your students to add weekly goals to their big goals, letting them pick the milestone tasks that they must complete. These smaller goals will fuel their energy and give them confidence to stay focused on their big goals. These are the "super-short-term micro-goals" that will keep them excited about continual progress. Have them zoom in and decide "Here's what I am going to get done *this* week"; then, from time to time (e.g., at the end of each week), help them notice the progress they are making toward the long-term big goal.

Being Culturally Responsive

The well-established "empathy gap" between teachers and students of different cultures creates a barrier to learning, one that is worthy of attention because the *majority of minority students* perceive they are discriminated against by their teachers. Because of this widespread perception, minority students commonly report feeling as though their academic efforts are pointless (D'Hondt, Eccles, Houtte, & Stevens, 2016).

Social inequity continues to be a real problem in our schools. African American students are suspended from school two to three times as often as students of other racial or ethnic groups (Gregory et al., 2016). And the data suggests a consistent trend of teacher bias against white females in math courses (Riegle-Crumb & Humphries, 2012). These are just two examples. There *are* training programs designed to reverse these implicit biases, and they have shown promising results. For example, in some schools, training teachers in non-discriminatory relationship-building skills and engagement strategies has eliminated the biased suspension of African American students, with lasting results (Gregory et al., 2016).

Recognizing and respecting all cultures in your classroom will yield high payoffs, both relationally and academically.

IN THE CLASSROOM

Do *your* homework to learn about your students and the cultures they come from. Ask parents at the beginning of the year to write you a letter or email explaining the uniqueness of their child and cultures they come from that are especially meaningful to them.

- Use culturally specific holidays or events as an opportunity to teach the rest of the class about a cultural tradition. Knowledge and awareness are the seeds from which tolerance and compassion grow.

- Always be on the lookout for any unintentional preferences or biases in your interactions with students. "Play it safe" by assuming that you do have biases, and make a point of noting them to yourself weekly. The research is too solid on this topic for teachers to pretend they are blind to their students' differences.

- Show students a new successful role model (who looks just like the other students) every month or so. They need to see an "older version" of themselves doing what they hope to one day achieve to know their expectations are truly within reach. Ask students to visualize being the success stories you know they can be.

Ensuring Access to Allies

For students, an ally is anyone who can offer them extended support and a feeling of hope, or any resource they can turn to in times of need. Students thrive when they know they have allies supporting them. An ally can be a specific person, such as a teacher, classmate, counselor, or coach. Textbooks, access to the internet, and subject-specific equipment or tools can also be allies. Let's explore the most accessible allies—teachers—and the impact they can have when students feel safe enough to ask them for help.

Help-Seeking

Students who ask for help perform better academically (Ryan & Shin, 2011). And low-achieving students are less likely to ask for help than their high-achieving classmates. With an effect size of 0.72, "help-seeking" demonstrates the huge advantage students have when they reach out and ask for help (Hattie, 2017). But in order for students to feel safe enough to ask you for help, they must believe you are their ally in learning.

When a trusting relationship exists between students and their teacher, students are more likely to ask for help and feel safe enough to make a mistake. They will feel confident that they won't be teased or looked down upon if they fail the first time they try something.

There is a prevailing mindset among students that asking questions means you are not smart (Hicks & Liu, 2016). This idea emerges in the early years of schooling and solidifies over time. Be diligent in shifting this belief. Celebrate the curiosity and the desire for understanding that drive people to seek help.

Create systems in your class that promote emotional safety for "help-seeking."

- Students can place a small object on their desk to indicate they need extra assistance. Maybe each student can have a wooden block on his or her table—one side painted red, the opposite side painted green. Red side up means "I need help!" Green side up means "I'm good right now."

- Use a digital messaging system, to allow students to ask for help in a way that is discreet and thus won't threaten their standing in the eyes of their peers.

IN THE CLASSROOM

Conclusion

A possible source for certain threads of non-conscious learning is via the brain's mirror neuron system. The shortest explanation of what mirror neurons help us do is "Monkey see, monkey do." It is all about imitation learning. Italian researchers Iaccomo Rizzolati and Vittorio Gallasse discovered these amazing subsets of brain cells by accident in the monkey brain (Rizzolatti, Fadiga, Fogassi, & Gallese, 1999). The researchers found a small number of neurons that fired or showed their greatest activity both when the individual performed a task and when they observed a task. A study published in 2010 recorded the activity of single neurons with mirror properties in the human brain (Mukamel, Ekstrom, Kaplan, Iacoboni, & Fried, 2010).

The significance of the mirror neuron system is profound. It is likely the basis for imitation learning, contagious yawning, social learning, mob behaviors, copycat crimes, and why kids pick up on the teacher's emotions. In short, it helps us understand why we are affected by the behaviors of people around us. But are these mirror neurons always on and working? Assuming that they are healthy, they are always on.

But our frontal lobes, as they mature, can step in to dampen the effects of the mirror neurons. So instead of copying another person's negative or seemingly irrational behavior, you might say to yourself that the action is crazy, irrelevant, or dangerous and choose to avoid it. However, many younger kids, and even teens, have not yet reached this point and thus will still copy the bad behavior. In fact, many adults with compromised frontal lobes (e.g., from brain injury, drugs, or depression) still make poor choices based on seeing others do the same.

In a classroom, because of the mirror neuron system, students may unconsciously pick up on the teacher's mood, facial expressions, and actions far more than previously thought. When teachers are happy, some of it can rub off on students (and vice versa), and a teacher's frown, scowl, or sarcastic comment may be more hurtful than we can know.

Being aware of the unconscious influence that you (as the teacher) and other elements of the environment have on learning can lead to improved decisions that impact learning.

Better Classroom Learning—Easy as R-C-C 10

Our world is full of acronyms: AD/HD, LGBT, GATE, NEA, ELL, TAG, and a few thousand more. We have one more acronym that might just be the most important, relevant one in the entire book: R-C-C.

Those three simple letters stand for the single best "keeper" idea from the whole book. Yes, the learning context is very important. And, yes, transfer into real world is critical, too. But, *inside the brain,* only three things matter: R-C-C. They are R for **readiness** to learn (receptivity), C for coherent **construction** of the learning, and C for **consolidation** (error-correction, storage, and transfer).

This chapter is all about classroom implementation of the things you are learning about in this book. Our brains are designed to keep us alive, and with some limits on the capacity we can learn and store, being selective is critical. To survive, you need a relatively small amount of highly relevant knowledge. Tailoring your instruction to meet these parameters requires an understanding of the peculiar "rules" for how our brains learn best, and this chapter will drill down to the classroom a bit deeper.

As an instructor, thinking about the learning process a bit backwards will help your learners understand it better and save you a lot of grief. One useful model is Understanding by Design, created by Grant Wiggins and Jay McTighe. One of their tenets is to plan backwards. Begin with formally designating your desired results. Next, state how will you know that you are getting from the students (when you do get it). That is your evidence of learning. Finally, you can start up with your learning plan. We are now, in this chapter, doing the learning planning.

Let's explore how the brain best learns new content and skills. Content, for the purposes of this book, includes declarative, factual knowledge that is typically taught in a school—science, language arts, math, history, and so on. We will also address skills that the brain can learn, such as active listening, problem-solving, responsibility, kindness, self-regulation, and empathy. Whether the brain is learning content or skills, the learning process is similar. The acquisition of knowledge in a brain-friendly way can be divided into three main stages, as illustrated in Figure 10.1.

Readiness provides a structural framework and the "emotional and psychological opening" for the new learning. It can also add, modify, or prime the brain with possible new or better connections. **Coherent construction** involves the creation of new neural networks, either through reorganizing existing networks or through building new ones. **Consolidation** provides certainty of accuracy, with enough latency and elaboration to ensure the new learning is stored and can be used.

This chapter is not meant to be an all-encompassing three-step process. Everything mentioned in the previous chapters on learning climates, motivation, relevance, emotions, physical activity, and more are still highly important. Hold on to all that previous learning as we add these three "timeline" continuum stages of brain-compatible learning.

10.1 The Stages of Optimal Learning: R-C-C

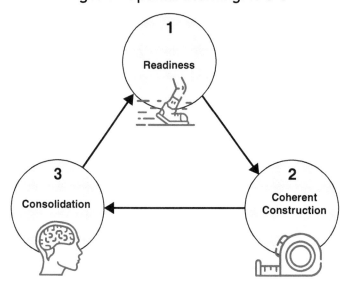

R: Readiness

For new learning—whether it involves content knowledge or a real-world ability—to be encoded in the brain, the brain needs to be "ready." What does that mean? There are certain pre-existing conditions that enhance the brain's capacity to learn new things. Do these conditions *always* need to be met? No.

Most episodic (e.g., "hand on hot stove" and other surprises) and implicit (non-conscious) learning occurs without any preparation. However, for the specific, school-based content and skill-based learning we are focusing on in this chapter, a certain level of readiness will boost attention, learning, and retention (Shing & Brod, 2016). Three key areas of readiness support both content- and skill-based learning:

1. Prior knowledge
2. Pre-exposure and priming
3. Behavioral relevance

Prior Knowledge

The more background learners have on a topic, the faster they will absorb and process the new information (Shing & Brod, 2016). The brain benefits if, in preparation for new learning, it gets opportunities to bring to the surface everything it currently "knows" about the content area or skill. Through reflection, or through outside support from another person (e.g., a teacher), learners can challenge and adjust their own misconceptions and false assumptions in preparation for more learning.

That's right—prior knowledge is sometimes false, misleading, or biased. Anyone who watches a variety of national evening news channels is likely to notice that the selection and treatment of identical news events varies dramatically, presumably depending on the biases of the news producers. Similarly, students may have absorbed the "news story" of the learning in a way that allows them to get certain facts right but leaves out some details, involves a misunderstanding of context or significance, or leads them to the wrong conclusions. In addition, they may have been given confusing or inaccurate information.

In a classroom, to prepare students for new learning, a teacher must guide their brains to assess their current prior knowledge and reexamine any potentially false knowledge. Let's say a teacher is going to be talking about guerrilla warfare in Central America. Prior to the lesson, some students might think the term "guerrilla warfare" refers to a battle with armed gorillas; others may believe that guerrilla warfare is acceptable because conflicts are best handled with violence; and yet others may be likely to propose unrealistic "win-win" solutions between the combatants. In each of these cases, there is a lot of "cleaning up" that needs to happen. Every educator has a fiduciary duty to share with students how to assess content, notice biases, and openly share personal prior misperceptions.

Pre-exposure and priming

Pre-exposure is any strategy that introduces content to the brain long before the formal learning occurs (Moravec, Williams, Aguilar-Roca, & O'Dowd, 2010). As a kid growing up, I (Eric) tried out a plastic car that was powered by pedals. When I was old enough for the ride, I drove small gas-powered cars in Disneyland. Those experiences were the "classic" pre-exposure for my someday getting a license and driving a real car.

Think of pre-exposure as a movie trailer—something that provides a big-picture overview of what is coming. Ideally, there is plenty of curiosity and anticipation built in, just as with a real movie trailer. Pre-exposure provides learners with a foundation on which to build connections. The more background you provide, the better and faster your students may learn (Shin, Dronjic, & Park, 2019). Displaying posters or a mind map of an upcoming unit are examples of pre-exposure.

Priming is similar to pre-exposure. It simply involves a preview of something more immediate—something that will happen in a matter of days, hours, or minutes (Weingarten, Chen, McAdams, Yi, Hepler, & Albarracín, 2016). One benefit of priming is it can activate a state of curiosity or anticipation—both of which enhance motivation and learning (Kidd & Hayden, 2015). Here's an example of priming. A teacher tells his students, "When we get back from recess, we'll be solving the great color mystery—why are trees green and not blue?" That simple question can have students already thinking about everything they know about color, trees, and mysteries by the time they file back into the classroom. Don't worry about spoiling the climax in your movie trailer—let learners be surprised by the process rather than the content.

Giving students prior exposure to a topic days (or even a week) ahead of time can reduce the cognitive load (Moos, 2013) of new learning. It helps students build schema and be ready to retrieve related information from their long-term memory during the actual lesson on the topic.

Behavioral Relevance

Behavioral relevance is a critical feature of learner readiness. Input that is behaviorally relevant involves a strong, real-world reason *to take action*. One way of determining whether something is behaviorally relevant to *you* is whether it makes it "relevant" for you to think and behave differently than you are right now. Let's say there's a large outdoor event happening with hungry people in attendance. The announcement of "Free food!" is very clearly behaviorally relevant, and the crowds will flock to the food source. Or, if you are fearful in an unsafe situation, the announced appearance of a police officer is behaviorally relevant, since it is an opportunity for increased safety. This is the key neuroplasticity rule for teachers: Before you start your instruction, *always* get behavioral relevance. Help your students understand *why* they should care about the information you're about to share. If their brains aren't "buying" the behavioral relevance of what you're "selling" in the classroom, their brains aren't changing (Kilgard & Merzenich, 1998).

When a learner recognizes the behavioral relevance of new content or a new skill, the chances of its being learned, remembered, and internalized increases (O'Keefe & Linnenbrink-Garcia, 2014). In addition, self-referencing ("how does this relate to me?") drives our attention and memory (Morel et al., 2014). Behavioral relevance can also be used to invoke autonomy in the learner (Vansteenkiste, Simons, Lens, Sheldon, & Deci, 2004), which is a strong factor in intrinsic motivation (Ryan, & Deci, 2000). What this means is that students, when they relate to the content, are more likely to take ownership for and direct their own learning.

Behavioral relevance is critical across all age groups—from youngsters through adulthood (Leshikar & Duarte, 2014). How it is utilized differs based on the learner's values, motivations, and desires. For a student who is interested in raising her grade in the class, communicating behavioral relevance might mean telling her, "If you do this, it will likely help you do better on your next test." A different student, with different values, might be more willing to put forth similar effort but only in order to please a teacher or impress her peers. In that case, to indicate behavioral relevance, a teacher could say, "You're going to get props and look cool to your friends when you learn this." For young students (K-2), who may strongly value having extra fun or making their parents happy, it may work wonders for them to hear "Your parents will be so happy to see you do well on this!"

IN THE
CLASSROOM

Content Acquisition

Remember, when teaching your students skills, just as when teaching them content, it's helpful to gear up their brains for that learning.

Here is an example of how to use prior knowledge and priming to ready your students for content acquisition, in a lesson on clouds: A week before your lesson, hang pictures of the three main types of clouds, to pre-expose students to the topic. The morning of the lesson, **prime** their thinking with a comment such as "Today you will all become master weather-tellers. It's like being a fortune-teller, just specifically about the weather." Make it relevant by reminding them of a time they might have accidentally worn clothes that didn't match the weather for the day. Assure them that with their new knowledge today, those days are over!

IN THE
CLASSROOM

Skill Building

You can use similar tools to prepare your students to learn new skills, in a lesson on how to offer a sincere apology: In the weeks leading up to your lesson, find opportunities to pre-expose the students to this life skill through overt modeling. (The power of modeling is discussed at length in another chapter.) On the day of the lesson, have students reflect on times someone told them "I'm sorry" but it didn't feel sincere or sufficient to heal the hurt. Share a story of a sincere apology that helped mend an important relationship in your life. To cement students' notion of its behavioral relevance, assure them that the communication tool you're about to teach them can be used to remedy nearly all situations in which they may have injured, offended, or insulted someone.

C: Coherent Construction

With a "ready" brain, the construction of new (or reorganizing of existing) neural networks is next. If our brain only "copied" new information on to its "hard drive" (long-term memory), things would be much simpler. But we rarely copy what we hear with 100% accuracy unless it is pretty short, brief and simple. An exception would be learning how to say or spell a simple vocabulary word. This leads us to our next stage.

"Coherent construction" is more than "constructing" our new learning. That suggests more than that we be active and mindful in the process. But unless what we piece together makes sense and has some meaning, it is not likely to be valuable or be recalled. In short, not all new learning is useful.

As our brains try to make sense of the new learning, we interweave it with our past experiences, biases, and context. Our new learning has to fit our identity, values, and expectations, or else we may be dismissive of the learning (Hutchinson, Pak, & Turk-Browne, 2016). Here are three tools that can help your students learn more thoroughly (and maybe more quickly).

1. Shift the size of the content chunks
2. Shifting the "bias filter"
3. Multisensory instruction

Shift the Size of the Content Chunks

There may be times a student appears to be disengaged and apathetic, perhaps even while nodding and saying "uh huh." But don't assign that student a label of "unmotivated" or "lazy" too quickly. What you're witnessing could be, instead, a cognitive mismatch.

Too much content, too fast, is unlikely to get processed correctly and saved accurately (Schacter, Guerin, & Jacques, 2011). Researchers agree that our immediate memory (both short-term and working memory) is naturally fairly limited. This memory (our mental workspace for the "now" moment) has a baseline capacity to process no more than four new chunks of information at a time, for up to 30 or so seconds (Paas, & Ayres, 2014). Sure, we can learn to extend and expand that capacity (with training or tools), but one to four chunks is where we generally start.

And to make sure you understand how small each of these "chunks" is, the algorithm for long division is *not* just one data chunk. It is a complex process that can consume all of a student's working memory, assuming the student already has a strong understanding of basic division, multiplication, and subtraction.

What happens when you try to learn something that has more than four parts? Use of your working memory takes up "cognitive space" in your brain. This drain on your resources is called a cognitive load. When there is too much on your mental "plate" (e.g., emotional issues, excess content, worries, and stress), this "excess cognitive load" impairs learning. If a math unit has eight parts (chunks to it), break it up into three chunks: a chunk of two smaller pieces and two chunks of three smaller pieces.

To mitigate the strain on your working memory when learning new content or skills, break the new information down into chunks (e.g., focus on just a few key words at a time) (Thalmann, Souza, & Oberauer, 2018). Small "portion sizes" will aid your "digestion" of the knowledge. Learn, rehearse, apply those new ideas, and then go back to the buffet and serve yourself another helping until the big picture is complete. You can "offload" concepts from your working memory by writing them down or using your hands to gesture (to "hold" the idea or concept in another memory pathway: the procedural route). Once the info is "offloaded," you will be better able to focus on the task at hand.

The "right" size of the "content chunk" varies. For some students, in some topics, the best way to keep them engaged is using aggregates of chunks (referencing the "big picture"). This type of student needs to constantly reference the "why" and the "gist" of the content. If a student is a ninth-grader, the tiny-chunk task might be doing tonight's homework properly. The bigger chunk might be fostering background knowledge for his or her desired area of study in college. Ultimately any of us can only do one small chunk at a time. But it is the back and forth and managing of the chunk size that helps manage the cognitive load.

Now you're ready for some practical tools that incorporate the brain-changing tools you've learned so far.

IN THE CLASSROOM

Building skills in any content area requires specific parameters in the brain in order to make changes. When you are trying to help students build a skill—whether it be the academic skill of reading, the social skill of kindness, or any other type of skill—here's the brain-based protocol:

Begin **priming** a few weeks in advance, to improve readiness. Define measurable and specific **goals** for the change being made. For example, "I want to see 75% of hands raised when I ask more compelling questions." Share an **example of excellence** with your students— either by modeling or sharing past student work. Invoke high levels of **behavioral relevance** for why this new skill is important. Focus intensely on the one new skill being learned, and do it until there is clear progress toward mastery.

The format for skill-learning is called **deliberate practice.** This is the process of practicing something that is just above (about 5% higher) your students' current skill level, so that it is hard but not impossible. Implement skills practice for 10 to 15 consecutive minutes a day. The task should be difficult, so that it cultivates occasional frustration in a deeper practice. To keep students in the optimal "learning zone," continually use your tools to tweak the process. Reactivate the behavioral relevance daily. Start with micro chunks, then use multisensory learning. Continuously check for understanding. Focus your questions more on "how" and "why" rather than lower-order right/wrong questions. Remember to allow for thinking time before you call on students to respond.

Overlearning means going beyond comfort to mastery; practicing the change is key to "locking" it in. New skills typically take 40 to 60 repetitions to become a habit, over a period of weeks and months (Lally, van Jaarsveld, Potts, & Wardle, 2010). You can use this time to reassess and tweak your instruction. There is rarely a straight line for learning, especially for skill learning. Figure 10.2 shows you the learning curve for skills practice.

While much of our daily interactions can be quick and simple, school can get pretty complex. For example, we hear complex sentences,

10.2   Deliberate Practice: Continual, Increasing

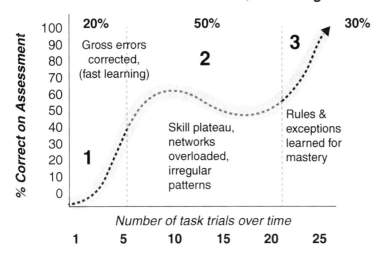

paragraphs, and stories. We get problems to solve, factual sequences and skills to learn. To manage that challenge, you'll always be weaving multiple feedback processes into the construction process, and each part of the learning processes can be more robust with quality feedback. Formative feedback is feedback a learner receives *during* the learning process, as opposed to at the end (i.e., summative feedback). So that your learners are constantly making minor corrections to their memory, you should ensure that they receive feedback *daily*. Formative feedback can be elicited via listening, answering, or demonstrating. It can be generated via think-pair-share strategies (with the teacher roaming to listen in on conversations), or it can be sparked by strategic questions that foster classroom dialogue. The best feedback is that which helps students learn to answer three important questions: "Where am I at now? Where am I going? How do I get there next?" (Hattie & Timperley, 2007).

IN THE CLASSROOM

Respond to giving and getting feedback without shaming, guilt, or judgment. Recognize feedback as simply guidelines for growth. **Change** your mental model after new learning has occurred. Both you and your students should now be able to describe the way in which your thinking has been shaped. An example would be when a student says, "I think I am finally getting this math. I'm starting to like it, too."

Shifting the "Bias Filter"

Teaching without any bias filter at all would be likely impossible. How *much* content is offered, *what* is added, and what is *never introduced* in our classes all depend on the biases we hold. In any classroom discussion, our biases also factor in to *which* questions we are trying to answer, the "rules of engagement" (what is allowed or not) and whose side we are on.

A bias may be identified as sexist, racist, classist, religious, or age-related. Such biases, although they have harmful potential, may most often be unconscious and subtle rather than intentional and overt. On the other hand, biases need not be related to people at all; they may relate to events, ideas, or the way things work. In professional writing, bias includes the perspective of the writer and the aims of the work. In short, assume that *everything* you read has a bias. Even a published scientific study or physics textbook can be rewritten with a different bias.

To boost classroom learning, you have many options for reducing bias. You might consider reorganizing the content with a new "filter." For example, you can study a war from multiple perspectives (the perspective of those in power, the perspective of the soldiers doing the fighting, the perspective of ethnic differences, the perspective of the aggressor country, the perspective of the oppressed, a social-class angle, the perspective of sheer economics, or a child's perspective). This kind of deep dive into the learning ensures the brain understands the wider or deeper context and not just isolated or rote facts (Spires, Kerkhoff, & Graham, 2016).

Shifting the bias filter provides students fresh opportunities to think about things differently. It can suggest which approach is best for *that* specific problem, thus better encoding the learning (Rohrer, Dedrick, & Stershic, 2015), because it helps the brain detect similarities and differences in the telling of the story.

Multisensory Instruction

Since memories are stored in different areas of the brain, teachers should aim to input new learning in different parts of the brain to improve the memory consolidation process. The once-touted "Learning Styles" theory claimed that a learner best learns through one favorite learning "pathway" (Cassidy, 2004; Pashler, McDaniel, Rohrer, & Bjork, 2008). Not only has the original theory never been scientifically validated or replicated, it contradicts our current understanding of how to best construct new learning (Willingham, Hughes, & Dobolyi, 2015; Newton & Miah, 2017).

Instead of a single "pathway," teachers should attempt to target multiple sensory cortices within each learning experience. The more widespread their brains' involvement, the clearer the picture and better the understanding will be when learners retrieve the information and reconsolidate it (Schneider, Beege, Nebel, & Rey, 2018). Following are some common ways of engaging different parts of students' brains in a single lesson:

- Visual cortex: visual aids, colors, mind maps, short video clips, and visual language ("Picture this . . ."; "Imagine . . .")

- Auditory cortex: callbacks, vocal dynamics (whispering, using an accent, shouting a key word), music, rhymes, singing, and rhythm

- Motor cortex: body motions, note-taking, gestures, and short skits

IN THE
CLASSROOM

Content Acquisition

In Chapter 5 (on neuroplasticity), you were reminded of the many ways you can approach the challenge of new content or skill acquisition. The formats included schema-based, immersion, deliberate practice, and self-regulated. This portion of the chapter applies perfectly (with just a touch of modification) to each of those formats.

Here's the schema-based format. When teaching the six steps of the photosynthesis process, help students master their recall of the first two steps before adding the next two steps to their knowledge. As you help students master each chunk, allow them to draw pictures, explain it to a neighbor, and act it out as a class, to make the learning multisensory. As students act out the photosynthesis process, have them take a different angle each time—from the perspective of the leaf, the sun, or the water.

Are you teaching math? Consider starting with a bare-bones overview of the learning or a story about a math discovery. Use the power of biases: Engage a new depth of learning when mathematics is learned through the filter of three separate famous mathematicians, such as Pythagoras, Newton, and Fermat (that's a bias filter).

Would you like your students to *really* understand how an electron behaves? Change your filter bias—personify an electron and learn about his/her *wild* life as a part of an atom!

IN THE
CLASSROOM

Skill Building

Teaching students to collaborate and work as a well-functioning team is a complex goal with many parts. Have students share what they believe makes a great team, including examples of high-performing teams. This will expose any bias they have regarding teamwork. Because there are many elements to a well-functioning team, focus on one element at a time: having a common goal/vision; trusting your teammates; giving/ receiving feedback; and so on.

Spend time delving into one element for that class period before introducing another in the next class period. Have students create icons to visually represent each element of an effective team, as well as a motion to anchor the learning to their bodies. (For having a common goal/vision, students might decide to draw a soccer goal with net and make a show of raising their hands in celebration as if they just scored a goal.) To round off their multisensory learning, students can create a motto or chant for their team that embraces the essential components of a high-functioning team.

C: Consolidation

Memories are not as "cast in stone" as we might hope. They are, by nature, dynamic, flexible, and thus prone to distortion (Schacter, Guerin, & Jacques, 2011). Because memories are stored in various cortical regions, when it comes time to retrieve (aka remember) something, it is common for us to make errors as we reassemble the pieces. This consolidation stage of learning ensures the accuracy and transfer of the new knowledge or skill. Let's look at three principles that support strong confirmation:

1. Getting it right
2. Spaced learning
3. Relevant transfer

Getting It Right

The act of "remembering" (or retrieval) is highly subject to inaccuracies. How can such an amazing organ as the human brain make so many errors? Keep in mind that retrieval includes the frontal lobe working with several other parts of the brain, bringing bits and pieces from numerous brain regions together to reconstruct a memory. Although sometimes errors in information recall–related performance are due to the wrong information being consolidated in the first place, most scientists agree it is the reconstructive process that is susceptible to distortion (Schacter, Guerin, & Jacques, 2011; Lacy & Stark, 2013). Two key solutions to this weakness are retrieval practices and formative feedback. We introduced formative assessment earlier; it is a mandatory part of every learning process. That type of feedback will reduce errors.

We first talked about retrieval practices in Chapter 5. **Retrieval** is any activity that challenges the learner to mentally, verbally, or visually retrieve information previously learned *without looking it up*. Retrieval practice is far more effective than "studying," which often involves staring at a book or reviewing less-than-perfect notes. Not only do retrieval practices facilitate error correction; they greatly enhance student learning (Karpicke, 2012). It is most effective to engage in retrieval practices both the same day new information is learned and at intervals for two weeks afterward (Roediger & Butler, 2011).

Examples of retrieval practices are practice tests, flash cards, partner quizzing, and learning stations. When students talk about what they have learned, it reactivates their memories and solidifies the learning (Sekeres et al., 2016). Before you have your class do any retrieval activity, it is imperative that you establish a system to "error-correct" so that students avoid reinforcing incorrect information. That is, ensure they have (and use) some means of confirming their answers. It is not in the *completion* of these tasks that students correct their memories. It is through the acquisition of **feedback** (from the teacher, a device, a peer, or an assessment) on these tasks that learning and memory can improve.

Spaced Learning

Although it may seem counterintuitive, time away (i.e., a break) from new learning can help the new information consolidate properly in students' brains. This concept of "spaced learning" allows the brain to thoroughly process the new information and consolidate it into a memory (Smolen, Zhang, & Byrne, 2016). In one study that may get your attention, students 13–15 years old were given either a spaced learning biology course with retrieval practice or the standard four-month biology lectures (Kelley & Whatson, 2013). The testing method was limited to high-stakes tests of a National Curriculum course in the specific context of school education. In fact, this process is so good that, when spaced learning is combined with retrieval tools, students not only learned the content better in a Biology course, they remembered it longer, too. The test scores for each of the experimental groups were significantly higher than random answers with an effect size of 4.97 (nearly a ten-to-one ratio). Other studies support spaced learning and found that learners consistently retained information better when they reengaged with the content periodically (Kang, 2016).

Relevant Transfer

Very few learning strategies are as important as behavior relevancy. To help students see actionable change in the content, educators

Review new information, if possible, within 30 minutes of when your students learn it. Review it again the next day, within a week, and then at longer intervals (based on difficulty). Aim to revisit new learning at least three times to effectively confirm the new learning. Create daily or weekly traditions around spaced retrieval, such as partner quizzes, bell ringers, ticket-out-the-door, and pop quizzes.

need to (1) connect the content "dots," (2) try out different bias filters, and (3) maybe mind-map the content to find new areas for a tie-in. When teachers help students do this part of the learning, student effort increases, because the "why" of the learning is reinforced.

Aside from in social-studies classwork that focuses on the current political climate, this part of the learning process is commonly ignored. Many students feel as though school is what they have to do to get a diploma. Teachers who are highly successful remember the importance of the three Rs: relevance, rigor, and relationships. They take extra time and thinking to put the puzzle pieces together for their students to increase their recognition of relevancy.

Let's close out this chapter with some examples of these consolidation strategies for you to follow in the classroom.

Content Acquisition

When teaching different literary devices such as simile, metaphor, alliteration, and personification, allow students multiple opportunities to "get it right." Use a variety of tools to check for understanding, such as having students match each device to an example, setting up a learning station for each device, and calling on students to create sentences that employ a device. Remember to circle back to this new learning the next day, a few days later, and a week after its introduction, to ensure proper encoding. Have students go on "treasure hunts" for these literary devices in news articles, social media posts, movies, and even their favorite YouTube channels.

IN THE CLASSROOM

Skill Building

To reinforce students' learning of a goal-setting frame, use multiple examples to help them understand how to create a goal that is specific, measurable, and realistic. Have them create a variety of sample goals to share with peers and receive feedback on. Use mini assignments or ticket-out-the-door strategies to provide even more formative feedback. To create relevant transfer, have students imagine they are a well-known individual striving to achieve the next level of success in their career. Guide them to set a goal as if they were that person. To make it even more personal, support them in using the goal-setting frame for their own personal, academic, and social goals.

Getting Your Brain to Work With You, Not Against You: Self-Care

11

It is no secret: Being a teacher is hard work. It can be physically exhausting, emotionally draining, and socially lonely. To make matters worse, the more stress teachers are under, the more it leads to poor student outcomes, such as lower grades and frequent behavior problems. Teachers who are highly stressed have higher rates of sickness, absenteeism, and accelerated signals of aging. All of these difficulties and their consequences can create a vicious circle, and at times you may be tempted to throw in the towel. We've all known teachers who say: "I can't do this any longer. I am out of here at the end of this year."

But it doesn't have to be that way. The work you are doing every day is too meaningful for it to be dragging you down. You have a lot more say in shaping your daily experiences than you think you do. Teaching can be a profession that is invigorating, soul-filling, and full of meaningful connections.

In this chapter, we'll be focusing on some things you can do to make a big difference to your learners. We're not talking about field trips. We're not talking about instruction-related preparations, lesson planning, or research. There are plenty of resources you can turn to for guidance and fresh ideas in these respects. We mean to focus instead on your underlying ability to keep up with the demands and the frantic pace of teaching, which all comes down to the habits you form in caring for your brain and your body. Everything you do impacts your brain and its ability to function at its best. In fact, to help you shift your mindset from how you conduct your class to how you can transform your personal life, we've renamed some of the advice sections "Out of the Classroom." We still emphasize one or two classroom elements of a brain-based approach, such as your relationships with your students.

This chapter guides you through the principles that will support you in sustaining your physical, emotional, and social health so that you can be the teacher you strive to be. In order to *give* your best to your students, you must *be* at your best. To be at your best, consider focusing on these three areas of your general well-being:

1. Vibrant health

2. Running your own brain (self-regulation)

3. Relationships

Rather than give you a long "to-do" list it makes more sense to focus on the fewest things that matter most. This illustration highlights the big three items.

11.1   Get Your Brain on Your Side

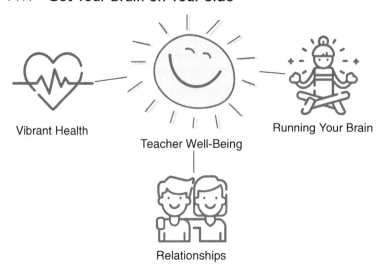

Vibrant Health

Teacher Well-Being

Running Your Brain

Relationships

Vibrant Health (Physical Well-Being)

You may be a teacher for the next 20 years, or you may not. Perhaps you'll go on to become an administrator or an author. Whatever you choose to do, few things are as important in this life as your physical health. If you're not doing well yourself, how can you hope to do anything well?

Nutrition

What does your diet have to do with your brain, or how you show up as a teacher? Everything! Simply put, your body and brain are inexplicably connected. What you put in your body affects your brain function. What you do to your brain affects your body.

The "gut-brain axis" is a term used to describe the two-way communication between the gut and the brain (Chianese et al., 2018). In fact, many researchers now refer to one's gut biome as the "second brain." Your gut bacteria stimulate the neurons of your enteric nervous system to communicate directly to your brain. This constant communication, driven by your diet, influences memory, mood, and cognition (Galland, 2014).

OUT OF THE CLASSROOM

To be at your best physically, fuel your body with foods that will boost your energy, mood, and overall health. The general guideline for optimal brain and body nutrition is to consume more natural foods (fruits, vegetables, healthy fats and whole grains) and fewer high-sugar, high-carb processed foods (white breads, candy, soda, chips, alcohol, etc.) (Beilharz, Maniam, & Morris, 2015).

Keep consuming foods rich in natural fats, such as avocado and nuts, while cutting back on foods high in trans fats, such as those that are fried. This type of diet may will increase neurogenesis—the production of new brain cells—and reduce chronic inflammation, a health problem that is connected to all chronic diseases (Netea et al., 2017).

Your goal is to keep your body at top biological functioning. That means enhancing the health of your mitochondria, strengthening your antioxidants and commit to the overall robustness of your immune system. Do whatever works for you in this regard.

Movement

In Chapter 7, you learned the power you can harness with movement and physical activity to improve your students' learning outcomes. As you might have guessed, much of the research and benefits apply to teachers. Physical activity impacts your brain function, mood, and health.

To recap, physical activity enhances both working memory and short-term memory (Chen, Zhu, Yan, & Yin, 2016). Exercise triggers the release of brain-derived neurotrophic factor (BDNF), a natural substance that enhances cognition by boosting the ability of neurons to communicate with each other (Griesbach, Hovda, Molteni, Wu, & Gomez-Pinilla, 2004). Daily exercise contributes to elevated BDNF levels in various areas of the brain, including the hippocampus, which is critical for memory processing.

Physical activity is linked to greater levels of happiness and self-worth (Reddon, Meyre, & Cairney, 2017). People report being in a better mood after engaging in moderate to vigorous physical activity (Wen et al., 2018).

OUT OF THE CLASSROOM

If you leave school in a foul mood or frequently wonder whether being a teacher is of any worth, try building your brain and body with regular exercise for a couple weeks and see if things change. This boosts a sense of control over your life. Start a morning walk/jog program at your school to keep you motivated and accountable. Use it as an opportunity to start your day off right and build connections with students. Or sign on as an assistant coach to one of the sports teams at your middle or high school and then join in the workouts.

Sleep

Most adults need seven to eight hours of sleep every night. Anything less (or even more) than that, and the risk of chronic inflammation increases. Inflammation is the immune system's natural response to the presence of foreign bacteria and viruses, as well as to wounds, other injuries, and toxins that can cause illness. Your acute inflammation response (pain, repairing a cut or wound, etc.) is temporary and critically helpful in restoring the body to health. However, chronic inflammation is the result of the immune system being in constant "fight mode." Over time, chronic inflammation directs your disease-fighting cells to attack innocent, healthy cells, tissues, and organs throughout your body, eventually damaging multiple systems. This is what can happen when your body does not regularly receive the proper amount of rest.

Poor sleep quality has also been linked to increased cancer risk (Xiao, Arem, Pfeiffer, & Matthews, 2017). The body works to heal itself during sleep, so limiting that time can deplete your body's resources for fighting off foreigners and keeping you in good condition.

How does a lack of sleep lead to inflammation? Sleep is regulated by circadian rhythms that cause you to drift between phases of sleep and wakefulness throughout the day. When your sleep pattern is disrupted (e.g., because you've been staying up too late grading papers for the past week), your circadian rhythms get out of sync. These same circadian rhythms are also responsible *for regulating your immune system* (Scheiermann, Kunisaki, & Frenette, 2013).

So, when your circadian rhythms are disrupted, your immune function is also compromised. Even one night of binge-watching your favorite TV show till early morning can trigger inflammation processes in the body (Irwin et al., 2008). People who habitually get less (or more) sleep than they need exhibit elevated CRP levels (a substance produced by the liver in response to inflammation)—an indicator of chronic inflammation (Irwin, Olmstead, & Carroll, 2016).

Going to bed at the same time each night and waking up at the same time every day reinforces healthy circadian rhythms, which in turn supports healthy immune function, including keeping inflammation to a minimum. So, set yourself a bedtime that will allow you to get the recommended amount of sleep. If you struggle with insomnia, stay away from the night-time medications (they are bad for the brain)—instead, focus on some simple things you can do to help you fall asleep, as well as improve the quality of your sleep. Try taking melatonin an hour before bedtime. Set an alarm on your phone for 30 minutes before bedtime to remind you to turn off all your screens (phones, tablets, laptops—anything that's brightly lit and interesting). Turn down the thermostat to between 62 and 68 degrees. Darken your sleeping area as much as possible, or wear a sleep mask. If the problem is that thoughts keep running through your head, try writing them down in a notepad on the nightstand or counting backward from 100 by threes, and enjoy some well-earned rest.

OUT OF THE CLASSROOM

Running Your Own Brain (Emotional Well-Being)

You are likely involved in daily conversations that revolve around one or more of these stress-inducing topics: high standards to meet, standardized tests to cram for, disrespectful students, angry parents, students experiencing trauma and/or poverty, and students with learning challenges. You may try to wish these things away, but they keep cropping up. At times, the situation may seem hopeless. Unless you take steps to maintain your mental health, you're likely to struggle with depression.

Though you may continue to do the best job you can for your students, the consequences of your troubles will extend to them as well. A negative state of mind can reduce your effectiveness as a teacher, even if the impact on students' learning isn't evident right away. One study, for example, found that teachers' depressive symptoms in the winter negatively predicted students' spring mathematics achievement. The classroom experiences of the affected teachers' students were of lower quality than those of their less-stressed peers. Finally, students with lower math ability made greater gains when they were in higher-quality classrooms with less depressed teachers (McLean & Connor, 2015).

The numbers of students in poverty, experiencing trauma, or faced with learning challenges are increasing. Teachers today need greater emotional resilience and self-regulation to manage the emotional stressors of being an educator. Coming up are three prominent ways to improve teacher well-being.

Choosing Serenity and Peace

Here's a secret about "stress." It is *your* brain that generates *your* stress response. Here's how it works. First, incoming sensory data arrives. At that moment, your brain's two "stress filters" (relevance and sense of control) take over (Godoy, Rossignoli, Delfino-Pereira, Garcia-Cairasco, & de Lima Umeoka, 2018). Based on how *you* filter and then process the information, you'll either get stressed (or not). In other words, you are in charge of the stress you feel. Again, stress is generated in your brain as a response ***to a perception*** of a loss of control of a person, event, or situation. That's why we may have differing responses to the same potential stressor. People are different, and people experience stress differently depending on their coping tools. Thinking that your students, principal, or parents stress you

11.2 Stressed Brains Underperform

Impact of Acute Stress on the Underside
of the Brain as Seen with a SPECT Scan

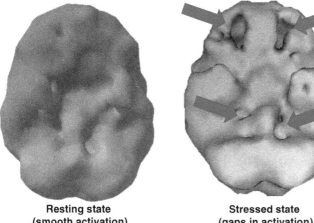

Resting state
(smooth activation)

Stressed state
(gaps in activation)

out is misplaced blame. They don't stress you out. You stress you out (Godoy et al., 2018). So how can you take back some of that control when the going gets tough?

Start by learning how to say no (long before you need it) when people ask you for help, whether in your work or your personal life. We're talking about students, other teachers, your friends, and your family members. It may not seem to fit your idea of yourself or the way you should behave, but you can have the best of intentions and still turn down obligations that would overextend your ability to meaningfully support others. Being the person who says "Yes!" to everything with a smile, only to turn around and feel a rush of stress as you realize you over-committed yourself does not serve you or your students. Practice saying, "Wow—that sounds interesting. Thanks for thinking of me. Unfortunately, my plate is seriously full right now. I'll let you know if things slow down a bit and I'm able to contribute at another time."

Here's another simple but effective technique. It only takes a second. The next time a student yells at you, a parent sends an angry email to you, or you learn of yet another student suffering from hunger, an abusive home, or suicidal thoughts, take a deep breath and pause.

For deeper and more lasting exercises in stress reduction, choose one of these proven stress reducers to take care of yourself as you work to care for others: meditation, journaling, praying, breathing exercises, or spending time talking and connecting with a loved one (Schnaider-Levi, Mitnik, Zafrani, Goldman, & Lev-Ari, 2017).

Extending Forgiveness

Many teachers get frustrated with a student early in a semester or the school year, then hold a grudge against him or her all year long. Some staff may even hold a grudge against a school leader who left the school years ago! But anger and resentment are dangerous "brain baggage," with serious costs.

To "resent" is to hold an emotional grudge against another. The grudge is an unresolved and unhealed hurt from something that another said or did where *you felt wronged*. For example, a student rolled her eyes at you, a colleague questioned your lesson plan, or your principal made a comment suggesting you consider another career. These can all lead to feelings of anger and resentment, whether or not the person truly meant to insult you.

People who carry grudges and resentment are prone to a long list of undesirable outcomes—heart disease, obesity, insulin resistance, high lipid ratio, excess triglycerides, increased alcohol consumption, and smoking behavior, just to name a few (Toussaint et al., 2018; Toussaint, Shields, & Slavich, 2016). Resentment is linked to depression and other mental health challenges (Ricciardi et al., 2013). People who harbor hostility toward others experience impaired cognitive function for up to 10 years or more (Toussaint et al., 2018). Ever heard someone say, "I'm so angry I just can't think straight?" All those angry feelings cloud your brain function and make it difficult to think, learn, and remember.

With all these troublesome outcomes, why do we often find it so hard to forgive? It's because resentment activates the reward systems in your brain—specifically the nucleus accumbens and caudate nucleus (Billingsley & Losin, 2017). This is the same reward system activated when someone uses hard drugs. In crude terms, we hold on to hurt feelings and get "high" off the hoped-for reward of punishing your adversary. Our perception is that by holding this hurt in our consciousness, we will eventually get some kind of revenge. But that is a costly lie people tell themselves.

Maybe you believe that forgiving the person you hold so much anger toward would trivialize the unfairness you have suffered or compromise your sense of justice. You might feel like you'd be "rolling over" or allowing that person to "get away with it." The truth is that letting go of resentment and grudges in no way condones or minimizes the behavior of those who have hurt you. Forgiveness *is a personal health skill* that puts you on a better life path. It can help you bring up the anchor you've been dragging while you struggle to row your boat.

Forgiveness involves (a) the reduction (or dissipation) of vengeful or angry thoughts, feelings, or motives and (b) a shift in thinking toward the perceived offender (Toussaint et al., 2016; Quintana-Orts & Rey, 2018).

Start by forgiving that *one* student or *one* family member for that *one* thing they did that *one* time. Letting go of just one resentment for a single, isolated, or situation-contingent, experience is called "state forgiveness," as in "For the moment, I can let it go." In a giving or kind "state" we all are more likely to do kinder things. The more often you can do this, the more often you will uphold your values of being a thoughtful and compassionate person. In the long run, what you want is to develop "trait forgiveness," which is a permanent skill set to forgive in all circumstances. This level of forgiveness *does not negate the gravity of the hurt created;* rather it acknowledges the pain and supports you taking control of the hurt and choosing forgiveness for yourself.

What are the benefits of developing trait forgiveness? People with trait forgiveness experience better physical health. Specifically, they have healthier hearts, live longer, sleep better, are less likely to turn to medications or alcohol for relief (Ricciardi et al., 2013). They also have better emotional health—less stress (which also improves physical health), happier, higher levels of overall well-being (Ricciardi et al., 2013).

When someone is being forgiving, fMRI scans show their prefrontal cortex is active (Billingsley & Losin, 2017). The prefrontal cortex is a region of the brain involved in critical thinking, planning, and decision-making. It is our reasoning center, which we can use to convince the amygdala, our reactive emotional center, to take a back seat and not override our behavior. The involvement of the prefrontal cortex is significant because it reminds us that you get to choose forgiveness. It can inhibit the revenge-seeking motives generated by the reward centers in the brain that drive resentment (Billingsley & Losin, 2017).

FIVE STEPS TOWARD FORGIVENESS

1. **Acknowledge the hurt.** Feeling disrespected never feels good. It is natural to be upset and hurt by these experiences. Label the feelings you are experiencing; allow yourself to feel them; express them in writing or to a trusted confidant. Ask yourself how motivated you are to be done with this painful experience.

2. **Recognize the powerlessness of resentment.** Refusing to forgive gives you a false feeling of power. You think you are powerful by withholding forgiveness, but in reality you are allowing the way someone else behaved to have power over you. This false sense of power is used to mask your own hurt and vulnerability or your frustration that someone did not live up to your expectations. Holding a grudge (or a grade) against that person will not offer you the healing you are looking for.

3. **Empathize with your offender.** See your offender as a human, with character and a personality beyond their choice that hurt you. Take the uncomfortable step into their shoes and see their choice from their perspective. What need were they seeking to fulfill with their choice? Find similarities between you and your offender (Ricciardi et al., 2013). If the offender was a student, remember that he or she is still a kid—with an immature brain, undeveloped social skills, and whatever else students may lack—and is driven by social needs that authorize rebellious behavior if it impresses his or her peers.

4. **Make a choice.** The pain you dredge up by dwelling in the past is your choice. Choose to no longer be a victim, and allow yourself to feel differently. Surrender your desire for justice to a higher power, and move on with your life. Life is too short. Even if a student cussed you out during class, why let this person's poor choices impact you?

5. **Renew or release the relationship.** It is up to you to decide whether the one who initiated the hurtful experience should be allowed to stay in your life. Do the person's positive attributes outweigh his or her negative ones? If so, work to renew the relationship and move forward; explicitly tell the person, "What you did was not okay, but I am still committed to having a positive relationship with you." Know that, while giving forgiveness to an offender is a one-time event, finding relief from your own pain is a process. Be kind to yourself as you take the time needed to fully heal. If, on the other hand, the relationship is no longer worth the struggle, either ask for support from school administration or remove the person from your personal life—and then move on.

Choosing Gratitude and Optimism

With all the stressors that teachers face, it is easy to get discouraged and feel like it's just not worth it. Depression, anxiety, and low job satisfaction are real issues in this line of employment. These factors are strongly connected to workload, student behavior, and employment conditions (Ferguson, Frost, & Hall, 2012). How can a passionate teacher manage all these feelings?

First, if you find yourself getting angry, discouraged, or depressed for more than a week or so, get professional help. See a counselor or doctor. Why? Because the longer you are in a negative state of mind, the more permanent it begins to feel and the harder it becomes to change it. Thus, sadly, only a small portion of those who get prescriptions for a long-standing depression ever get any relief (Bschor & Kilarski, 2016).

The challenges you face in your chosen profession—the seemingly endless responsibilities, setbacks, and obstacles to student learning—are unlikely to go away. The key to handling the emotional drain that can accompany this challenging, yet meaningful, work is to fill your emotional reserves with enough positive deposits to keep your well from running dry. This is where gratitude and optimism can help.

Making gratitude a life habit is one of the greatest gifts you can give yourself. Gratitude is an orientation of noticing and appreciating the positive role that others have played in your life (Wood, Froh, & Geraghty, 2010). Gratitude is proven to be connected to a wide array of benefits—improved relationships, physical health, self-esteem, high levels of work satisfaction, lower levels of stress and depression, and more (Rusk, Vella-Brodrick, & Waters, 2016).

How can you get a "foothold" and start this process? One way is to keep a paper on your desk to write just two phrases every day. First, as you enter your classroom every morning, jot down a few words that express one thing you are looking forward to that day. Second, as you leave each day, write one thing you are grateful for that happened that day.

Relationships (Social Well-Being)

Humans are social creatures who depend on each other for survival. Yes, that includes surviving the world of teaching. Remember our discussion in Chapter 4, on the significance of relationships: Lack of connection is associated with physical pain (Eisenberger, 2012), emotion distress such as anxiety and depression (Stanley & Adolphs, 2013), and reduced gray matter in the brain (Gianaros et al., 2007).

Teachers have a variety of relationship dynamics to navigate that impact performance and overall well-being. Let's focus in on three of those relationships: your relationships with your students, your relationships with your colleagues, and your personal relationships.

With Your Students

Have you ever noticed how a negative interaction with one student can impact your mood and teaching for the rest of the day? Working to improve your relationships with all your students will not only help you be at your best, it will improve their learning too. Do you have a student (or two) who just drives you crazy? That's the student you might consider spending more time with. There is evidence that spending just a few minutes a day with individual at-risk students can improve the teacher's view of that student (Driscoll & Pianta, 2010).

Building strong relationships with your students takes time, effort, and, preferably, a plan. We recommend that you commit to eating lunch with students one day a week. Make it a habit to greet them at the door every day. Make eye contact with them, greet them by name, and connect with them through a high-five, handshake, or other greeting.

With Your Colleagues

Teaching has, unfortunately, evolved in some areas to be a very isolated profession. If this is true at your school, consider being the one to disrupt the cultural norm of "closed door" teaching. Create time to collaborate with your colleagues. Ask them what is working well for them, and share where you are finding success.

If the teachers' lounge has traditionally been a space to "vent" about students, stakes, and scores, work to shift that norm. Do your part to transform it into a place where teachers celebrate successes, admit mistakes, and ask for support. Your strategies might include the following:

1. Every day of the school year, make it a point to say, text, or give a note to a colleague of appreciation for the contributions he or she makes to the school, the kids, or you.

2. Celebrate a "staff of the week" (or month, if your school is small) so that every staff member gets acknowledged.

3. Do a favor for another staff: give them a box of tissue, buy them lunch, or, if they need help moving over a weekend, jump in to lend a hand!

Your Personal Relationships

As you know, your relationships outside of school have an impact on your life *in school* (Gonzalez, Ragins, Ehrhardt, & Singh, 2018). In order to feel "whole" and be effective at work, use the following tools to handle or prevent conflicts and to keep issues from one sphere of your life from crossing over into the other.

1. If you are angry with someone, ask yourself, "How might my anger be inappropriate?" In short, it might be that you have made an accidental faulty assumption or judgment.

2. Make it a point to forgive and heal broken relationships. Schedule time to spend with the people most important to you. Create a standing "date night" with your partner, child, or best friend to ensure you are strengthening your key relationships.

3. Use your commute to help manage your feelings. Before you get out of your car at work, take a deep breath and visualize your students' faces, feel their needs, and put a smile on your face. Tell yourself, "I can be my best, for them, for just these hours today." After you drive home and park, sit in your car and clear your head. Let go of any work stressors. Remember the good things in your relationships; remember what makes you happy and how you can fuel your own joy. Take a deep breath, and walk into your home calm and ready to feel relaxed and connected with those you love.

In everything you do, remember that short, brief stress is unavoidable. But the more nasty, chronic stress, the kind that damages your health, is optional.

Conclusion

Brain-based learning is the pursuit of learning through the brain's natural learning processes. It begins by understanding how the brain (and thus learning) is impacted by the factors outlined in this book. As you reflect on your teaching, perhaps you have realized you naturally teach in ways that are "brain-friendly." And perhaps you have come to learn of new habits you would like to adopt in your teaching. We appreciate you and your efforts, and we wish you well on this amazing adventure of brain-based teaching and learning.

References

Chapter 1

Anderson, A. A., Parsa, K., Geiger, S., Zaragoza, R., Kermanian, R., Miguel, H., . . . Gandjbakhche, A. H. (2018). Exploring the role of task performance and learning style on prefrontal hemodynamics during a working memory task. *PLoS One, 13*(6), e0198257.

Barr, R., & Brito, N. (2013). From specificity to flexibility: Developmental changes during infancy. In P. Bauer & R. Fivush (Eds.), *Wiley-Blackwell Handbook on the Development of Children's Memory* (pp. 453–479). Chichester: John Wiley and Sons.

Bogdanov, P., Dereli, N., Dang, X., Bassett, D. S., Wymbs, N. F., Grafton, S. T., & Singh, A. K. (2017). Learning about learning: Mining human brain sub-network biomarkers from fMRI data. *PLoS One, 12*(10), e0184344. doi:10.1371/journal.pone.0184344

Camina, E., & Güell, F. (2017). The neuroanatomical, neurophysiological and psychological basis of memory: Current models and their origins. *Frontiers in Pharmacology, 8*, 438.

Carhart-Harris, R. L., & Nutt, D. J. (2017). Serotonin and brain function: A tale of two receptors. *Journal of Psychopharmacology (Oxford, England), 31*, 1091–1120.

Carpenter, K. L., Wills, A. J., Benattayallah, A., & Milton, F. (2016). A comparison of the neural correlates that underlie rule-based and information-integration category learning. *Human Brain Mapping, 37*(10), 3557–3574.

Chaddock-Heyman, L., Erickson, K. I., Chappell, M. A., Johnson, C. L., Kienzler, C., Knecht, A., . . . Kramer, A. F. (2016). Aerobic fitness is associated with greater hippocampal cerebral blood flow in children. *Developmental Cognitive Neuroscience, 20*, 52–58.

Coffield, F. (2013). *Learning styles: Time to move on.* Nottingham, England: National College for School Leadership. Retrieved from http://www.learnersfirst.net/private/wp-content/uploads/Opinion-Piece-Learning-styles-time-to-move-on-Coffield.pdf

de Schotten, M. T., Urbanski, M., Valabregue, R., Bayle, D. J., & Volle, E. (2014). Subdivision of the occipital lobes: An anatomical and functional MRI connectivity study. *Cortex, 56*, 121–137.

Dang, L. C., O'Neil, J. P., & Jagust, W. J. (2012). Genetic effects on behavior are mediated by neurotransmitters and large-scale neural networks. *NeuroImage, 66*, 203–214.

Dekker, S., Lee, N. C., Howard-Jones, P., & Jolles, J. (2012). Neuromyths in education: Prevalence and predictors of misconceptions among teachers. *Frontiers in Psychology, 3*, 429. doi:10.3389/fpsyg.2012.00429

Eichenbaum, H., & Cohen, N. J. (2014). Can we reconcile the declarative memory and spatial navigation views on hippocampal function? *Neuron, 83*(4), 764–770.

Fletcher, M. L., Ogg, M. C., Lu, L., Ogg, R. J., & Boughter, J. D. (2017). Overlapping representation of primary tastes in a defined region of the gustatory cortex. *Journal of Neuroscience*, *37*(32), 7595–7605.

Friederici, A. D. (2017). Evolution of the neural language network. *Psychonomic Bulletin & Review*, *24*(1), 41–47.

Gross, R. (2012). *Psychology: The science of mind and behaviour* (6th ed.). Abingdon, Oxfordshire, England: Hodder Education.

Hamill, R. W., Shapiro, R. E., & Vizzard, M. A. (2012). Peripheral autonomic nervous system. In D. Robertson, I. Biaggioni, G. Burnstock, P. A. Low, & J. F. R. Paton (Eds.), *Primer on the autonomic nervous system* (3rd ed., pp. 17–20). London, England: Academic Press.

Herman, J. P. (2012). Neural pathways of stress integration: Relevance to alcohol abuse. *Alcohol Research: Current Reviews*, *34*(4), 441–447.

Kump, B., Moskaliuk, J., Cress, U., & Kimmerle, J. (2015). Cognitive foundations of organizational learning: Re-introducing the distinction between declarative and non-declarative knowledge. *Frontiers in Psychology*, *6*, 1489.

Loonis, R. F., Brincat, S. L., Antzoulatos, E. G., & Miller, E. K. (2017). A meta-analysis suggests different neural correlates for implicit and explicit learning. *Neuron, 96*(2), 521–534.e7.

Moscovitch, M., Cabeza, R., Winocur, G., & Nadel, L. (2016). Episodic memory and beyond: The hippocampus and neocortex in transformation. *Annual Review of Psychology*, *67*, 105–134.

Newton, P. M., & Miah, M. (2017). Evidence-based higher education—is the learning styles "myth" important? *Frontiers in Psychology*, *8*, 444. doi:10.3389/fpsyg.2017.00444

Oakes, L. M. (2017). Plasticity may change inputs as well as processes, structures, and responses. *Cognitive Development, 42*, 4–14.

Osada, T., Adachi, Y., Kimura, H. M., & Miyashita, Y. (2008). Towards understanding of the cortical network underlying associative memory. *Philosophical Transactions of the Royal Society of London. Series B, Biological Sciences, 363*, 2187–2199.

Oudiette, D., Antony, J. W., Creery, J. D., & Paller, K. A. (2013). The role of memory reactivation during wakefulness and sleep in determining which memories endure. *Journal of Neuroscience, 33*(15), 6672–6678.

Pearson-Fuhrhop, K. M., Minton, B., Acevedo, D., Shahbaba, B., & Cramer, S. C. (2013). Genetic variation in the human brain dopamine system influences motor learning and its modulation by L-dopa. *PLoS One*, *8*(4), e61197. doi:10.1371/journal.pone.0061197

Reber, P. J. (2013). The neural basis of implicit learning and memory: A review of neuropsychological and neuroimaging research. *Neuropsychologia, 51*(10), 2026–2042.

Ritchey, M., Murty, V. P., & Dunsmoor, J. E. (2016). Adaptive memory systems for remembering the salient and the seemingly mundane. *Behavioral and Brain Sciences, 39*, e221. doi:10.1017/S0140525X15001922

Robertson, J. (2018). The gliocentric brain. *International Journal of Molecular Sciences, 19*(10), 3033. doi:10.3390/ijms19103033

Schneider, S., Beege, M., Nebel, S., & Rey, G. D. (2018). A meta-analysis of how signaling affects learning with media. *Educational Research Review, 23*, 1–24.

Taylor, J. A., Krakauer, J. W., & Ivry, R. B. (2014). Explicit and implicit contributions to learning in a sensorimotor adaptation task. *Journal of Neuroscience*, *34*(8), 3023–3032.

Wang, Y., Mao, X., Li, B., Lu, B., & Guo, C. (2016). Semantic memory influences episodic retrieval by increased familiarity. *NeuroReport, 27*(10), 774–782.

Xie, Y., & Dorsky, R. I. (2017). Development of the hypothalamus: Conservation, modification and innovation. *Development (Cambridge, England), 144*(9), 1588–1599.

Yang, J., & Li, P. (2012). Brain networks of explicit and implicit learning. *PLoS One, 7*(8), e42993.

Zatorre, R. J., Fields, R. D., & Johansen-Berg, H. (2012). Plasticity in gray and white: Neuroimaging changes in brain structure during learning. *Nature Neuroscience, 15*(4), 528–536.

Zeidman, P., & Maguire, E. A. (2016). Anterior hippocampus: The anatomy of perception, imagination and episodic memory. *Nature Reviews Neuroscience, 17*(3), 173–182.

Chapter 2

Abel, T., Havekes, R., Saletin, J. M., & Walker, M. P. (2013). Sleep, plasticity and memory from molecules to whole-brain networks. *Current Biology, 23*(17), R774–R788.

Anand, P., Kunnumakkara, A. B., Sundaram, C., Harikumar, K. B., Tharakan, S. T., Lai, O. S., . . . Aggarwal, B. B. (2008). Cancer is a preventable disease that requires major lifestyle changes. *Pharmaceutical Research, 25*(9), 2097–2116. doi:10.1007/s11095-008-9661-9

Anand, S., Nath, B., & Saraswathy, R. (2014). Diabetes—increased risk for cancers through chromosomal aberrations. *Asian Pacific Journal of Cancer Prevention, 15*(11), 4571–4573.

Anderson, M. L., Nokia, M. S., Govindaraju, K. P., & Shors, T. J. (2012). Moderate drinking? Alcohol consumption significantly decreases neurogenesis in the adult hippocampus. *Neuroscience, 224*, 202–209.

Beilharz, J., Maniam, J., & Morris, M. (2015). Diet-induced cognitive deficits: The role of fat and sugar, potential mechanisms and nutritional interventions. *Nutrients, 7*(8), 6719–6738.

Crews, D., Gore, A. C., Hsu, T. S., Dangleben, N. L., Spinetta, M., Schallert, T., Anway, M. D., … Skinner, M. K. (2007). Transgenerational epigenetic imprints on mate preference. *Proceedings of the National Academy of Sciences of the United States of America, 104*, 5942–5946.

Chang, C. Y., Ke, D. S., & Chen, J. Y. (2009). Essential fatty acids and human brain. *Acta Neurologica Taiwanica, 18*(4), 231–241.

Goldstein, A. N., & Walker, M. P. (2014). The role of sleep in emotional brain function. *Annual Review of Clinical Psychology, 10*, 679–708.

Gottesman, I. I., & Hanson, D. R. (2005). Human development: Biological and genetic processes. *Annual Review of Psychology, 56*, 263–286.

Gu, J., & Kanai, R. (2014). What contributes to individual differences in brain structure? *Frontiers in Human Neuroscience, 8*, 262.

Hutcherson, C. A., Seppala, E. M., & Gross, J. J. (2014). The neural correlates of social connection. *Cognitive, Affective, & Behavioral Neuroscience, 15*(1), 1–14.

Jäncke, L., Mérillat, S., Liem, F., & Hänggi, J. (2014). Brain size, sex, and the aging brain. *Human Brain Mapping, 36*(1), 150–169.

Jeon, Y. K., & Ha, C. H. (2017). The effect of exercise intensity on brain derived neurotrophic factor and memory in adolescents. *Environmental Health and Preventive Medicine, 22*(1), 27.

Kanherkar, R. R. Bhatia-Dey, N., & Csoka, A. B. (2014). Epigenetics across the human lifespan. *Frontiers in Cell and Developmental Biology, 2*, 49. doi:10.3389/fcell.2014.00049

Killgore, W. D. (2010). Effects of sleep deprivation on cognition. *Progress in Brain Research*, 105–129.

Ma, N., Dinges, D. F., Basner, M., & Rao, H. (2015). How acute total sleep loss affects the attending brain: A meta-analysis of neuroimaging studies. *Sleep, 38*(2), 233–240.

Maguire, E. A., Gadian, D. G., Johnsrude, I. S., Good, C. D., Ashburner, J., Frackowiak, R. S. J., et al. (2000). Navigation-related structural change in the hippocampi of taxi drivers. *Proceedings of the National Academy of Sciences of the United States of America, 97*, 4398–4403.

Masento, N. A., Golightly, M., Field, D. T., Butler, L. T., & van Reekum, C. M. (2014). Effects of hydration status on cognitive performance and mood. *British Journal of Nutrition, 111*(10), 1841–1852.

Matos, A. M., Macedo, M. P., & Rauter, A. P. (2017). Bridging type 2 diabetes and Alzheimer's disease: Assembling the puzzle pieces in the quest for the molecules with therapeutic and preventive potential. *Medicinal Research Reviews, 38*(1), 261–324.

Mazziotta, J. C., Woods, R., Iacoboni, M., Sicotte, N., Yaden, K., Tran, M., . . . Toga, A. W. (2009). The myth of the normal, average human brain— The ICBM experience: (1) Subject screening and eligibility. *Neuroimage, 44*, 914–922.

Michael, S. L., Merlo, C. L., Basch, C. E., Wentzel, K. R., & Wechsler, H. (2015). Critical connections: Health and academics. *Journal of School Health, 85*(11), 740–758.

Mueller, A. D., Meerlo, P., McGinty, D., & Mistlberger, R. E. (2013). Sleep and adult neurogenesis: Implications for cognition and mood. *Current Topics in Behavioral Neurosciences, 25*, 151–181.

Ong, C. K., Lirk, P., Tan, C. H., & Seymour, R. A. (2007). An evidence-based update on nonsteroidal anti-inflammatory drugs. *Clinical Medicine & Research, 5*, 19–34.

Ota, M., Matsuo, J., Ishida, I., Hattori, K., Teraishi, T., Tonouchi, H., . . . Kunugi, H. (2016). Effect of a ketogenic meal on cognitive function in elderly adults: Potential for cognitive enhancement. *Psychopharmacology, 233*(21–22), 3797–3802.

Oudiette, D., Antony, J. W., Creery, J. D., & Paller, K. A. (2013). The role of memory reactivation during wakefulness and sleep in determining which memories endure. *Journal of Neuroscience, 33*(15), 6672–6678.

Plomin, R., DeFries, J. C., Knopik, V. S., & Neiderhiser, J. M. (2016). Top 10 replicated findings from behavioral genetics. *Perspectives on Psychological Science, 11*(1), 3–23.

Roselli, C. E. (2018). Neurobiology of gender identity and sexual orientation. *Journal of Neuroendocrinology, 30*(7), e12562.

Ruigrok, A. N., Salimi-Khorshidi, G., Lai, M., Baron-Cohen, S., Lombardo, M. V., Tait, R. J., & Suckling, J. (2014). A meta-analysis of sex differences in human brain structure. *Neuroscience & Biobehavioral Reviews, 39*, 34–50.

Ryan, A. M., & Shin, H. (2011). Help-seeking tendencies during early adolescence: An examination of motivational correlates and consequences for achievement. *Learning and Instruction, 21*(2), 247–256.

Savic, I., & Arver, S. (2011). Sex dimorphism of the brain in male-to-female transsexuals. *Cerebral Cortex, 21*(11), 2525–2533.

Sachdeva, A., Chandra, M., Choudhary, M., Dayal, P., & Anand, K. S. (2016). Alcohol-related dementia and neurocognitive impairment: A review study. *International Journal of High-Risk Behaviors & Addiction, 5*(3), e27976.

Smith, E. S., Junger, J., Derntl, B., & Habel, U. (2015). The transsexual brain–A review of findings on the neural basis of transsexualism. *Neuroscience & Biobehavioral Reviews, 59*, 251–266.

Stanley, D. A., & Adolphs, R. (2013). Toward a neural basis for social behavior. *Neuron, 80*(3), 816–826.

Tucker-Drob, E. M., Rhemtulla, M., Harden, K. P., Turkheimer, E., & Fask, D. (2011). Emergence of a Gene x socioeconomic status interaction on infant mental ability between 10 months and 2 years. *Psychological Science, 22*(1), 125–133.

Tucker-Drob, E. M., & Bates, T. C. (2016). Large cross-national differences in Gene x socioeconomic status interaction on intelligence. *Psychological Science, 27*(2), 138–149.

Volkow, N., & Morales, M. (2015). The brain on drugs: From reward to addiction. *Cell, 162*(4), 712–725.

Wood, W., Quinn, J. M., & Kashy, D. A. (2002). Habits in everyday life: Thought, emotion, and action. *Journal of Personality and Social Psychology, 83*, 1281–1297.

Chapter 3

Anderson, D. I., Campos, J. J., Witherington, D. C., Dahl, A., Rivera, M., He, M., . . . Barbu-Roth, M. (2013). The role of locomotion in psychological development. *Frontiers in Psychology, 4*, 440. doi:10.3389/fpsyg.2013.00440

Canbeyli, R. (2013). Sensorimotor modulation of mood and depression: In search of an optimal mode of stimulation. *Frontiers in Human Neuroscience, 7*, 428.

Carstensen, L. L. (2006). The influence of a sense of time on human development. *Science (New York, NY), 312*(5782), 1913–1915.

Cedeño Laurent, J. G., Williams, A., Outlhote, Y., Zanobetti, A., Allen, J. G., & Spengler, J. D. (2018). Reduced cognitive function during a heat wave among residents of non-air-conditioned buildings: An observational study of young adults in the summer of 2016. *PLoS Medicine, 15*(7), e1002605. https://doi.org/10.1371/journal.pmed.1002605

Choi, H., Merriënboer, J. J., & Paas, F. (2014). Effects of the physical environment on cognitive load and learning: Towards a new model of cognitive load. *Educational Psychology Review, 26*(2), 225–244.

Daisey, J. M., Angell, W. J., & Apte, M. G. (2003). Indoor air quality, ventilation and health symptoms in schools: An analysis of existing information. *Indoor Air, 13*(1), 53–64.

Ekkel, E. D., & de Vries, S. (2017). Nearby green space and human health: Evaluating accessibility metrics. *Landscape and Urban Planning, 157*, 214–220.

Evans, G. W., Lepore, S. J., Shejwal, B. R., & Palsane, M. N. (1998). Chronic residential crowding and children's well-being: An ecological perspective. *Child Development, 69*(6), 1514–1523.

Fisher, A. V., Godwin, K. E., & Seltman, H. (2014). Visual environment, attention allocation, and learning in young children. *Psychological Science, 25*(7), 1362–1370.

Gaoua, N., Racinais, S., Grantham, J., El Massioui, F. (2011). Alterations in cognitive performance during passive hyperthermia are task dependent. *International Journal of Hyperthermia, 27*, 1–9.

Goodman, J., Hurwitz, M., Park, R. J., & Smith, J. (2019). *Heat and learning* (EdWorkingPaper No. 19-30). Retrieved from Annenberg Institute at Brown University: http://edworkingpapers.com/ai19-30

Han, J., Waddington, G., Adams, R., Anson, J., & Liu, Y. (2015). Assessing proprioception: A critical review of methods. *Journal of Sport and Health Science, 5*(1), 80–90.

Haslinger, B., Erhard, P., Altenmüller, E., Schroeder, U., Boecker, H., & Ceballos-Baumann, A. O. (2005). Transmodal sensorimotor networks during action observation in professional pianists. *Journal of Cognitive Neuroscience, 17*(2), 282–293.

Hattie, J. (2017, December). *Hattie's 2018 updated list of factors related to student achievement: 252 influences and effect sizes (Cohen's d)*. Retrieved from http://www.visiblelearning.org

Heschong, L. (2001). *CALIFORNIA ENERGY COMMISSION Daylighting in schools: Reanalysis report*. White Salmon, WA: New Buildings Institute.

Hjordt, L. V., Stenbæk, D. S., Ozenne, B., Mc Mahon, B., Hageman, I., Hasselbalch, S. G., & Knudsen, G. M. (2017). Season-independent cognitive deficits in seasonal affective disorder and their relation to depressive symptoms. *Psychiatry Research, 257*, 219–226.

Jean-Louis, G., Kripke, D., Cohen, C., Zizi, F., & Wolintz, A. (2005). Associations of ambient illumination with mood: Contribution of ophthalmic dysfunctions. *Physiology & Behavior, 84*(3), 479–487.

Johnson, A. J. (2011). Cognitive facilitation following intentional odor exposure. *Sensors, 11*(5), 5469–5488.

Klatte, M., Meis, M., Sukowski, H., & Schick, A. (2007). Effects of irrelevant speech and traffic noise on speech perception and cognitive performance in elementary school children. *Noise and Health, 9*(36), 64.

Lamb, R., Akmal, T., & Petrie, K. (2015). Development of a cognition-priming model describing learning in a STEM classroom. *Journal of Research in Science Teaching, 52*(3), 410–437.

Mahnert, A., Moissl-Eichinger, C., & Berg, G. (2015). Microbiome interplay: Plants alter microbial abundance and diversity within the built environment. *Frontiers in Microbiology, 6*, 887.

Martin, A. A., Hamill, L. R., Davies, S., Rogers, P. J., & Brunstrom, J. M. (2015). Energy-dense snacks can have the same expected satiation as sugar-containing beverages. *Appetite, 95*, 81–88.

Meamarbashi, A., & Rajabi, A. (2013). The effects of peppermint on exercise performance. *Journal of the International Society of Sports Nutrition, 10*(1), 15.

Meijs, N., Cillessen, A. H., Scholte, R. H., Segers, E., & Spijkerman, R. (2008). Social intelligence and academic achievement as predictors of adolescent popularity. *Journal of Youth and Adolescence, 39*(1), 62–72.

Mihelčič, M., & Podlesek, A. (2017). The influence of proprioception on reading performance. *Clinical and Experimental Optometry, 100*(2), 138–143.

Nussbaumer, B., Kaminski-Hartenthaler, A., Forneris, C. A., Morgan, L. C., Sonis, J. H., Gaynes, B. N., . . . Van Noord, M. G. (2015). Light therapy for preventing seasonal affective disorder. *Cochrane Database of Systematic Reviews* (11), CD011269.

Oudeyer, P., Gottlieb, J., & Lopes, M. (2016). Intrinsic motivation, curiosity, and learning: Theory and applications in educational technologies. *Progress in Brain Research, 229*, 257–284.

Perera, F. (2017). Pollution from fossil-fuel combustion is the leading environmental threat to global pediatric health and equity: Solutions exist. *International Journal of Environmental Research and Public Health, 15*(1), 16.

Pilcher, J. J., Nadler, E., & Busch, C. (2002). Effects of hot and cold temperature exposure on performance: A meta-analytic review. *Ergonomics, 45*(10), 682–698.

Rhind, J. P. (2012). *Essential oils: A handbook for aromatherapy practice* (2nd ed.). London, England: Singing Dragon.

Russell, J., Vidal-Gadea, A. G., Makay, A., Lanam, C., & Pierce-Shimomura, J. T. (2014). Humidity sensation requires both mechanosensory and thermosensory pathways in *Caenorhabditis elegans*. *Proceedings of the National Academy of Sciences of the United States of America, 111*(22), 8269–8274.

Sellaro, R., & Colzato, L. S. (2017). Aromas. In L. S. Colzato, *Theory-driven approaches to cognitive enhancement* (pp. 243–255). New York, NY: Springer Berlin Heidelberg.

Sellaro, R., van Dijk, W. W., Paccani, C. R., Hommel, B., & Colzato, L. S. (2015). A question of scent: Lavender aroma promotes interpersonal trust. *Frontiers in Psychology, 5*, 1486.

Sengupta, P., & Garrity, P. (2013). Sensing temperature. *Current Biology, 23*(8), R304–R307.

Seppänen, O. A., & Fisk, W. (2006). Some quantitative relations between indoor environmental quality and work performance or health. *HVAC&R Research, 12*(4), 957–973.

Shah, J., & Inamullah, M. (2012). The impact of overcrowded classroom on the academic performance of the students at secondary level. *International Journal of Research in Commerce, Economics and Management, 2*(6), 9–11.

Siuda-Krzywicka, K., Bola, Ł., Paplińska, M., Sumera, E., Jednoróg, K., Marchewka, A., … Szwed, M. (2016). Massive cortical reorganization in sighted Braille readers. *Elife, 5*, e10762.

Sunyer, J., Esnaola, M., Alvarez-Pedrerol, M., Forns, J., Rivas, I., López-Vicente, M., … Viana, M. (2015). Association between traffic-related air pollution in schools and cognitive development in primary school children: A prospective cohort study. *PLoS Medicine, 12*(3), e1001792.

Sutton, T. M., & Altarriba, J. (2016). Color associations to emotion and emotion-laden words: A collection of norms for stimulus construction and selection. *Behavior Research Methods, 48*(2), 686–728.

Taylor, L., Watkins, S. L., Marshall, H., Dascombe, B. J., & Foster, J. (2016). The impact of different environmental conditions on cognitive function: A focused review. *Frontiers in Physiology, 6*, 372.

Wallner, P., Kundi, M., Panny, M., Tappler, P., & Hutter, H. P. (2015). Exposure to air ions in indoor environments: Experimental study with healthy adults. *International Journal of Environmental Research and Public Health, 12*(11), 14301–14311. doi:10.3390/ijerph121114301

Woo, C. W., Koban, L., Kross, E., Lindquist, M. A., Banich, M. T., Ruzic, L., . . . Wager, T. D. (2014). Separate neural representations for physical pain and social rejection. *Nature Communications, 5*, 5380. doi:10.1038/ncomms6380

Wood, R. A., Burchett, M. D., Orwell, R. A., Tarran, J., & Torpy, F. (2002). *Plant/soil capacities to remove harmful substances from polluted indoor air.* Gore Hill, NSW, Australia: Plants and Environmental Quality Group, Centre for Ecotoxicology, UTS.

Wolverton, B. C., Johnson, A., & Bounds, K. (1989). *Interior landscape plants for indoor air pollution abatement.* Bay Saint Louis, MS: NASA John C. Stennis Space Center.

Wolverton, B. C., & Wolverton, J. D. (1993). Plants and soil microorganisms: Removal of formaldehyde, xylene, and ammonia from the indoor environment. *Journal of the Mississippi Academy of Sciences, 38*(2), 11–15.

Xiong, L., Huang, X., Li, J., Mao, P., Wang, X., Wang, R., & Tang, M. (2018). Impact of indoor physical environment on learning efficiency in different types of tasks: A 3× 4× 3 full factorial design analysis. *International Journal of Environmental Research and Public Health, 15*(6), 1256. doi:10.3390/ijerph15061256

Chapter 4

Alcott, B. (2017). Does teacher encouragement influence students' educational progress? A propensity-score matching analysis. *Research in Higher Education, 58*(7), 773–804.

Benner, A. D., & Mistry, R. S. (2007). Congruence of mother and teacher educational expectations and low-income youth's academic competence. *Journal of Educational Psychology, 99*(1), 140–153.

Cooper, K. M., Haney, B., Krieg, A., & Brownell, S. E. (2017). What's in a name? The importance of students perceiving that an instructor knows their names in a high-enrollment biology classroom. *CBE—Life Sciences Education, 16*(1), ar8.

DeWall, C. N., MacDonald, G., Webster, G. D., Masten, C. L., Baumeister, R. F., Powell, C., ... & Eisenberger, N. I. (2010). Acetaminophen reduces social pain: Behavioral and neural evidence. *Psychological Science, 21*(7), 931–937.

Domes, G., Heinrichs, M., Michel, A., Berger, C., & Herpertz, S. C. (2007). Oxytocin improves "mind-reading" in humans. *Biological Psychiatry, 61*(6), 731–733.

Driscoll, K. C., & Pianta, R. C. (2010). Banking time in Head Start: Early efficacy of an intervention designed to promote supportive teacher–child relationships. *Early Education & Development, 21*(1), 38–64.

Eisenberger, N. I. (2012). The pain of social disconnection: Examining the shared neural underpinnings of physical and social pain. *Nature Reviews Neuroscience, 13*(6), 421–434.

Frijling, J. L., van Zuiden, M., Koch, S. B., Nawijn, L., Veltman, D. J., & Olff, M. (2016). Intranasal oxytocin affects amygdala functional connectivity after trauma script-driven imagery in distressed recently trauma-exposed individuals. *Neuropsychopharmacology, 41*(5), 1286–1296.

Gianaros, P. J., Horenstein, J. A., Cohen, S., Matthews, K. A., Brown, S. M., Flory, J. D., . . . Hariri, A. R. (2007). Perigenual anterior cingulate morphology covaries with perceived social standing. *Social Cognitive and Affective Neuroscience, 2*(3), 161–173.

Gillies, R. (2016). Cooperative learning: Review of research and practice. *Australian Journal of Teacher Education, 41*(3), 39–54.

Goodman, J. F. (2017). The shame of shaming. *Phi Delta Kappan, 99*(2), 26–31.

Gottman, J. M., & Peluso, P. R. (2018). Dynamic models of social interaction. In *Mathematical modeling of social relationships: What mathematics can tell us about people* (pp. 17–29). New York, NY: Springer Science+Business Media.

Groh, A. M., Fearon, R. P., Bakermans-Kranenburg, M. J., Van IJzendoorn, M. H., Steele, R. D., & Roisman, G. I. (2014). The significance of attachment security for children's social competence with peers: A meta-analytic study. *Attachment & Human Development, 16*(2), 103–136.

Herrenkohl, T. I., Sousa, C., Tajima, E. A., Herrenkohl, R. C., & Moylan, C. A. (2008). Intersection of child abuse and children's exposure to domestic violence. *Trauma, Violence, & Abuse, 9*(2), 84–99.

Holt-Lunstad, J., Smith, T. B., & Layton, J. B. (2010). Social relationships and mortality risk: A meta-analytic review. *PLoS Medicine 7*(7): e1000316. https://doi.org/10.1371/journal.pmed.1000316

Hueston, C. M., Cryan, J. F., & Nolan, Y. M. (2017). Stress and adolescent hippocampal neurogenesis: Diet and exercise as cognitive modulators. *Translational Psychiatry, 7*(4), e1081.

Hutcherson, C. A., Seppala, E. M., & Gross, J. J. (2014). The neural correlates of social connection. *Cognitive, Affective, & Behavioral Neuroscience, 15*(1), 1–14.

Kendrick, K. M. (2004). The neurobiology of social bonds. *Journal of Neuroendocrinology, 16*(12), 1007–1008.

Kidd, C., Palmeri, H., & Aslin, R. N. (2013). Rational snacking: Young children's decision-making on the marshmallow task is moderated by beliefs about environmental reliability. *Cognition, 126*(1), 109–114.

Liu, M. W., Zhu, Q., & Yuan, Y. (2018). The role of the face itself in the face effect: Sensitivity, expressiveness, and anticipated feedback in individual compliance. *Frontiers in Psychology, 9*, 2499.

Magon, N., & Kalra, S. (2011). The orgasmic history of oxytocin: Love, lust, and labor. *Indian Journal of Endocrinology and Metabolism, 15*(Suppl3), S156.

Mikami, A. Y., Ruzek, E. A., Hafen, C. A., Gregory, A., & Allen, J. P. (2017). Perceptions of relatedness with classroom peers promote adolescents' behavioral engagement and achievement in secondary school. *Journal of Youth and Adolescence, 46*(11), 2341–2354.

Pritchett, R., Pritchett, J., Marshall, E., Davidson, C., & Minnis, H. (2013). Reactive attachment disorder in the general population: A hidden ESSENCE disorder. *The Scientific World Journal.* doi: 10.1155/2013/818157

Ruggiero, G., Frassinetti, F., Coello, Y., Rapuano, M., Di Cola, A. S., & Iachini, T. (2017). The effect of facial expressions on peripersonal and interpersonal spaces. *Psychological Research, 81*(6), 1232–1240.

Ryan, A. M., & Shin, H. (2011). Help-seeking tendencies during early adolescence: An examination of motivational correlates and consequences for achievement. *Learning and Instruction, 21*(2), 247–256.

Seltzer, L. J., Ziegler, T. E., & Pollak, S. D. (2010). Social vocalizations can release oxytocin in humans. *Proceedings of the Royal Society B: Biological Sciences, 277*(1694), 2661–2666.

Shively, C. A., Musselman, D. L., & Willard, S. L. (2009). Stress, depression, and coronary artery disease: Modeling comorbidity in female primates. *Neuroscience & Biobehavioral Reviews, 33*(2), 133–144.

Stanley, D. A., & Adolphs, R. (2013). Toward a neural basis for social behavior. *Neuron, 80*(3), 816–826.

Ueda, Y., Nagoya, K., Yoshikawa, S., & Nomura, M. (2017). Forming facial expressions influences assessment of others' dominance but not trustworthiness. *Frontiers in Psychology, 8,* 2097.

Wärnmark, A., Treuter, E., Wright, A. P., & Gustafsson, J. A. (2003). Activation functions 1 and 2 of nuclear receptors: Molecular strategies for transcriptional activation. *Molecular Endocrinology, 17*(10), 1901–1909.

Wildeman, C., & Emanuel, N. (2014). Cumulative risks of foster care placement by age 18 for US children, 2000–2011. *PLoS One, 9*(3), e92785.

Chapter 5

Barber, S. J., Rajaram, S., & Marsh, E. J. (2008). Fact learning: How information accuracy, delay, and repeated testing change retention and retrieval experience. *Memory, 16*(8), 934–946.

Butler, A. C. (2010). Repeated testing produces superior transfer of learning relative to repeated studying. *Journal of Experimental Psychology: Learning, Memory, and Cognition, 36*(5), 1118–1133.

Conrad, C. D. (2010). A critical review of chronic stress effects on spatial learning and memory. *Progress in Neuro-Psychopharmacology and Biological Psychiatry, 34*(5), 742–755.

Del Giudice, M. (2015). Plasticity as a developing trait: Exploring the implications. *Frontiers in Zoology, 12*(S1), S4.

Eichenbaum, H. (2017). Memory: Organization and control. *Annual Review of Psychology, 68,* 19–45.

Fazio, L. K., Huelser, B. J., Johnson, A., & Marsh, E. J. (2010). Receiving right/wrong feedback: Consequences for learning. *Memory (Hove, England), 18*(3), 335–350.

Girardeau, G., Benchenane, K., Wiener, S. I., Buzsáki, G., & Zugaro, M. B. (2009). Selective suppression of hippocampal ripples impairs spatial memory. *Nature Neuroscience, 12*(10), 1222–1223.

Gourévitch, B., Edeline, J. M., Occelli, F., & Eggermont, J. J. (2014). Is the din really harmless? Long-term effects of non-traumatic noise on the adult auditory system. *Nature Reviews Neuroscience, 15*(7), 483–491.

Gu, J., & Kanai, R. (2014). What contributes to individual differences in brain structure? *Frontiers in Human Neuroscience, 8,* 262.

Hattie, J. A., & Timperley, H. (2007). The power of feedback. *Review of Educational Research, 77,* 81–112.

Karpicke, J. D. (2012). Retrieval-based learning. *Current Directions in Psychological Science, 21*(3), 157–163.

Kelley, P., & Whatson, T. (2013). Making long-term memories in minutes: A spaced learning pattern from memory research in education. *Frontiers in Human Neuroscience, 7,* 589.

Klatte, M., Meis, M., Sukowski, H., & Schick, A. (2007). Effects of irrelevant speech and traffic noise on speech perception and cognitive performance in elementary school children. *Noise and Health, 9*(36), 64.

Knudsen, E. I. (2004). Sensitive periods in the development of the brain and behavior. *Journal of Cognitive Neuroscience*, *16*(8), 1412–1425.

Lacy, J. W., & Stark, C. E. (2013). The neuroscience of memory: Implications for the courtroom. *Nature Reviews Neuroscience, 14*(9), 649–658.

Lloyd, K., & Dayan, P. (2015). Tamping ramping: Algorithmic, implementational, and computational explanations of phasic dopamine signals in the accumbens. *PLoS Computational Biology*, *11*(12), e1004622.

Mather, M., Clewett, D., Sakaki, M., & Harley, C. W. (2016). Norepinephrine ignites local hotspots of neuronal excitation: How arousal amplifies selectivity in perception and memory. *Behavioral and Brain Sciences*, *39*, e200. doi: 10.1017/S0140525X15000667

Morewedge, C. K., & Kahneman, D. (2010). Associative processes in intuitive judgment. *Trends in Cognitive Sciences*, *14*(10), 435–440.

Olcese, U., Oude Lohuis, M., & Pennartz, C. (2018). Sensory processing across conscious and nonconscious brain states: From single neurons to distributed networks for inferential representation. *Frontiers in Systems Neuroscience*, *12*, 49.

Patton, M. H., Blundon, J. A., & Zakharenko, S. S. (2019). Rejuvenation of plasticity in the brain: Opening the critical period. *Current Opinion in Neurobiology*, *54*, 83–89.

Rangel-Gomez, M., & Meeter, M. (2016). Neurotransmitters and novelty: A systematic review. *Journal of Psychopharmacology*, *30*(1), 3–12.

Rimmele, U., Davachi, L., Petrov, R., Dougal, S., & Phelps, E. A. (2011). Emotion enhances the subjective feeling of remembering, despite lower accuracy for contextual details. *Emotion*, *11*(3), 553–562.

Roediger, H. L., & Butler, A. C. (2011). The critical role of retrieval practice in long-term retention. *Trends in Cognitive Sciences, 15*(1), 20–27.

Sampaio-Baptista, C., & Johansen-Berg, H. (2017). White matter plasticity in the adult brain. *Neuron*, *96*(6), 1239–1251.

Sasmita, A. O., Kuruvilla, J., & Ling, A. P. K. (2018). Harnessing neuroplasticity: Modern approaches and clinical future. *International Journal of Neuroscience*, *128*(11), 1061–1077.

Schacter, D. L., Guerin, S. A., & Jacques, P. L. (2011). Memory distortion: An adaptive perspective. *Trends in Cognitive Sciences, 15*(10), 467–474.

Schaefer, N., Rotermund, C., Blumrich, E. M., Lourenco, M. V., Joshi, P., Hegemann, R. U., . . . Ghosh, S. (2017). The malleable brain: Plasticity of neural circuits and behavior—A review from students to students. *Journal of Neurochemistry*, *142*(6), 790–811.

Sehgal, M., Song, C., Ehlers, V. L., & Moyer, J. R. Jr. (2013). Learning to learn—Intrinsic plasticity as a metaplasticity mechanism for memory formation. *Neurobiology of Learning and Memory*, *105*, 186–199.

Sharot, T., Delgado, M. R., & Phelps, E. A. (2004). How emotion enhances the feeling of remembering. *Nature Neuroscience, 7*(12), 1376–1380.

Talarico, J. M., & Rubin, D. C. (2003). Confidence, not consistency, characterizes flashbulb memories. *Psychological Science, 14*(5), 455–461.

Tovar-Moll, F., & Lent, R. (2016). The various forms of neuroplasticity: Biological bases of learning and teaching. *Prospects*, *46*(2), 199–213.

Voss, P., Thomas, M. E., Cisneros-Franco, J. M., & de Villers-Sidani, É. (2017). Dynamic brains and the changing rules of neuroplasticity: Implications for learning and recovery. *Frontiers in Psychology*, *8*, 1657.

Walker, M. P., & Stickgold, R. (2010). Overnight alchemy: Sleep-dependent memory evolution. *Nature Reviews Neuroscience*, *11*(3), 218.

Walter, N., Nikoleizig, L., & Alfermann, D. (2019). Effects of self-talk training on competitive anxiety, self-efficacy, volitional skills, and performance: An intervention study with junior sub-elite athletes. *Sports*, *7*(6), 148.

Wierzynski, C. M., Lubenov, E. V., Gu, M., & Siapas, A. G. (2009). State-dependent spike-timing relationships between hippocampal and prefrontal circuits during sleep. *Neuron*, *61*(4), 587–596.

Chapter 6

Celeghin, A., Diano, M., Bagnis, A., Viola, M., & Tamietto, M. (2017). Basic emotions in human neuroscience: Neuroimaging and beyond. *Frontiers in Psychology*, *8*, 1432.

Ekman, P. (n.d.). *The atlas of emotions*. Retrieved from https://www.atlasofemotions.org

Ekman, P. (2016). What scientists who study emotion agree about. *Perspectives on Psychological Science*, *11*(1), 31–34.

Fox, A. S., Oler, J. A., Tromp, D. P., Fudge, J. L., & Kalin, N. H. (2015). Extending the amygdala in theories of threat processing. *Trends in Neurosciences*, *38*(5), 319–329.

Frühholz, S., Hofstetter, C., Cristinzio, C., Saj, A., Seeck, M., Vuilleumier, P., & Grandjean, D. (2015). Asymmetrical effects of unilateral right or left amygdala damage on auditory cortical processing of vocal emotions. *Proceedings of the National Academy of Sciences*, *112*(5), 1583–1588.

Hallam, G. P., Webb, T. L., Sheeran, P., Miles, E., Wilkinson, I. D., Hunter, M. D., . . . Farrow, T. F. (2015). The neural correlates of emotion regulation by implementation intentions. *PLoS One*, *10*(3), e0119500.

Hudson, N. W., Lucas, R. E., & Donnellan, M. B. (2017). Day-to-day affect is surprisingly stable: A 2-year longitudinal study of well-being. *Social Psychological and Personality Science*, *8*(1), 45–54.

Immordino-Yang, M. H., & Damasio, A. (2007). We feel, therefore we learn: The relevance of affective and social neuroscience to education. *Mind, Brain, and Education*, *1*(1), 3–10.

Janak, P. H., & Tye, K. M. (2015). From circuits to behaviour in the amygdala. *Nature*, *517*(7534), 284–292.

Kragel, P. A., Knodt, A. R., Hariri, A. R., & LaBar, K. S. (2016). Decoding spontaneous emotional states in the human brain. *PLoS Biology*, *14*(9), e2000106.

McGarry, L. M., & Carter, A. G. (2016). Inhibitory gating of basolateral amygdala inputs to the prefrontal cortex. *Journal of Neuroscience*, *36*(36), 9391–9406.

Madan, C. R., Fujiwara, E., Caplan, J. B., & Sommer, T. (2017). Emotional arousal impairs association-memory: Roles of amygdala and hippocampus. *NeuroImage*, *156*, 14–28.

Oosterwijk, S., Lindquist, K. A., Anderson, E., Dautoff, R., Moriguchi, Y., & Barrett, L. F. (2012). States of mind: Emotions, body feelings, and thoughts share distributed neural networks. *NeuroImage*, *62*(3), 2110–2128.

Oudiette, D., Antony, J. W., Creery, J. D., & Paller, K. A. (2013). The role of memory reactivation during wakefulness and sleep in determining which memories endure. *Journal of Neuroscience*, *33*(15), 6672–6678.

Pessoa, L., & McMenamin, B. (2017). Dynamic networks in the emotional brain. *The Neuroscientist*, *23*(4), 383–396.

Sakaki, M., Nga, L., & Mather, M. (2013). Amygdala functional connectivity with medial prefrontal cortex at rest predicts the positivity effect in older adults' memory. *Journal of Cognitive Neuroscience*, *25*(8), 1206–1224.

Scarantino, A., & Griffiths, P. (2011). Don't give up on basic emotions. *Emotion Review*, *3*(4), 444–454.

Shariff, A. F., & Tracy, J. L. (2011). What are emotion expressions for? *Current Directions in Psychological Science*, *20*(6), 395–399.

Touroutoglou, A., Lindquist, K. A., Dickerson, B. C., & Barrett, L. F. (2015). Intrinsic connectivity in the human brain does not reveal networks for "basic" emotions. *Social Cognitive and Affective Neuroscience, 10*(9), 1257–1265. doi:10.1093/scan/nsv013

Trampe, D., Quoidbach, J., & Taquet, M. (2015). Emotions in everyday life. *PLoS One, 10*(12), e0145450.

Tyng, C. M., Amin, H. U., Saad, M. N., & Malik, A. S. (2017). The influences of emotion on learning and memory. *Frontiers in Psychology, 8,* 1454.

Chapter 7

Álvarez-Bueno, C., Pesce, C., Cavero-Redondo, I., Sánchez-López, M., Garrido-Miguel, M., & Martínez-Vizcaíno, V. (2017). Academic achievement and physical activity: A meta-analysis. *Pediatrics, 140*(6), e20171498.

Bermon, S., Petriz, B., Kajeniene, A., Prestes, J., Castell, L., & Franco, O. L. (2015). The microbiota: An exercise immunology perspective. *Exercise Immunology Review, 21,* 70–79.

Burns, R. D., Brusseau, T. A., Fu, Y., Myrer, R. S., & Hannon, J. C. (2016). Comprehensive school physical activity programming and classroom behavior. *American Journal of Health Behavior, 40*(1), 100–107.

Carlson, J. A., Engelberg, J. K., Cain, K. L., Conway, T. L., Mignano, A. M., Bonilla, E. A., … Sallis, J. F. (2015). Implementing classroom physical activity breaks: Associations with student physical activity and classroom behavior. *Preventive Medicine, 81,* 67–72.

Chen, A. G., Zhu, L. N., Yan, J., & Yin, H. C. (2016). Neural basis of working memory enhancement after acute aerobic exercise: fMRI study of preadolescent children. *Frontiers in Psychology, 7,* 1804.

D'Agostino, E. M., Day, S. E., Konty, K. J., Larkin, M., Saha, S., & Wyka, K. (2018). Peer reviewed: Individual-level fitness and absenteeism in New York City middle school youths, 2006–2013.

Preventing Chronic Disease, 15, 170152. doi:http://dx.doi.org/10.5888/pcd15.170152

De Groot, R., Van Dijk, M., Savelberg, H., Van Acker, F., & Kirschner, P. (2017). Physical activity and school absenteeism due to illness in adolescents. *Journal of School Health, 87*(9), 658–664.

Donnelly, J. E., Hillman, C. H., Castelli, D., Etnier, J. L., Lee, S., Tomporowski, P., . . . Szabo-Reed, A. N. (2016). Physical activity, fitness, cognitive function, and academic achievement in children: A systematic review. *Medicine and Science in Sports and Exercise, 48,* 1197–1222.

Eriksson, P. S., Perfilieva, E., Björk-Eriksson, T., Alborn, A., Nordborg, C., Peterson, D. A., & Gage, F. H. (1998). Neurogenesis in the adult human hippocampus. *Nature Medicine, 4*(11), 1313–1317.

Esteban-Cornejo, I., Tejero-Gonzalez, C. M., Sallis, J. F., & Veiga, O. L. (2015). Physical activity and cognition in adolescents: A systematic review. *Journal of Science and Medicine in Sport, 18*(5), 534–539.

Grazioli, E., Dimauro, I., Mercatelli, N., Wang, G., Pitsiladis, Y., Di Luigi, L., & Caporossi, D. (2017). Physical activity in the prevention of human diseases: Role of epigenetic modifications. *BMC Genomics, 18*(Suppl. 8), 802.

de Greeff, J. W., Bosker, R. J., Oosterlaan, J., Visscher, C., & Hartman, E. (2018). Effects of physical activity on executive functions, attention and academic performance in preadolescent children: A meta-analysis. *Journal of Science and Medicine in Sport, 21*(5), 501–507.

Griesbach, G. S., Hovda, D. A., Molteni, R., Wu, A., & Gomez-Pinilla, F. (2004). Voluntary exercise following traumatic brain injury: Brain-derived neurotrophic factor upregulation and recovery of function. *Neuroscience, 125*(1), 129–139.

Hueston, C. M., Cryan, J. F., & Nolan, Y. M. (2017). Stress and adolescent hippocampal neurogenesis: Diet and exercise as cognitive modulators. *Translational Psychiatry, 7*(4), e1081.

Ivey-Stephenson, A. Z., Crosby, A. E., Jack, S. P., Haileyesus, T., & Kresnow-Sedacca, M. J. (2017). Suicide trends among and within urbanization levels by sex, race/ethnicity, age group, and mechanism of death—United States, 2001–2015. *Morbidity and Mortality Weekly Report: Surveillance Summaries, 66*(18), 1–16.

Jeon, Y. K., & Ha, C. H. (2017). The effect of exercise intensity on brain derived neurotrophic factor and memory in adolescents. *Environmental Health and Preventive Medicine, 22*(1), 27.

Knecht, S., Breitenstein, C., Bushuven, S., Wailke, S., Kamping, S., Flöel, A., . . . Ringelstein, E. B. (2004). Levodopa: Faster and better word learning in normal humans. *Annals of Neurology, 56*(1), 20–26.

Kvam, S., Kleppe, C. L., Nordhus, I. H., & Hovland, A. (2016). Exercise as a treatment for depression: A meta-analysis. *Journal of Affective Disorders, 202*, 67–86.

Lee, I. M., Shiroma, E. J., Lobelo, F., Puska, P., Blair, S. N., Katzmarzyk, P. T., & Lancet Physical Activity Series Working Group. (2012). Effect of physical inactivity on major non-communicable diseases worldwide: An analysis of burden of disease and life expectancy. *The Lancet, 380*(9838), 219–229.

Lloyd, K., & Dayan, P. (2015). Tamping ramping: Algorithmic, implementational, and computational explanations of phasic dopamine signals in the accumbens. *PLoS Computational Biology, 11*(12), e1004622.

López-Vicente, M., Garcia-Aymerich, J., Torrent-Pallicer, J., Forns, J., Ibarluzea, J., Lertxundi, N., . . . Vrijheid, M. (2017). Are early physical activity and sedentary behaviors related to working memory at 7 and 14 years of age? *Journal of Pediatrics, 188*, 35–41.

Lowe, S. R., & Galea, S. (2017). The mental health consequences of mass shootings. *Trauma, Violence, & Abuse, 18*(1), 62–82.

McClelland, M. M., Tominey, S. L., Schmitt, S. A., Hatfield, B., Purpura, D., Gonzales, C., & Tracy, A. (2019). Red light, purple light! Results of an intervention to promote school readiness for children from low-income backgrounds. *Frontiers in Psychology, 10*, 2365.

McEwen, B. S. (2017). Neurobiological and systemic effects of chronic stress. *Chronic Stress* (Jan./Dec.), 1. doi:10.1177.2470547017692328

Michael, S. L., Merlo, C. L., Basch, C. E., Wentzel, K. R., & Wechsler, H. (2015). Critical connections: Health and academics. *Journal of School Health, 85*(11), 740–758.

Nathan, N., Elton, B., Babic, M., McCarthy, N., Sutherland, R., Presseau, J., . . . Wolfenden, L. (2018). Barriers and facilitators to the implementation of physical activity policies in schools: A systematic review. *Preventive Medicine, 107*, 45–53.

Nyberg, M., Gliemann, L., & Hellsten, Y. (2015). Vascular function in health, hypertension, and diabetes: Effect of physical activity on skeletal muscle microcirculation. *Scandinavian Journal of Medicine & Science in Sports, 25*, 60–73.

Phillips, C. (2017). Brain-derived neurotrophic factor, depression, and physical activity: Making the neuroplastic connection. *Neural Plasticity, 2017*, Article ID 7260130, 17 pages. doi:10.1155/2017/7260130

Phillips, C., & Fahimi, A. (2018). Immune and neuroprotective effects of physical activity on the brain in depression. *Frontiers in Neuroscience, 12*, 498. doi:10.3389/fnins.2018.00498

Ponitz, C. E. C., McClelland, M. M., Jewkes, A. M., Connor, C. M., Farris, C. L., & Morrison, F. J. (2008). Touch your toes! Developing a direct measure of behavioral regulation in early childhood. *Early Childhood Research Quarterly, 23*(2), 141–158.

Pontifex, M. B., Gwizdala, K. L., Parks, A. C., Pfeiffer, K. A., & Fenn, K. M. (2016). The association between physical activity during the day and long-term memory stability. *Scientific Reports, 6*, 38148.

Poulose, S. M., Miller, M. G., Scott, T., & Shukitt-Hale, B. (2017). Nutritional factors affecting adult neurogenesis and cognitive function. *Advances in Nutrition, 8*(6), 804–811.

Raffington, L., Prindle, J., Keresztes, A., Binder, J., Heim, C., & Shing, Y. L. (2018). Blunted cortisol stress reactivity in low-income children relates to lower memory function. *Psychoneuroendocrinology*, *90*, 110–121.

Ratey, J. (2008). *Spark: The revolutionary new science of exercise and the brain*. School TIMSS data on page 12. New York, NY: Little, Brown.

Reddon, H., Meyre, D., & Cairney, J. (2017). Physical activity and global self-worth in a longitudinal study of children. *Medicine and Science in Sports and Exercise*, *49*(8), 1606–1613.

Sapolsky, R. M. (2015). Stress and the brain: Individual variability and the inverted-U. *Nature Neuroscience*, *18*(10), 1344–1346.

Spalding, K., Bergmann, O., Alkass, K., Bernard, S., Salehpour, M., Huttner, H., . . . Frisén, J. (2013). Dynamics of hippocampal neurogenesis in adult humans. *Cell, 153*(6), 1219–1227.

Varga, I., Kyselovič, J., Galfiova, P., & Danisovic, L. (2017). The non-cardiomyocyte cells of the heart. Their possible roles in exercise-induced cardiac regeneration and remodeling. In J. Xiao (Ed.), *Exercise for cardiovascular disease prevention and treatment: From molecular to clinical, Part 1* (pp. 117–136). Singapore: Springer.

Venezia, A. C., Quinlan, E., & Roth, S. M. (2017). A single bout of exercise increases hippocampal BDNF: Influence of chronic exercise and noradrenaline. *Genes, Brain and Behavior, 16*(8), 800–811.

Vignoli, B., Battistini, G., Melani, R., Blum, R., Santi, S., Berardi, N., & Canossa, M. (2016). Peri-synaptic glia recycles brain-derived neurotrophic factor for LTP stabilization and memory retention. *Neuron*, *92*(4), 873–887.

Vos, T., Abajobir, A. A., Abate, K. H., Abbafati, C., Abbas, K. M., Abd-Allah, F., … Aboyans, V. (2017). Global, regional, and national incidence, prevalence, and years lived with disability for 328 diseases and injuries for 195 countries, 1990–2016: A systematic analysis for the Global Burden of Disease Study 2016. *The Lancet*, *390*(10100), 1211–1259.

Voss, J. L., Bridge, D. J., Cohen, N. J., & Walker, J. A. (2017). A closer look at the hippocampus and memory. *Trends in Cognitive Sciences*, *21*(8), 577–588.

Wen, C. K. F., Liao, Y., Maher, J. P., Huh, J., Belcher, B. R., Dzubur, E., & Dunton, G. F. (2018). Relationships among affective states, physical activity, and sedentary behavior in children: Moderation by perceived stress. *Health Psychology*, *37*(10), 904–914.

Yang, X., Ru, W., Wang, B., Gao, X., Yang, L., Li, S., . . . Gong, P. (2016). Investigating the genetic basis of attention to facial expressions: The role of the norepinephrine transporter gene. *Psychiatric Genetics*, *26*(6), 266–271.

Yau, S. Y., Li, A., & So, K. F. (2015). Involvement of adult hippocampal neurogenesis in learning and forgetting. *Neural Plasticity, 2015,* Article ID 717958, 13 pages. doi:10.1155/2015/717958

Zoladz, P. R., Park, C. R., & Diamond, D. M. (2011). Neurobiological basis of the complex effects of stress on memory and synaptic plasticity. In C. D. Conrad (Ed.), *The handbook of stress: Neuropsychological effects on the brain* (pp. 157–178). Chichester, England: Wiley-Blackwell.

Chapter 8

Bechtold, J., Simpson, T., White, H. R., & Pardini, D. (2015). Chronic adolescent marijuana use as a risk factor for physical and mental health problems in young adult men. *Psychology of Addictive Behaviors*, *29*(3), 552–563.

Brechwald, W. A., & Prinstein, M. J. (2011). Beyond homophily: A decade of advances in understanding peer influence processes. *Journal of Research on Adolescence, 21*(1), 166–179.

Burrow, A. L., & Hill, P. L. (2011). Purpose as a form of identity capital for positive youth adjustment. *Developmental Psychology, 47*(4), 1196–1206.

Casto, K. V., & Edwards, D. A. (2016). Testosterone, cortisol, and human competition. *Hormones and Behavior, 82*, 21–37.

Cheon, S. H., & Reeve, J. (2015). A classroom-based intervention to help teachers decrease students' amotivation. *Contemporary Educational Psychology, 40*, 99–111.

Cillessen, A. H., & Rose, A. J. (2005). Understanding popularity in the peer system. *Current Directions in Psychological Science, 14*(2), 102–105.

Clayton, N. S., Salwiczek, L. H., & Dickinson, A. (2007). Episodic memory. *Current Biology, 17*(6), R189–R191.

Corbett, B., Weinberg, L., & Duarte, A. (2017). The effect of mild acute stress during memory consolidation on emotional recognition memory. *Neurobiology of Learning and Memory, 145*, 34–44.

Damon, W., Menon, J., & Cotton Bronk, K. (2003). The development of purpose during adolescence. *Applied Developmental Science, 7*(3), 119–128.

Filbey, F. M., McQueeny, T., Kadamangudi, S., Bice, C., & Ketcherside, A. (2015). Combined effects of marijuana and nicotine on memory performance and hippocampal volume. *Behavioural Brain Research, 293*, 46–53.

Geurts, B. (2018). Making sense of self-talk. *Review of Philosophy and Psychology, 9*(2), 271–285.

Guyer, A. E., Silk, J. S., & Nelson, E. E. (2016). The neurobiology of the emotional adolescent: From the inside out. *Neuroscience & Biobehavioral Reviews, 70*, 74–85.

Hatzigeorgiadis, A., & Galanis, E. (2017). Self-talk effectiveness and attention. *Current Opinion in Psychology, 16*, 138–142.

Hochanadel, A., & Finamore, D. (2015). Fixed and growth mindset in education and how grit helps students persist in the face of adversity. *Journal of International Education Research, 11*(1), 47–50.

Kidd, C., & Hayden, B. Y. (2015). The Psychology and Neuroscience of Curiosity. *Neuron, 88*(3), 449–460.

Kim, B. R., Chow, S. M., Bray, B., & Teti, D. M. (2017). Trajectories of mothers' emotional availability: Relations with infant temperament in predicting attachment security. *Attachment & Human Development, 19*(1), 38–57.

Lazowski, R. A., & Hulleman, C. S. (2016). Motivation interventions in education. *Review of Educational Research, 86*(2), 602–640.

Levy, D. E., Riis, J., Sonnenberg, L. M., Barraclough, S. J., & Thorndike, A. N. (2012). Food choices of minority and low-income employees: A cafeteria intervention. *American Journal of Preventive Medicine, 43*(3), 240–248.

Lim, L., Hart, H., Mehta, M. A., Simmons, A., Mirza, K., & Rubia, K. (2016). Neurofunctional abnormalities during sustained attention in severe childhood abuse. *PLoS One, 11*(11), e0165547.

Lloyd, K., & Dayan, P. (2015). Tamping ramping: Algorithmic, implementational, and computational explanations of phasic dopamine signals in the accumbens. *PLoS Computational Biology, 11*(12), e1004622.

Lubman, D. I., Cheetham, A., & Yücel, M. (2015). Cannabis and adolescent brain development. *Pharmacology & Therapeutics, 148*, 1–16.

Mahler, D., Großschedl, J., & Harms, U. (2018). Does motivation matter?–The relationship between teachers' self-efficacy and enthusiasm and students' performance. *PLoS One, 13*(11), e0207252.

Maier, S. F., & Seligman, M. E. P. (2016). Learned helplessness at fifty: Insights from neuroscience. *Psychological Review, 123*(4), 349–367.

Marques, S. C., Lopez, S. J., Fontaine, A. M., Coimbra, S., & Mitchell, J. (2015). How much hope is enough? Levels of hope and students' psychological and school functioning. *Psychology in the Schools, 52*(4), 325–334.

Meece, J. L., Anderman, E. M., & Anderman, L. H. (2006). Classroom goal structure, student motivation, and academic achievement. *Annual Review of Psychology*, 57 487–503.

Mikami, A. Y., Ruzek, E. A., Hafen, C. A., Gregory, A., & Allen, J. P. (2017). Perceptions of relatedness with classroom peers promote adolescents' behavioral engagement and achievement in secondary school. *Journal of Youth and Adolescence, 46*(11), 2341–2354.

Nelson, B. D., & Hajcak, G. (2017). Defensive motivation and attention in anticipation of different types of predictable and unpredictable threat: A startle and event-related potential investigation. *Psychophysiology, 54*(8), 1180–1194.

Nugent, F. S., Penick, E. C., & Kauer, J. A. (2007). Opioids block long-term potentiation of inhibitory synapses. *Nature, 446*(7139), 1086.

Nuthall, G. (2005). The cultural myths and realities of classroom teaching and learning: A personal journey. *Teachers College Record, 107*(5), 895–934.

Ojanen, T., Grönroos, M., & Salmivalli, C. (2005). An interpersonal circumplex model of children's social goals: Links with peer-reported behavior and sociometric status. *Developmental Psychology, 41*(5), 699–710.

Oosterwijk, S., Lindquist, K. A., Anderson, E., Dautoff, R., Moriguchi, Y., & Barrett, L. F. (2012). States of mind: Emotions, body feelings, and thoughts share distributed neural networks. *NeuroImage, 62*(3), 2110–2128.

Oudiette, D., Antony, J. W., Creery, J. D., & Paller, K. A. (2013). The role of memory reactivation during wakefulness and sleep in determining which memories endure. *Journal of Neuroscience, 33*(15), 6672–6678.

Reyna, V. F., & Farley, F. (2006). Risk and rationality in adolescent decision making: Implications

for theory, practice, and public policy. *Psychological Science in the Public Interest, 7*(1), 1–44.

Ryan, R. M., & Deci, E. L. (2013). Toward a social psychology of assimilation: Self-determination theory in cognitive development and education. In B. W. Sokol, F. M. E. Grouzet, & U. Muller (Eds.), *Self-regulation and autonomy: Social and developmental dimensions of human conduct* (pp. 191–207). Cambridge, England: Cambridge University Press.

Schacter, D. L., Gilbert, D. T., & Wegner, D. M. (2009). *Introducing psychology*. New York, NY: Palgrave Macmillan.

Shan, Z. Y., Kwiatek, R., Burnet, R., Del Fante, P., Staines, D. R., Marshall-Gradisnik, S. M., & Barnden, L. R. (2016). Progressive brain changes in patients with chronic fatigue syndrome: A longitudinal MRI study. *Journal of Magnetic Resonance Imaging, 44*(5), 1301–1311.

Thaler, R. H., & Sunstein, C. R. (2009). *Nudge: Improving decisions about health, wealth, and happiness* (rev. and expanded ed.). New York, NY: Penguin.

Unsworth, N., & Robison, M. K. (2017). A locus coeruleus-norepinephrine account of individual differences in working memory capacity and attention control. *Psychonomic Bulletin & Review, 24*(4), 1282–1311.

Urhahne, D. (2015). Teacher behavior as a mediator of the relationship between teacher judgment and students' motivation and emotion. *Teaching and Teacher Education, 45*, 73–82.

Zhang, Y., Loh, H. H., & Law, P. Y. (2016). Effect of opioid on adult hippocampal neurogenesis. *Scientific World Journal*, 2601264. doi:10.1155/2016/260126

Chapter 9

Adolphs, R. (2010). What does the amygdala contribute to social cognition? *Annals of the New York Academy of Sciences, 1191*(1), 42–61.

Ahmed, W., Minnaert, A., Werf, G. V., & Kuyper, H. (2008). Perceived social support and early adolescents' achievement: The mediational roles of motivational beliefs and emotions. *Journal of Youth and Adolescence, 39*(1), 36–46.

Babad, E., Avni-Babad, D., & Rosenthal, R. (2003). Teachers' brief nonverbal behaviors in defined instructional situations can predict students' evaluations. *Journal of Educational Psychology, 95*(3), 553–562.

Benner, A. D., & Mistry, R. S. (2007). Congruence of mother and teacher educational expectations and low-income youth's academic competence. *Journal of Educational Psychology, 99*(1), 140–153.

Casas, J., & Steinmann, T. (2014). Predator-induced flow disturbances alert prey, from the onset of an attack. *Proceedings of the Royal Society B: Biological Sciences, 281*(1790), 20141083.

Casey, B. J., Jones, R. M., Levita, L., Libby, V., Pattwell, S. S., Ruberry E. J., . . . Somerville, L. H. (2010). The storm and stress of adolescence: Insights from human imaging and mouse genetics. *Developmental Psychobiology, 52*, 225–235.

Casto, K. V., & Edwards, D. A. (2016). Testosterone, cortisol, and human competition. *Hormones and Behavior, 82*, 21–37.

Cheon, S. H., & Reeve, J. (2015). A classroom-based intervention to help teachers decrease students' amotivation. *Contemporary Educational Psychology, 40*, 99–111.

Czekala, C., Mauguière, F., Mazza, S., Jackson, P. L., & Frot, M. (2015). My brain reads pain in your face, before knowing your gender. *Journal of Pain, 16*(12), 1342–1352.

D'Hondt, F., Eccles, J. S., Houtte, M. V., & Stevens, P. A. (2016). Perceived ethnic discrimination by teachers and ethnic minority students' academic futility: Can parents prepare their youth for better or for worse? *Journal of Youth and Adolescence, 45*(6), 1075–1089.

Dehaene, S., Changeux, J. P., Naccache, L., Sackur, J., & Sergent, C. (2006). Conscious, preconscious, and subliminal processing: A testable taxonomy. *Trends in Cognitive Sciences, 10*(5), 204–211.

Dumont, H., Protsch, P., Jansen, M., & Becker, M. (2017). Fish swimming into the ocean: How tracking relates to students' self-beliefs and school disengagement at the end of schooling. *Journal of Educational Psychology, 109*(6), 855–870.

Eisenberger, N. I. (2012). The pain of social disconnection: Examining the shared neural underpinnings of physical and social pain. *Nature Reviews Neuroscience, 13*(6), 421–434.

Farmer, T. W., Lines, M. M., & Hamm, J. V. (2011). Revealing the invisible hand: The role of teachers in children's peer experiences. *Journal of Applied Developmental Psychology, 32*(5), 247–256.

Farrington, C. A., Roderick, M., Allensworth, E. A., Nagaoka, J., Johnson, D. W., Keyes, T. S., & Beechum, N. (2012). *Teaching adolescents to become learners: The role of noncognitive factors in academic performance—A critical literature review.* Chicago, IL: Consortium on Chicago School Research.

Farrington, C. (2013). *Academic mindsets as critical component of deeper learning.* Chicago, IL: Consortium on Chicago School Research.

Fox, A. S., Oler, J. A., Tromp, D. P., Fudge, J. L., & Kalin, N. H. (2015). Extending the amygdala in theories of threat processing. *Trends in Neurosciences, 38*(5), 319–329.

Gianaros, P. J., Horenstein, J. A., Cohen, S., Matthews, K. A., Brown, S. M., Flory, J. D., . . . Hariri, A. R. (2007). Perigenual anterior cingulate morphology covaries with perceived social standing. *Social Cognitive and Affective Neuroscience, 2*(3), 161–173.

Gregory, A., Hafen, C. A., Ruzek, E., Mikami, A. Y., Allen, J. P., & Pianta, R. C. (2016). Closing the racial discipline gap in classrooms by changing teacher practice. *School Psychology Review, 45*(2), 171–191.

Hattie, J. (2017, December). *Hattie's 2018 updated list of factors related to student achievement: 252 influences and effect sizes (Cohen's d).* Retrieved from http://www.visiblelearning.org

Hicks, C. M., & Liu, D. (2016). Young children selectively expect failure disclosure to high-achieving peers. *Infant and Child Development, 26*(2), e1978.

Holt-Lunstad, J., & Smith, T. (2010). Social relationships and mortality risk: A meta-analytic review. *PLoS Medicine, 7*(7), e1000316.

Hutcherson, C. A., Seppala, E. M., & Gross, J. J. (2014). The neural correlates of social connection. *Cognitive, Affective, & Behavioral Neuroscience, 15*(1), 1–14.

Jenkins, L. N., Floress, M. T., & Reinke, W. (2015). Rates and types of teacher praise: A review and future directions. *Psychology in the Schools, 52*(5), 463–476.

Jensen, K., Vaish, A., & Schmidt, M. F. (2014). The emergence of human prosociality: Aligning with others through feelings, concerns, and norms. *Frontiers in Psychology, 5,* 822. doi:10.3389/fpsyg.2014.00822

Kok, B. E., Coffey, K. A., Cohn, M. A., Catalino, L. I., Vacharkulksemsuk, T., Algoe, S. B., . . . Fredrickson, B. L. (2013). How positive emotions build physical health. *Psychological Science, 24*(7), 1123–1132.

Lei, H., Cui, Y., & Chiu, M. M. (2018). The relationship between teacher support and students academic emotions: A meta-analysis. *Frontiers in Psychology, 8,* 2288.

McDonald, L., Flint, A., Rubie-Davies, C. M., Peterson, E. R., Watson, P., & Garrett, L. (2014). Teaching high-expectation strategies to teachers through an intervention process. *Professional Development in Education, 42*(2), 290–307.

Maier, S. F., & Seligman, M. E. P. (2016). Learned helplessness at fifty: Insights from neuroscience. *Psychological Review, 123*(4), 349–367.

Marques, S. C., Gallagher, M. W., & Lopez, S. J. (2017). Hope- and academic-related outcomes: A meta-analysis. *School Mental Health, 9*(3), 250–262.

Marques, S. C., Lopez, S. J., Fontaine, A. M., Coimbra, S., & Mitchell, J. (2015). How much hope is enough? Levels of hope and students' psychological and school functioning. *Psychology in the Schools, 52*(4), 325–334.

Mikami, A. Y., Ruzek, E. A., Hafen, C. A., Gregory, A., & Allen, J. P. (2017). Perceptions of relatedness with classroom peers promote adolescents' behavioral engagement and achievement in secondary school. *Journal of Youth and Adolescence, 46*(11), 2341–2354.

Mobbs, D., Marchant, J. L., Hassabis, D., Seymour, B., Tan, G., Gray, M., . . . Frith, C. D. (2009). From threat to fear: The neural organization of defensive fear systems in humans. *The Journal of Neuroscience: The Official Journal of the Society for Neuroscience, 29*(39), 12236–12243. doi:10.1523/JNEUROSCI.2378-09.2009

Mukamel, R., Ekstrom, A. D., Kaplan, J., Iacoboni, M., & Fried, I. (2010). Single-neuron responses in humans during execution and observation of actions. *Current Biology, 20*(8), 750–756.

Osterman, K. F. (2000). Students' need for belonging in the school community. *Review of Educational Research, 70*(3), 323–367.

Pianta, R. C., Hamre, B. K., & Allen, J. P. (2012). Teacher-student relationships and engagement: Conceptualizing, measuring, and improving the capacity of classroom interactions. In S. L. Christenson, A. L. Reschly, & C. Wylie (Eds.), *Handbook of research on student engagement* (pp. 365–386). New York, NY: Springer.

Rand, K. L. (2017). Hope, self-efficacy, and optimism: Conceptual and empirical differences. In M. W. Gallagher & S. J. Lopez (Eds.), *The Oxford handbook of hope* (pp. 45–58). New York, NY: Oxford University Press.

Reichard, R. J., Avey, J. B., Lopez, S., & Dollwet, M. (2013). Having the will and finding the way: A review and meta-analysis of hope at work. *The Journal of Positive Psychology, 8*(4), 292–304.

Riegle-Crumb, C., & Humphries, M. (2012). Exploring bias in math teachers' perceptions of students' ability by gender and race/ethnicity. *Gender & Society, 26*(2), 290–322.

Rizzolatti, G., Fadiga, L., Fogassi, L., & Gallese, V. (1999). Resonance behaviors and mirror neurons. *Archives italiennes de biologie, 137*(2), 85–100.

Rosenthal, R. & Jacobson, L. (1969). Pygmalion in the classroom: Teacher expectation and pupils' intellectual development. *Psychology in the Schools, 6*(2), 212–214.

Rubie-Davies, C. M., & Rosenthal, R. (2016). Intervening in teachers' expectations: A random effects meta-analytic approach to examining the effectiveness of an intervention. *Learning and Individual Differences, 50*, 83–92.

Ryan, R. M., & Deci, E. L. (2013). Toward a social psychology of assimilation: Self-determination theory in cognitive development and education. In B. W. Sokol, F. M. E. Grouzet, & U. Muller (Eds.), *Self-regulation and autonomy: Social and developmental dimensions of human conduct* (pp. 191–207). Cambridge, England: Cambridge University Press.

Ryan, A. M., & Shim, S. S. (2012). Changes in help seeking from peers during early adolescence: Associations with changes in achievement and perceptions of teachers. *Journal of Educational Psychology, 104*(4), 1122–1134.

Ryan, A. M., & Shin, H. (2011). Help-seeking tendencies during early adolescence: An examination of motivational correlates and consequences for achievement. *Learning and Instruction, 21*(2), 247–256.

Satici, S. A., & Uysal, R. (2016). Psychological vulnerability and subjective happiness: The mediating role of hopelessness. *Stress and Health, 33*(2), 111–118.

Silk, J. S., Lee, K. H., Kerestes, R., Griffith, J. M., Dahl, R. E., & Ladouceur, C. D. (2017). "Loser" or "Popular"? Neural response to social status words in adolescents with major depressive disorder. *Developmental Cognitive Neuroscience, 28*, 1–11. doi:10.1016/j.dcn.2017.09.005

Smythies, J. (2003). Space, time and consciousness. *Journal of Consciousness Studies, 10*(3), 47–56.

Snyder, C. R., Rand, K. L., & Sigmon, D. R. (2005). Hope theory: A member of the positive psychology family. In C. R. Snyder & S. J. Lopez (Eds.), *Handbook of positive psychology* (pp. 257–278). New York, NY: Oxford University Press.

Stanley, D. A., & Adolphs, R. (2013). Toward a neural basis for social behavior. *Neuron, 80*(3), 816–826.

Stoddard, S. A., & Pierce, J. (2015). Promoting positive future expectations during adolescence: The role of assets. *American Journal of Community Psychology, 56*(3–4), 332–341. doi:10.1007/s10464-015-9754-7

Travers, C., Morisano, D., & Locke, E. (2015). Self-reflection, growth goals, and academic outcomes: A qualitative study. *British Journal of Educational Psychology, 85*(2), 224–241.

Utevsky, A. V., & Platt, M. L. (2014). Status and the brain. *PLoS Biology, 12*(9), e1001941. doi:10.1371/journal.pbio.1001941

Chapter 10

Cassidy, S. (2004). Learning styles: An overview of theories, models, and measures. *Educational Psychology, 24*(4), 419–444.

Hutchinson, J. B., Pak, S. S., & Turk-Browne, N. B. (2016). Biased competition during long-term memory formation. *Journal of Cognitive Neuroscience, 28*(1), 187–197.

Kang, S. H. (2016). Spaced repetition promotes efficient and effective learning. *Policy Insights from the Behavioral and Brain Sciences, 3*(1), 12–19.

Karpicke, J. D. (2012). Retrieval-based learning. *Current Directions in Psychological Science, 21*(3), 157–163.

Kelley, P., & Whatson, T. (2013). Making long-term memories in minutes: A spaced learning pattern from memory research in education. *Frontiers in Human Neuroscience, 7*, 589.

Kidd, C., & Hayden, B. Y. (2015). The psychology and neuroscience of curiosity. *Neuron, 88*(3), 449–460.

Lacy, J. W., & Stark, C. E. (2013). The neuroscience of memory: Implications for the courtroom. *Nature Reviews Neuroscience, 14*(9), 649–658.

Lally, P., van Jaarsveld, C. H. M., Potts, H. W. W., & Wardle, J. (2010). How are habits formed: Modelling habit formation in the real world. *European Journal of Social Psychology, 40*(6), 998–1009.

Leshikar, E. D., & Duarte, A. (2014). Medial prefrontal cortex supports source memory for self-referenced materials in young and older adults. *Cognitive, Affective, & Behavioral Neuroscience, 14*(1), 236–252.

Moos, D. (2013). Examining hypermedia learning: The role of cognitive load and self-regulated learning. *Journal of Educational Multimedia and Hypermedia, 22*(1), 39–61.

Moravec, M., Williams, A., Aguilar-Roca, N., & O'Dowd, D. K. (2010). Learn before lecture: A strategy that improves learning outcomes in a large introductory biology class. *CBE—Life Sciences Education, 9*(4), 473–481.

Morel, N., Villain, N., Rauchs, G., Gaubert, M., Piolino, P., Landeau, B., . . . Chételat, G. (2014). Brain activity and functional coupling changes associated with self-reference effect during both encoding and retrieval. *PLoS One, 9*(3), e90488.

Newton, P. M., & Miah, M. (2017). Evidence-based higher education—is the learning styles "myth" important? *Frontiers in Psychology, 8*, 444.

O'Keefe, P. A., & Linnenbrink-Garcia, L. (2014). The role of interest in optimizing performance and self-regulation. *Journal of Experimental Social Psychology, 53*, 70–78.

Oudiette, D., Antony, J. W., Creery, J. D., & Paller, K. A. (2013). The role of memory reactivation during wakefulness and sleep in determining which memories endure. *Journal of Neuroscience, 33*(15), 6672–6678.

Paas, F., & Ayres, P. (2014). Cognitive load theory: A broader view on the role of memory in learning and education. *Educational Psychology Review, 26*(2), 191–195.

Pashler, H., McDaniel, M., Rohrer, D., & Bjork, R. (2008). Learning styles: Concepts and evidence. *Psychological Science in the Public Interest, 9*(3), 105–119.

Roediger, H. L., & Butler, A. C. (2011). The critical role of retrieval practice in long-term retention. *Trends in Cognitive Sciences, 15*(1), 20–27.

Rohrer, D., Dedrick, R. F., & Stershic, S. (2015). Interleaved practice improves mathematics learning. *Journal of Educational Psychology, 107*(3), 900–908.

Ryan, R. M., & Deci, E. L. (2000). Self-determination theory and the facilitation of intrinsic motivation, social development, and well-being. *American Psychologist, 55*(1), 68–78.

Schacter, D. L., Guerin, S. A., & Jacques, P. L. (2011). Memory distortion: An adaptive perspective. *Trends in Cognitive Sciences, 15*(10), 467–474.

Schneider, S., Beege, M., Nebel, S., & Rey, G. D. (2018). A meta-analysis of how signaling affects learning with media. *Educational Research Review, 23*, 1–24.

Sekeres, M. J., Bonasia, K., St-Laurent, M., Pishdadian, S., Winocur, G., Grady, C., & Moscovitch, M. (2016). Recovering and preventing loss of detailed memory: Differential rates of forgetting for detail types in episodic memory. *Learning & Memory, 23*(2), 72–82.

Shin, J., Dronjic, V., & Park, B. (2019). The interplay between working memory and background knowledge in L2 reading comprehension. *TESOL Quarterly, 53*(2), 320–347.

Shing, Y. L., & Brod, G. (2016). Effects of prior knowledge on memory: Implications for education. *Mind, Brain, and Education*, *10*(3), 153–161.

Smolen, P., Zhang, Y., & Byrne, J. H. (2016). The right time to learn: Mechanisms and optimization of spaced learning. *Nature Reviews Neuroscience*, *17*(2), 77–88.

Spires, H. A., Kerkhoff, S. N., & Graham, A. C. (2016). Disciplinary literacy and inquiry: Teaching for deeper content learning. *Journal of Adolescent & Adult Literacy*, *60*(2), 151–161.

Thalmann, M., Souza, A. S., & Oberauer, K. (2019). How does chunking help working memory? *Journal of Experimental Psychology: Learning, Memory, and Cognition*, *45*(1), 37–55.

Vansteenkiste, M., Simons, J., Lens, W., Sheldon, K. M., & Deci, E. L. (2004). Motivating learning, performance, and persistence: The synergistic effects of intrinsic goal contents and autonomy-supportive contexts. *Journal of Personality and Social Psychology*, *87*(2), 246–260.

Weingarten, E., Chen, Q., McAdams, M., Yi, J., Hepler, J., & Albarracín, D. (2016). From primed concepts to action: A meta-analysis of the behavioral effects of incidentally presented words. *Psychological Bulletin*, *142*(5), 472–497.

Willingham, D. T., Hughes, E. M., & Dobolyi, D. G. (2015). The scientific status of learning styles theories. *Teaching of Psychology*, *42*(3), 266–271.

Chapter 11

Beilharz, J., Maniam, J., & Morris, M. (2015). Diet-induced cognitive deficits: The role of fat and sugar, potential mechanisms and nutritional interventions. *Nutrients, 7*(8), 6719–6738.

Billingsley, J., & Losin, E. A. (2017). The neural systems of forgiveness: An evolutionary psychological perspective. *Frontiers in Psychology, 8*, 737.

Bschor, T., & Kilarski, L. L. (2016). Are antidepressants effective? A debate on their efficacy for the treatment of major depression in adults. *Expert Review of Neurotherapeutics, 16*(4), 367–374.

Chianese, R., Coccurello, R., Viggiano, A., Scafuro, M., Fiore, M., Coppola, G., . . . Meccariello, R. (2018). Impact of dietary fats on brain functions. *Current Neuropharmacology*, *16*(7), 1059–1085.

Chen, A. G., Zhu, L. N., Yan, J., & Yin, H. C. (2016). Neural basis of working memory enhancement after acute aerobic exercise: fMRI study of preadolescent children. *Frontiers in Psychology*, *7*, 1804.

Driscoll, K. C., & Pianta, R. C. (2010). Banking time in Head Start: Early efficacy of an intervention designed to promote supportive teacher–child relationships. *Early Education & Development*, *21*(1), 38–64.

Eisenberger, N. I. (2012). The pain of social disconnection: Examining the shared neural underpinnings of physical and social pain. *Nature Reviews Neuroscience*, *13*(6), 421–434.

Ferguson, K., Frost, L., & Hall, D. (2012). Predicting teacher anxiety, depression, and job satisfaction. *Journal of Teaching and Learning*, *8*(1), 27–42.

Galland, L. (2014). The gut microbiome and the brain. *Journal of Medicinal Food*, *17*(12), 1261–1272.

Gianaros, P. J., Horenstein, J. A., Cohen, S., Matthews, K. A., Brown, S. M., Flory, J. D., . . . Hariri, A. R. (2007). Perigenual anterior cingulate morphology covaries with perceived social standing. *Social Cognitive and Affective Neuroscience*, *2*(3), 161–173.

Godoy, L. D., Rossignoli, M. T., Delfino-Pereira, P., Garcia-Cairasco, N., & de Lima Umeoka, E. H. (2018). A comprehensive overview on stress neurobiology: Basic concepts and clinical implications. *Frontiers in Behavioral Neuroscience*, *12*, 127.

Gonzalez, J. A., Ragins, B. R., Ehrhardt, K., & Singh, R. (2018). Friends and family: The role of relationships in community and workplace attachment. *Journal of Business and Psychology*, *33*(1), 89–104.

Griesbach, G. S., Hovda, D. A., Molteni, R., Wu, A., & Gomez-Pinilla, F. (2004). Voluntary exercise following traumatic brain injury: Brain-derived neurotrophic factor upregulation and recovery of function. *Neuroscience, 125*(1), 129–139.

Irwin, M. R., Olmstead, R., & Carroll, J. E. (2016). Sleep disturbance, sleep duration, and inflammation: A systematic review and meta-analysis of cohort studies and experimental sleep deprivation. *Biological Psychiatry, 80*(1), 40–52.

Irwin, M. R., Wang, M., Ribeiro, D., Cho, H. J., Olmstead, R., Breen, E. C., … Cole, S. (2008). Sleep loss activates cellular inflammatory signaling. *Biological Psychiatry, 64*(6), 538–540.

McLean, L., & Connor, C. M. (2015). Depressive symptoms in third-grade teachers: Relations to classroom quality and student achievement. *Child Development, 86*(3), 945–954.

Netea, M. G., Balkwill, F., Chonchol, M., Cominelli, F., Donath, M. Y., Giamarellos-Bourboulis, E. J., . . . Hotchkiss, R. (2017). A guiding map for inflammation. *Nature Immunology, 18*(8), 826.

Quintana-Orts, C., & Rey, L. (2018). Traditional bullying, cyberbullying and mental health in early adolescents: Forgiveness as a protective factor of peer victimisation. *International Journal of Environmental Research and Public Health, 15*(11), 2389.

Reddon, H., Meyre, D., & Cairney, J. (2017). Physical activity and global self-worth in a longitudinal study of children. *Medicine and Science in Sports and Exercise, 49*(8), 1606–1613.

Ricciardi, E., Rota, G., Sani, L., Gentili, C., Gaglianese, A., Guazzelli, M., & Pietrini, P. (2013). How the brain heals emotional wounds: The functional neuroanatomy of forgiveness. *Frontiers in Human Neuroscience, 7*, 839.

Rusk, R. D., Vella-Brodrick, D. A., & Waters, L. (2016). Gratitude or gratefulness? A conceptual review and proposal of the system of appreciative functioning. *Journal of Happiness Studies, 17*(5), 2191–2212.

Scheiermann, C., Kunisaki, Y., & Frenette, P. S. (2013). Circadian control of the immune system. *Nature Reviews Immunology, 13*(3), 190–198.

Schnaider-Levi, L., Mitnik, I., Zafrani, K., Goldman, Z., & Lev-Ari, S. (2017). Inquiry-based stress reduction meditation technique for teacher burnout: A qualitative study. *Mind, Brain, and Education, 11*(2), 75–84.

Stanley, D. A., & Adolphs, R. (2013). Toward a neural basis for social behavior. *Neuron, 80*(3), 816–826.

Toussaint, L. L., Shields, G. S., & Slavich, G. M. (2016). Forgiveness, stress, and health: A 5-week dynamic parallel process study. *Annals of Behavioral Medicine, 50*(5), 727–735.

Toussaint, L. L., Shields, G. S., Green, E., Kennedy, K., Travers, S., & Slavich, G. M. (2018). Hostility, forgiveness, and cognitive impairment over 10 years in a national sample of American adults. *Health Psychology, 37*(12), 1102–1106.

Wen, C. K. F., Liao, Y., Maher, J. P., Huh, J., Belcher, B. R., Dzubur, E., & Dunton, G. F. (2018). Relationships among affective states, physical activity, and sedentary behavior in children: Moderation by perceived stress. *Health Psychology, 37*(10), 904–914.

Wood, A. M., Froh, J. J., & Geraghty, A. W. (2010). Gratitude and well-being: A review and theoretical integration. *Clinical Psychology Review, 30*(7), 890–905.

Xiao, Q., Arem, H., Pfeiffer, R., & Matthews, C. (2017). Prediagnosis sleep duration, napping, and mortality among colorectal cancer survivors in a large US cohort. *Sleep, 40*(4). doi:10.1093/sleep/zsx010

Index

A SAGE Publishing Company

Helping educators make the greatest impact

CORWIN HAS ONE MISSION: to enhance education through intentional professional learning.

We build long-term relationships with our authors, educators, clients, and associations who partner with us to develop and continuously improve the best evidence-based practices that establish and support lifelong learning.

Solutions YOU WANT | Experts YOU TRUST | Results YOU NEED

EVENTS

>>> **INSTITUTES**

Corwin Institutes provide large regional events where educators collaborate with peers and learn from industry experts. Prepare to be recharged and motivated!

corwin.com/institutes

ON-SITE PD

>>> **ON-SITE PROFESSIONAL LEARNING**

Corwin on-site PD is delivered through high-energy keynotes, practical workshops, and custom coaching services designed to support knowledge development and implementation.

corwin.com/pd

>>> **PROFESSIONAL DEVELOPMENT RESOURCE CENTER**

The PD Resource Center provides school and district PD facilitators with the tools and resources needed to deliver effective PD.

corwin.com/pdrc

ONLINE

>>> **ADVANCE**

Designed for K–12 teachers, Advance offers a range of online learning options that can qualify for graduate-level credit and apply toward license renewal.

corwin.com/advance

Contact a PD Advisor at (800) 831-6640 or visit www.corwin.com for more information